COMPLETELY AWESOME!

RIPLEY
PUBLISHING

a Jim Pattison Company

PUBLISHING

Publisher Anne Marshall
Editorial Director Rebecca Miles
Project Editor Charlotte Howell
Text Geoff Tibballs
Proofreader Judy Barratt
Researchers Charlotte Howell, Dominic Lill, James Proud
Indexer Hilary Bird
Art Director Sam South
Project Design Rocket Design (East Anglia) Ltd
Cover Design Michelle Foster
Reprographics Juice Creative
Executive Vice President Norm Deska
Vice President, Archives and Exhibits Edward Meyer

PUBLISHER'S NOTE
While every effort has been made to verify the accuracy of the entries in this book, the Publishers cannot be held responsible for any errors contained in the work. They would be glad to receive any information from readers.

WARNING
Some of the stunts and activities in this book are undertaken by experts and should not be attempted by anyone without adequate training and supervision.

Cover image: Peg man, Kelvin Mercado, pinned 161 pegs to his face, more than anyone has ever done before.

Published by Ripley Publishing 2014

Ripley Publishing, Suite 188, 7576 Kingspointe Parkway, Orlando, Florida 32819, USA

2 4 6 8 10 9 7 5 3 1

Copyright © 2014 by Ripley Entertainment Inc.

ISBN 978-1-60991-101-0

Some of this material first appeared in *Ripley's Believe It or Not! Strikingly True!*

Library of Congress Control Number: 2013037047

Manufactured in China in November/2013
1st printing

First published in Great Britain in 2014 by Random House Books, Random House, 20 Vauxhall Bridge Road, London SW1V 2SA
www.rbooks.co.uk

Addresses for companies within The Random House Group Limited can be found at
www.randomhouse.co.uk/offices/htm

The Random House Group Limited Reg. No. 954009

A CIP catalogue record for this book is available from the British Library

ISBN 9780099568223 (UK)

Ripley's Legacy Lives On

Here at Ripley's, we're inquisitive. Every second of every day, we've got our ears to the ground, eyes peeled and fingers flicking through files and every kind of social media—only stopping short of sniffer dogs—in the pursuit of a barely believable truth, or a person with a life more extraordinary—continuing the legacy of Robert Ripley.

We have researchers, curators, archivists and model-makers, as well as editors and correspondents, who compile articles and write for the Ripley's Believe It or Not! books. Dedicated and passionate about what we do, we never tire in our mission to uncover and preserve the unbelievable side of life.

Robert Ripley always encouraged his dedicated readers to submit material and photographs—a tradition that exists to this day. With a huge database of incredible stories, a massive photo archive, and a warehouse stuffed with exhibits, Ripley's celebrates our amazing world, without ever passing judgment.

Daily cartoons are still produced and printed to this day, and appear online and in a number of newspapers around the world. Ripley's Believe It or Not! is the longest running syndicated cartoon in the world.

Contents

Ripley's World

Marco Polo, Christopher Columbus, Neil Armstrong... there are few true adventurers that can be compared to such great men—but Robert Ripley just might be one of them! In 1918, considering the limited forms of travel, Ripley's determination to visit countries barely known back home showed a pioneering spirit no less extraordinary than those intrepid explorers.

With style, in bow tie and spats, Ripley traveled to Papua New Guinea, Armenia, Tibet and beyond—his aim was to uncover the world's wonders and weird-ities, miracles and monstrosities and feature them in the Believe It or Not! cartoon he drew daily for *The New York Globe*.

Americans couldn't get enough of Ripley and he rocketed into radio and television—broadcasting from places such as the bottom of a shark tank. Soon he was said to be more popular than the U.S. President!

By 1933, Ripley had opened an Odditorium (museum) in Chicago to display the artifacts he'd collected. Today, Ripley's is a global empire with 32 Odditoriums, three aquariums, a warehouse packed with artifacts, and an archive of more than 25,000 photos and 100,000 cartoons.

Ripley's Believe It or Not! daily cartoon was an instant success and the phrase "believe it or not" soon entered everyday speech.

During a NBC 1936 live broadcast from Silver Springs, Florida, Ripley and his co-host Ross Allen entered into a pit full of poisonous snakes.

Robert Ripley with Arjan Desur Dangar, one of the performers at Ripley's Odditorium exhibition at the 1933 Chicago World's Fair.

Ripley enlisted the help of yaks to pull his car out of a snowdrift when it got stuck in a snowy mountain pass in Georgia in 1934. By 1940, Ripley had visited no fewer than 201 countries.

Available now! The first ever biography of Robert Ripley, *A Curious Man.*
Visit www.ripleys.com for details.

6

We've been out and about!

Ripley's archivist Edward Meyer bought this bike made from road kill bones by artist Rasha "Reese" Moore from Florida. Rasha brought his creations to the Ripley's St. Augustine "Bizarre Buying Bazaar" in July 2013, an event that encouraged people to bring along their "Believe It or Nots!"

There have been lots of changes going on at the Mrytle Beach Odditorium in South Carolina (below)—with over 40 new exhibits! This Captain America Superhero collage (right) was made by Cristiam Ramos, and represents comic book characters—both Marvel and DC, hero and villain. Cristiam made the entire sculpture by hand.

Ripley's Aquarium of Canada

Over 15,000 marine and freshwater fish, including some of the most amazing underwater creatures on the planet, have taken up residence in Ripley's new aquarium in downtown Toronto, Canada.

A total of 450 species enjoy 1½ million gallons (5.7 million liters) of water in 45 different habitats, ranging from the majestic kelp forests of Canada's Pacific Northwest to the spectacular color of a tropical Indo-Pacific reef. The aquarium features the longest underwater moving walkway of its kind in North America, which takes visitors through Dangerous Lagoon where turtles, sawfish, stingrays and sharks—including 9-ft-long (2.7 m) sand tigers—swim overhead.

Ripley's Believe It or Not!

Download the Ripley's Believe It or Not! app and access Ripley's content wherever you are. Head to the app store now to download and experience the world of Ripley's!

This is your one-stop portal into the incredible world of Ripley's. Download the world's weirdest phenomena onto your mobile device, including the latest Believe It or Not! photos, videos, stories and facts. This app features Ripley's image recognition technology, oddSCAN™, giving you the ability to scan real-world targets in Ripley's Odditoriums and some Ripley's books with your phone camera to unlock exclusive hidden content. It also offers live feeds, a guide to Ripley's attractions worldwide, Ripleyzines and more!

Unlock exclusive videos, photos and more using your smartphone.

POINT - SCAN - REVEAL
IT'S THAT EASY!

Some of the amazing features in our new app

cartoons

Ripleyzines

▲ *Why not also download Ripley iSword on the app store now! The world's first ever sword swallowing app!*

facebook   twitter   Odditoriums

SEND US YOUR BELIEVE IT OR NOT!

Contribute via our website: www.ripleybooks.com

Send your stories to www.ripleys.com/submit

Send an email to bionresearch@ripleys.com

Or write to us: BION Research, Ripley Entertainment Inc., 7576 Kingspointe Parkway, 188, Orlando, Florida 32819, U.S.A.

The Great Inferno

Tim Cockerill, aka The Great Inferno, happily gargles hot molten lead until it cools and hardens into solid metal in his mouth. During the day, Tim is a zoologist at Cambridge University in the U.K.

When he is not working in the lab, or trekking through a jungle to study insects, Tim wows audiences with such stunts as hammering nails into his head, heating his tongue with a blowtorch and swallowing fire. The Great Inferno has been amazing audiences for more than 15 years with his extremely painful-looking acts.

TIM ON CHEWING MOLTEN LEAD

"Fire-eaters have been doing this stunt for over 200 years, and the technique is still a closely guarded secret. Just like fire-eating, it takes years of practice before you can be ready to perform, and even then it is still highly dangerous. First, the metal is melted in a small furnace, and then a small amount (about a tablespoon) is transferred to a spoon. I then take this into my mouth and keep it there until it solidifies completely. After about 30 seconds I spit the nugget out onto a tray or catch it with a pair of thick gloves."

TIM ON THE BLOCKHEAD STUNT

"The Human Blockhead was invented in the 1930s by sideshow performer Melvin Burkhart, 'The Anatomical Wonder.' What you see is what you get with this stunt—a solid steel nail is hammered all the way into the face. This is not something to be tried by anyone—get the angle wrong and the nail would go straight through the skull and into the brain!"

High Horse

From the 1880s through to the 1970s, one of the most popular shows on the Steel Pier in Atlantic City, New Jersey, was the horse high dive. Highly trained horses, usually ridden by girls, would leap from heights of up to 60 ft (18 m) into a pool 10 ft (3 m) deep. Riders asserted at the time that the horses enjoyed diving, were excellent swimmers, and were never forced to jump. However, owing to public pressure, diving horse shows died out in the 1970s and only one show remains—in a scaled-down form—in New York, where a riderless horse named Lightning will jump 10 ft (3 m) into water for a bucket of oats.

Lottery Luck

Since 1993, Joan Ginther of Las Vegas, Nevada, has won the Texas Lottery four times, each time scooping at least $1 million, with total prize money of more than $20 million. She bought two of her winning tickets at the same store in Bishop, Texas, while visiting her father. Her chances of winning four lottery jackpots were put at more than 200-million-to-one.

Roar Deal

A thief in Germany stole a circus trailer unaware that there was a five-year-old lion in the back. The vehicle was later abandoned with its engine running after crashing into a road sign. Police believe the driver may have panicked on hearing the lion—named Caesar—let out a hungry roar.

Dump Dig

Sanitation workers in Parsippany, New Jersey, dug through 10 tons of trash at a city dump to successfully recover a wedding ring that had been accidentally thrown away by a couple. Bridget Pericolo had placed the ring in a cup, but her husband of 55 years, Angelo, mistakenly threw it out with the garbage before leaving for work.

Spelling Mistake

The general manager of the Chilean mint was fired after the country's name was spelt incorrectly on thousands of coins. The 2008 batch of 50-peso coins bore the stamp CHIIE, but amazingly no one spotted the spelling mistake until late 2009.

Classroom Relic

In June 2010, while cleaning up her classroom before a move, schoolteacher Michelle Eugenio of Peabody, Massachusetts, discovered a colonial-era document dating back to April 1792 among a pile of old books and scraps of paper.

Mistaken Identity

The dead body of a 75-year-old man slumped over a chair on the balcony of his third-floor Los Angeles, California, apartment was left undisturbed for several days one October as his neighbors thought it was a Halloween dummy.

Incriminating Evidence

An 18-year-old from Philadelphia, Pennsylvania, turned himself in to police in December 2009 for stealing a cell phone—after he took a photo of himself with it and it automatically sent a copy to the owner's e-mail!

Double Take

When Helen MacGregor was sent a 21-year-old postcard of the town in Yorkshire, England, where she grew up, she was amazed to see herself in the center of the photo as a toddler. A friend had sent her the postcard of Otley, unaware that the child pictured in the street scene was Miss MacGregor, then aged three.

Close Relatives

Adopted by different families at a young age, biological brothers Stephen Goosney and Tommy Larkin finally found each other nearly 30 years later—and discovered that for the past seven months they had been living almost directly across the street from each other in Corner Brook, Newfoundland, Canada.

Unexpected Mourner

Brazilian bricklayer Ademir Jorge Goncalves gave friends and family a surprise in November 2009 by turning up at his own funeral. Relatives had identified him as the disfigured victim of a car crash in Parana state, but actually he had been out on a drinking spree and did not hear about his death until his funeral was already underway.

Party Bug

Bug-eating parties are all the rage in Tokyo, Japan, where guests chow down on dishes such as grilled cockroaches, fried grasshoppers, cricket pie, and this red moth larvae soup.

Giant Pumpkin

Christy Harp of Jackson Township, Ohio, took first place at the 2009 Ohio Valley Giant Pumpkin Growers' annual weigh-off with a pumpkin that weighed 1,725 lb (783 kg)— nearly ten times the weight of an average man. At one point her prizewinning pumpkin grew at a rate of 33 lb (15 kg) per day.

Curry Favor

Feeding curry to sheep could help save the planet by lowering methane emissions. The spices used in curry kill the "bad" bacteria in a sheep's gut, reducing the amount of methane the sheep produce by up to 40 percent.

Salsa Bowl

During the 2010 Jacksonville Tomato Fest in Texas, a team of 20 volunteers made a 2,672-lb (1,212-kg) bowl of salsa.

Chocolate Landmark

A team of Chinese confectioners built a 33-ft-long (10-m) replica of the Great Wall of China entirely out of chocolate. The wall was made of dark-chocolate bricks held together with layers of white chocolate. It was unveiled at the 2010 World Chocolate Wonderland exhibition, which also featured 560 chocolate replicas of China's 2,200-year-old famous Terracotta Army.

Earthy Taste

Thuli Malindzi, 22, of Cape Town, South Africa, is addicted to eating soil and consumes a chunk every day. She has been eating earth for more than ten years. Although she has tried to give up, she cannot resist hard lumps of clay, which she says to her taste like fudge.

Chocolate Wall

To mark the 20th anniversary of the fall of the Berlin Wall, French chocolate-maker Patrick Roger constructed a 49-ft-long (15-m) replica of the landmark in chocolate. Over a period of three weeks, he used 1,980 lb (900 kg) of chocolate to build the wall, and even added graffiti and artwork to the surface by spraying it with cocoa butter mixed with food coloring.

Scorpion Snack

Li Liuqun of Hunan Province, China, is addicted to eating live scorpions and estimates he has eaten more than 10,000 of them over the last 30 years. Stung by a huge scorpion one day, he angrily bit off its head and enjoyed the taste so much that he now eats up to 30 in a single sitting. Luckily, he appears immune to the venom, which can paralyze and even kill.

1821 Bun

A hot-cross bun baked on Good Friday, 1821, has been kept in a Lincolnshire, England, family for 190 years—and still shows no sign of mold. The fruity bun, which has the date March 1821 on its base, was made by Nancy Titman's great- great-great-grandfather, William Skinner, who owned a bakery in London. It was not eaten at the time and has been preserved in a box ever since, passed down through generations of the family as an unusual heirloom. The bun is now rock hard and the currants have disintegrated, but the shape of the cross is still visible.

Creative Cakes

Debbie Goard of Oakland, California, has created hundreds of incredibly lifelike custom-made cakes in the shape of animals, foodstuffs and everyday objects. Her cake designs include dogs, a scorpion, a warthog, a burger, popcorn, spaghetti, sneakers, a Blackberry, a camera and a baby giraffe that was nearly 2 ft (60 cm) tall. Her life-sized Chihuahua cake was so realistic that restaurant patrons were concerned there was a real dog on the table!

Buoyancy Castle

Three men from London, England, invented a bizarre new water sport when they fulfilled an ambition to ride a full-sized bouncy castle across Lake Garda in Italy. After drifting into the path of a sailing regatta and being redirected by a police launch, adventurers Jack Watkins, Chris Hayes, and Dave Sibley completed the 5-mi (8-km) voyage in two hours.

Yoga Queen

At the age of 87, Bette Calman of Williamstown, Victoria, Australia, still teaches up to 11 yoga classes per week. She can perform headstands and "bridges," and, from lying on her front, can raise her whole body off the ground using only her arms.

Mighty Pen

Three men in Hyderabad, India, have created a pen that is not only mightier than a sword but is the size of a giraffe! The brass pen, which cost more than $5,000 to make, stands 16 ft (4.9 m) tall, 1 ft (30 cm) wide, weighs 88 lb (40 kg), and is embossed with Indian cultural illustrations.

Remote Patrol

Burglars who broke into a man's apartment in Midwest City, Oklahoma, were caught via webcam by the man's wife more than 8,000 mi (12,875 km) away in the Philippines. Jim and Maribel Chouinard used the webcam to communicate face-to-face when they were apart.

Bike Jump

At Reno, Nevada, in 2009, U.S. motorcyclist Ryan Capes soared an astonishing 316 ft (96.3 m) through the air from one ramp to another.

Maggot Transfer

In May 2009, Charlie Bell of London, England, moved 37½ lb (17 kg) of live maggots from one container to another—in his mouth. He practiced at home with rice for months before finally replacing the grains with the "revolting" maggots.

Late Appointment

Reynolds Smith Jr. was appointed by the Alabama Democratic Party to sit on a party panel in October 2009—even though he had in fact died 11 months earlier!

Secret Stash

Calin Tarescu of Alba Iulia, Romania, discovered that his wife had thrown away a pair of his old shoes in which he had stashed $64,000. Police helped him to recover the majority of the money.

Hand Stolen

The mummified hand of a cheating gambler was stolen from a locked cabinet at a pub in Wiltshire, England, in March 2010. The hand, said to have been cut off a gambler caught cheating at the card game whist, was clutching a pack of 18th-century playing cards and is rumored to be cursed.

King Board

Californians Joe Ciaglia and Rob Dyrdek built a giant skateboard that measures 36 ft 7 in (11.15 m) long, 8 ft 8 in (2.6 m) wide, 3 ft 7 in (1.09 m) tall, and weighs more than 3,600 lb (1,634 kg). It is 12 times larger than a standard board and is so big it is fitted with car tires and has to be transported on a flatbed truck.

Edible Plates

To save on washing up after school dinners, catering boss Tiziano Vicentini from Milan, Italy, has devised a range of edible plates made from a kind of dough that is tough enough to last a lunchtime, but tasty enough to eat afterward.

Big Dipper

Students from Miami-Dade, Florida, filled a 13-gal (49-l) bucket with homemade guacamole. The dip weighed 4,114 lb (1,866 kg) and was made from 3,500 lb (1,588 kg) of avocados, 500 lb (227 kg) of tomatoes, 100 lb (45 kg) of mayonnaise, and 500 limes.

Triple Yolker

Bob Harrop from Devon, England, beat odds of 25 million to one when he found a triple-yolk egg while preparing his breakfast. The former hotelier has fried more than 155,000 eggs over the years and has seen hundreds of double yolkers, but this was the first time he had ever come across an egg with three yolks.

Chocolate Fashion

At the 15th Paris Salon du Chocolat in Shanghai, China, chefs and clothes designers from across the world combined their talents to create dresses, jackets, shoes and handbags all made from chocolate.

Expensive Bottle

In London, England, in 2009, jeweler Donald Edge unveiled a gold, pearl and diamond-encrusted bottle of Chambord raspberry liqueur that was valued at more than $2 million. The bottle featured 1,100 individual diamonds.

Pizza Chain

A chain of 2,200 pizzas stretching 1,630 ft (496 m) was laid out in 14 rows at Bucharest, Romania, in 2009. The pizza chain required 1,320 lb (600 kg) of flour, 880 lb (400 kg) of mozzarella, 440 lb (200 kg) of tomato sauce, 4 gal (15 l) of olive oil, and 6 lb 10 oz (3 kg) of yeast.

Moon Beer

In its thirst to create even better beer, the family-owned Brewery Caulier in Péruwelz, Belgium, has begun producing beer made by the light of a full moon. The full moon speeds up the fermentation process, shortening it from seven days to five, which can add extra punch to the beer, giving it a stronger flavor.

Frog's Heart

Customers in Japan who order Frog Sashimi eat the still-beating heart of a freshly killed American bullfrog. The rest of the frog is eaten as a raw dish, with any leftovers, including the feet, turned into soup.

Mummies

ANCIENT TATTOOS

In 2006, a 1,500-year-old, heavily tattooed, and very well-preserved female mummy was discovered in a mud-brick pyramid in northern Peru. She was buried with many weapons, leading experts to believe that she could have been a rare warrior queen of the warlike Moche people.

EGYPTIAN CAT

The ancient Egyptians, who practiced mummification on royal personages, also mummified animals. These underwent the same elaborate treatment as human corpses, with cloth wraps, a large amount of salt, and resin. This Egyptian cat is more than 2,000 years old.

THE ICE MAIDEN OF AMPATO

The frozen, mummified body of a teenage Inca girl was discovered near the 20,700-ft (6,310-m) summit of Mount Ampato, Peru, in 1995. It is thought that she was ritually sacrificed more than 500 years ago. Other mummified children have also been found on the mountain. The "Ice Maiden," as she is known, was removed from the site and is kept under controlled conditions in a Peruvian museum.

BABY MUMMY

This incredibly well-preserved, mummified body of a young Peruvian child, who died some 6,500 years ago, is one of the oldest mummies ever found, and is hundreds of years older than the earliest known Egyptian mummies. It formed part of the largest collection of mummies ever assembled, which went on display at the California Science Center in Los Angeles in 2010.

ANCIENT BEAUTY

In 1934, a Swedish archeologist discovered hundreds of ancient mummies buried under boats in a mysterious cemetery in a remote desert in the Xinjiang region of China. The location, which featured rivers and lakes thousands of years ago, was lost until 2000, and researchers began to excavate the area in 2003. They found the body of a woman thought to have died almost 4,000 years ago, who has become known as the most beautiful mummy in the world, owing to incredibly well-preserved features that even include her eyelashes.

Ant Arsonists

A house fire in Daytona Beach, Florida, was started by ants. Dozens of carpenter ants had built their nest around an electrical box and, when the insects came in contact with the live wiring, they ignited. The resulting flames burst out of the box, set fire to an adjacent desk, and then spread to the rest of the house.

Dead Candidate

Carl Robin Geary Sr. was elected mayor of Tracy City, Tennessee, on April 13, 2010, several weeks after he had died.

Parallel Lives

Identical twins Jim Lewis and Jim Springer from Ohio were separated a month after birth, then reunited at age 39. Both had divorced a Linda, married a Betty, had sons named James, driven blue Chevrolets, and owned dogs named Toy.

Lennon's Toilet

A toilet once owned by Beatle John Lennon was sold for the grand sum of $14,740. The builder who had removed the lavatory from Lennon's Berkshire, England, home in 1971 kept it in his shed for almost 40 years.

Granny Auction

Ten-year-old Zoe Pemberton of Essex, England, put her grandmother Marion Goodall up for sale on eBay in 2009, describing her as "cuddly" but "annoying." Although the listing was meant as a joke, bidding for the granny reached $30,000 before the auction website took it down.

Lot of Dough

Using a secret 1950s sourdough recipe involving Somerset flour, Cotswolds spring water, and Cornish sea salt, baker Tom Herbert from Gloucestershire, England, creates loaves of bread that cost more than $30 per loaf. Each 4½-lb (2-kg) hand-crafted shepherd loaf takes him two days to make from start to finish.

Unique Stamp

The one-of-a-kind Treskilling Yellow postage stamp is worth about $7.4 million. First issued in Sweden in 1855, it owes its value to the fact that it was printed in yellow by mistake, when the rest of the batch was green. It survives today thanks only to a 14-year-old Swedish schoolboy who rescued it from his grandmother's garbage bin in 1885 and sold it to a dealer for about $1.

Soap Drama

A wife from Pune, Maharashtra, India, divorced her husband on the grounds that his refusal to allow her to watch her favorite soap operas on TV amounted to a form of domestic cruelty.

Ear Wig

Radhakant Bajpai has a striking claim to fame: magnificent ear tufts that are longer than the hair on most men's heads, and probably the longest ear hair in the world. When Radhakant's hair was officially measured last, it stretched 5.2 in (13.2 cm), but since then it has more than doubled to a reported 11 in (28 cm). Although some think that his extreme ear hair is odd, Radhakant is very proud of his achievement.

Completely Hooked

Massachusetts stuntman Ses Carny, "the American Madman," entertains audiences by inserting two stainless-steel fishing hooks into his eyes. With the sharp hooks resting on the orbital bones at the base of the eyes, he then pulls down on the hooks to reveal what it looks like under his eyeballs!

Top of the World

Jordan Romero of Big Bear Lake, California, reached the summit of Mount Everest—at the age of just 13. He climbed with his father and three Sherpa guides, and on getting to the peak of the world's highest mountain he telephoned his mother and said: "Mom, I'm calling you from the top of the world." Jordan has conquered many of the world's highest mountains, and climbed Africa's Mount Kilimanjaro when he was only ten.

Limbo Queen

Shemika Charles from Buffalo, New York State, weighs 140 lb (63.5 kg) and stands 5 ft 9 in (1.75 m) tall, but can limbo under a bar just 8½ in (22 cm) off the ground—while carrying a tray with three fuel canisters in each hand.

Happy Meals

Kelvin Baines of Devon, England, began his collection of McDonald's Happy Meal toys in the 1980s and he now has more than 7,500.

Rubber Bands

Allison Coach, 11, from Chesterfield Township, Michigan, has created a rubber band chain that measures more than 1.3 mi (2.1 km) long. She keeps the chain, which consists of more than 22,000 rubber bands, wrapped around a wooden stand made by her grandfather.

Clog Dance

More than 2,500 people in Pella, Iowa, took part in a mass clog dance in May 2010. To ease the discomfort of the wooden shoes they were wearing, many of the dancers put on extra-thick socks or stuffed their clogs with sponges.

Blind Speedster

Turkish pop singer Metin Senturk drove a car at 182 mph (292.9 km/h)—even though he is blind. He drove a Ferrari F430 unaccompanied along the runway at Urfa airport, with a co-driver giving him instructions through an earpiece in his helmet from a car following behind.

Tower Leap

In May 2010, Algerian-born rollerblader Taig Khris leaped from the 131-ft-high (40-m) first floor of Paris's Eiffel Tower and landed safely onto a 98-ft-high (30-m) ramp.

Serpent Queen

While working for Ringling Bros. Circus in the 1880s, petite American Millie Betra, billed as the "Serpent Queen," regularly handled dozens of huge pythons that were almost twice her size, even wrapping many of the snakes around her body simultaneously.

Lucky Numbers

Beating astronomical odds, Ernest Pullen of Bonne Terre, Missouri, won $3 million in two separate lotteries in the space of three months. After picking up $1 million in June 2010, he won another $2 million in September, combining his lucky numbers with numbers he had dreamed about six years earlier when foreseeing that he would one day win a lot of money.

Mattress Mishap

After accidentally throwing away a mattress that her mother had stuffed with $1 million, a Tel Aviv woman searched in vain through Israeli landfill sites containing thousands of tons of garbage. She had bought her mother a new mattress as a surprise.

Own Phone

After his cell phone was stolen, a Californian man bought a new one on classifieds website Craigslist, choosing it because it looked just like his old phone. When it arrived, it actually was his old phone and still had his numbers stored. Luckily for the police, the thief had put his return address on the package.

Battle Dead

In 2010, Brian Freeman, a former Australian army captain, uncovered the forgotten site of a World-War-II battle in Papua New Guinea, with the bodies of three Japanese soldiers still lying where they fell in 1942. Local villagers led him to Eora Creek—the biggest single battle of the Kokoda campaign—where he found the remains of the soldiers, along with their weapons and equipment.

Balloon Daredevils

Early balloonists used highly flammable hydrogen gas instead of hot air or helium. In 1785, the French inventor Jean-Pierre Blanchard and American John Jeffries used an early hydrogen gas balloon to fly across the English Channel between England and France. When Jean-François Pilâtre de Rozier attempted to do the same, his balloon exploded and he became the first person to die in an air accident.

Delayed Delivery

Gill Smeathers of Northamptonshire, England, received a package in February 2010 that was postmarked November 4, 1982.

Inflated Numbers

During World War II, the 1,100 men of the U.S. Army's 23rd Headquarters Special Troops used inflatable vehicles, sound recordings, and fake radio broadcasts to deceive the enemy into thinking they were an army of 30,000 soldiers.

High Tea

Waiters serve lunch to two steel workers perched on a girder high above New York City in 1930. The men were working on the construction of the 47-story, 625-ft-high (190-m) Waldorf-Astoria Hotel on Park Avenue.

Faithful Feet

Hua Chi, a monk at a monastery near Tongren, China, has been coming to exactly the same spot to kowtow at the temple for so many years that perfect footprints have been worn into the wooden floor. For nearly 20 years he has carefully placed his feet to bend down, and lie prostrate, 2,000–3,000 times a day, although now that he's over 70 years old, he can manage only a thousand!

Four Babies

Four sisters from one family each gave birth within four days in 2010. The same obstetrician delivered the babies of Lilian Sepulveda, Saby Pazos and Leslie Pazos at the same Chicago, Illinois, hospital on August 6 and 7, and a fourth sister, Heidi Lopez, gave birth in California on August 9.

200 Grandkids

During her life, Yitta Schwartz (1917–2010) of Kiryas Joel, New York, had 15 children, more than 200 grandchildren, and a staggering total of more than 2,000 living descendants.

Cash Bonfire

Infamous Colombian drug baron Pablo Escobar once burned more than $1.5 million in cash to keep his daughter Manuela warm during a single night on the run. When he realized she was suffering from hypothermia at his mountain hideout, he lit a bonfire using wads of U.S. dollars.

Document Leak

A 2,400-page restricted document from the U.K.'s Ministry of Defence giving advice on how to stop documents leaking onto the Internet was itself leaked onto the Internet in 2009.

Fake Workers

After adding biometric scanning to record employee attendance, the city of Delhi, India, discovered 22,853 fake workers on its payroll.

Extra Time

A Thai man spent three extra years behind bars in an Indonesian prison because of a typo in his paperwork. Kamjai Khong Thavorn should have been released in 2007 after serving a 20-year sentence for possessing heroin, but a clerical error wrongly stated his first year in prison as 1997 instead of 1987. No one spotted the error until 2010.

End of War

Although fighting in World War I finished in 1918, the war did not officially end until October 3, 2010—92 years later—when Germany finally settled its war debt by paying $90 million, which was the last instalment of the reparations imposed on it by the Allies. Germany was forced to pay compensation toward the cost of the war by the 1919 Treaty of Versailles—the bill would have been settled much earlier but Adolf Hitler had reneged on the agreement.

Croc Monsieur

After receiving reports of a 12-ft-long (3.6-m) crocodile circling boats in the English Channel, French authorities banned swimming near Boulogne and broadcast warnings to vacationers in both French and English—only to discover that the reptile was nothing more dangerous than a floating piece of wood.

What Fire?

A man in Pittsburgh, Pennsylvania, slept while his house caught fire and part of the roof collapsed. It was not until fire crews did a walk-through of the house more than two hours later that he woke up.

Working Flat Out

Hurrying to impose new parking restrictions ahead of the 2010 Tall Ships sailing races, council workers in Hartlepool, England, painted yellow lines right over a squashed, dead hedgehog in the road rather than move the animal.

Slice of Luck

A restaurant in Hankou, China, selected from 15 applicants for the post of chef by asking the candidates to slice a melon on a woman's stomach. The successful candidate, Hu Gua, chopped up his melon in less than a minute without hurting the woman who was protected from the blade by just a thin sheet of plastic.

Taste Test

As a designer and tester with Fox's Biscuits, Simon Pope of West Yorkshire, England, is paid to eat more than 7,000 cookies every year.

Chicken Feast

At the 2010 Canoefest in Brookville, Indiana, 1,654 lb (750 kg) of fried chicken was served up in a donated canoe. Up to 200 volunteers had cooked the 2,700 lb (1,225 kg) of raw meat.

Lime Pie

During the Key West, Florida, 2010 Conch Republic independence celebration, locals used 1,080 Key limes to prepare a 450-lb (204-kg), 7-ft-wide (2.1-m) Key lime pie.

Margarine Marge

Restaurant owner Simon Smith of Staffordshire, England, celebrated the 20th birthday of *The Simpsons* by making a 4-ft-high (1.2-m) bust of his favorite character, Marge, out of margarine. He used 26 lb (12 kg) of special heat-resistant puff pastry margarine on the sculpture and achieved the shape by wrapping it around chicken wire.

Headless Chickens

In parts of Asia, no part of the chicken goes to waste. In Bangkok, the capital of Thailand, barbecued chicken-head kebabs are available to buy as fast food. Once cooked, the brain and soft tissue can be eaten. Roasted, boiled and deep-fried chicken heads are also popular.

Fiery Sauce

Eight teenagers in Augsburg, Germany, were treated in a hospital after a test of courage in which they drank chili sauce that was more than 200 times hotter than Tabasco sauce. The sauce reached 535,000 on the Scoville scale, which measures the hotness of sauce, compared to 2,500 for regular Tabasco sauce.

Haute Dog

New York City restaurant Serendipity 3 introduced a $69 hot dog in 2010. The Haute Dog comes with white truffle oil, a salted pretzel bed, truffle butter, duck foie gras, Dijon mustard, Vidalia onions and ketchup.

Locust Topping

When a plague of millions of locusts hit the town of Mildura, Victoria, Australia, pizza café owner Joe Carrazza put dozens of the dead insects on his pizzas as a topping.

A Bug's Life

Artist Chris Trueman of Claremont, California, came up with an unusual way to make this portrait of his younger brother dressed up as a cowboy look like an old, yellowed photograph—he used 200,000 dead ants.

At first Chris tried to catch the harvester ants himself, but he soon realized that it would take him years to catch enough for the painting. So, he bought the ants live over the Internet and, after killing them, incorporated their bodies into the painting with tweezers and a resin called Galkyd, which has a yellowish color. It took him about two weeks to apply each batch of 40,000 ants to the portrait. The painting was first exhibited at the Alexander Salazar gallery in San Diego, but is now owned by Ripley's and is on display in Ripley's Odditorium in Baltimore.

RIPLEY'S ASK

What is the story behind the original photograph?
I staged and photographed my youngest brother Bryce when he was six or seven. I had him dress up in my old cowboy outfit and hold my father's unloaded rifle. He was in my parents' suburban backyard. It was a menacing image, as he pretended to be a cowboy, but was holding a real gun.

Why did you decide to use ants for the image?
I was revisiting a specific experience from my childhood. When I was five years old, my younger brother and I attacked an anthill and were bitten by red ants. That was the first time I intentionally tried to harm intelligent life and, more than 25 years later, I decided to return to that experience. Ants ride the line of what we consider intelligent life—if we see them in the kitchen, many of us think little of killing them all. But if we take the time to look at them closely, they are in fact remarkable creatures.

How long did it take to complete?
It took several years, not because of the actual labor, but because at one point I started to feel bad about killing all of the ants and I stopped the project for over a year. Then I decided that because I was most of the way done, the first ants would have died in vain if I didn't finish the work, so I decided to continue. It was also quite an expensive work to produce as each shipment of ants would cost $500.

Red harvester ants are native to the southwestern U.S.A. and are relatively large, measuring ½ in (1.3 cm) long. They are venomous and will give a painful bite!

Nose for Trouble

An anti-landmine organization based in Belgium uses African giant pouched rats to sniff out deadly landmines in Mozambique and Tanzania. The rats' relatively light weight means they are unlikely to explode the mines, even when scratching at the ground to indicate their whereabouts. These super rats, trained with food rewards, are also able to smell the life-threatening disease tuberculosis, analyzing samples more than 50 times quicker than a laboratory scientist.

Surprise Visit

After nine-year-old Beatrice Delap wrote to Captain Jack Sparrow—Johnny Depp's character in the *Pirates of the Caribbean* movies—asking for help with an uprising against teachers at her school in Greenwich, London, Depp responded by turning up at the school in full pirate costume. The Hollywood star was in the area filming the fourth movie in the series and gave the school 10 minutes' notice that he was on his way.

Sold Soul

More than 7,000 online shoppers unwittingly agreed to sell their souls in 2010, thanks to a clause in the terms and conditions of a British computer-game retailer. As an April Fool's Day joke to highlight the fact that online shoppers do not read the small print, GameStation added a clause to its contract granting it a "non transferable option to claim, for now and for ever more, your immortal soul."

Unlucky Number

Superstitious phone company bosses in Bulgaria suspended a jinxed cell phone number—0888 888 888—after all three customers to whom it had been assigned over the previous ten years suffered untimely deaths.

Identical Couples

Identical twin brothers married identical twin sisters in a joint wedding ceremony in China. Grooms Yang Kang and Yang Jian sported different haircuts for the ceremony so that people could tell them apart, while brides Zhang Lanxiang and Jiang Juxiang wore differently colored wedding dresses.

Ghostly Sale

Two vials said to contain the spirits of ghosts exorcised from a house in Christchurch, New Zealand, were sold on an online auction site for more than $1,500 in March 2010. The sales pitch claimed that the "holy water" in the vials had dulled the spirits' energy and put them to sleep. To revive them, the buyer would need to pour the contents into a dish and let them "evaporate into your house." The seller, Avie Woodbury, said that once an exorcist's fee had been deducted, the proceeds of the spirit sale would go to an animal welfare group.

Dead Ringer

Biker David Morales Colón of San Juan, Puerto Rico, became a dead ringer for his idol Meat Loaf by attending his own funeral in 2010 on the back of his beloved Honda motorcycle. So that friends could pay their respects at his wake, undertakers mounted his embalmed body carefully on the machine, hiding a series of body braces beneath his clothes and covering his eyes with wraparound sunglasses.

Watch the Beardie

Charles Earnshaw of Anchorage, Alaska, displays his "Beards of a Feather" facial hair sculpture at the 2010 U.S. National Beard and Mustache Championships in Bend, Oregon. There were over 200 entrants, and this creation earned him a prize in the freestyle section.

Satan Image

A family in Budapest, Hungary, abandoned their new-look bathroom after an image of Satan appeared overnight in a tile. Emerging from her first shower in the freshly decorated room, Andrea Csrefko fled in horror when she noticed the horned head of the devil in one of the tiles. The spooky image had not been there when husband Laszlo had put the tiles up and no cleaning detergent was able to remove it.

Long Fry

John Benbenek of Buffalo, New York, was eating lunch at Taffy's Hot Dog Stand when he found a massive 34-in-long (85-cm) French fry in his meal.

Go Slow

Road safety campaigners in Canada encouraged motorists to reduce their speed by painting a large 3-D image of a child on to the road outside an elementary school in West Vancouver, British Columbia. The picture of a girl chasing after a ball appeared to come alive when drivers were 100 ft (30 m) away, giving them time to slow down.

Dummy Guard

In July 2010, two prisoners escaped from a jail in Argentina that, because of a lack of resources, was using a dummy to man one of its guard towers. Staff had put a prison officer's cap on a football to try to fool the convicts into thinking they were being watched from the tower by a real person.

Frozen Assets

In May 2010, the Iowa Court of Appeals ordered the family of Orville Richardson, who died in February 2009 at age 81, to exhume his body so that his head could be cut off and frozen. In 2004, he had signed a contract with an Arizona company and paid $53,500 to have his head placed in cryogenic suspension after his death, but his siblings had buried him instead.

Gold Rush

A huge 220-lb (100-kg) Canadian gold coin was sold at auction to a Spanish company for $4 million. One of only five $1 million Maple Leaf coins ever produced by the Royal Canadian Mint, it measures 21 in (53 cm) in diameter and is 1¼ in (3 cm) thick.

Changing Fortunes

Brothers Zsolt and Geza Peladi were homeless and living in a cave outside Budapest, Hungary, when they discovered in December 2009 that they were due to inherit part of their grandmother's multi-billion euro fortune.

Blood Match

Eight years after breaking into a house in rural Tasmania, Australia, Peter Cannon was convicted of armed robbery because his DNA matched that of blood found inside a leech at the scene of the crime.

Picture Perfect

When Royal Dutch Navy sergeant Dick de Bruin lost his camera while scuba diving off the Caribbean island of Aruba, he thought he would never see it again. However, seven months later the camera was found 1,130 mi (1,800 km) away by a coastguard at Key West, Florida—and although it was covered in crusty sea growth, it still worked.

Old Student

A woman in China became an elementary school pupil at age 102. Ma Xiuxian from Jinan, Shandong Province, started work in a cotton mill at age 13, but had always longed for a proper education. Eighty-nine years after leaving school, the grandmother went back, joining the grade one class at Weishan Road Elementary School. She used hearing aids to make sure she could hear the teacher and a magnifying glass to help read text books.

All the Nines

Henry Michael Berendes of Wisconsin was born at 9.09 a.m. on 9-9-09 and weighed 9 lb 9 oz (4.3 kg).

Piglet Bank

An Internet site is selling a piggy bank made from a real piglet! The brainchild of designer Colin Hart from Belfast, Northern Ireland, the taxidermied pig with a slot in its back costs $4,000 and must be ordered 12 months in advance.

Tattooed Ladies

The tattooed lady was an astonishing and beautiful addition to the circus sideshows, dime museums, and carnivals that were found in North America and Europe in the late 19th century.

They featured in such shows for around a hundred years, when the last tattooed lady retired, aged 80, in 1995.

DISOWNED

Betty was born in 1909. During a girls' weekend in Atlantic City, New Jersey, she got a small tattoo and, as a result, her family disowned her. She claimed she had no other choice but to get more tattoos and make a career out of them. Betty worked with many circuses and was an attraction at the 1939 New York World's Fair with the "John Hix Strange as it Seems" sideshow.

INK REPELLANT

One of the first Western women to be significantly tattooed was Irene Woodward. On her debut in 1882, she scandalized the public with her tattoos—until then tattoos had previously only been seen on sailors. Inked by her father, Irene maintained (probably not truthfully) that he did it to protect her from being captured by American Indians. Described on one show billboard as "A pretty picturesque specimen of punctured purity," Irene was a shy and dignified performer.

SHOCKING STORY

Every great tattooed lady had a sensational story, and Nora Hildebrandt dramatically claimed that she'd been forcibly tattooed by American Indians while tied to a tree for a year. She even said that Sitting Bull was involved in the murky affair. The truth was a little less scandalous—Nora's father tattooed soldiers fighting in the Civil War and used to practice his designs on his daughter. By the time she began to exhibit herself in 1882, she had 365 tattoos.

Name Game

Les Cool and Les Hot (above) once worked together as radio repairmen for the Babeck Music Company in Olympia, Washington State. And in another curious name twist, I.M. Wiser and his wife May B. Wiser lived in Washington, D.C., in the 1940s. Mr. Wiser is seen here with "a little Wiser."

Last Post

A postcard bringing holiday news to a couple in West Yorkshire, England, was delivered 40 years after it was posted.

Thumb Find

When fisherman Blake Robinson caught a 6½-lb (2.9-kg) lake trout at Flaming Gorge Reservoir, Wyoming, he discovered a human thumb inside it.

Small World

In 1980, when Alex and Donna Voutsinas lived in different countries and long before they met and married, they were captured in the same photo at Walt Disney World, Orlando, Florida. Five-year-old Donna was photographed at the same moment as three-year-old Alex, who then lived in Montreal, Canada, was being pushed down Main Street in a stroller by his father.

Shoe Thief

A second-hand shoe store owner stole more than 1,200 pairs of designer shoes by posing as a mourner at hospitals and funeral homes in South Korea. His victims were genuine friends and relatives of the deceased, who had slipped off their shoes in a traditional demonstration of respect. The thief would remove his own footwear, pay his respects, then put on a more expensive pair and walk off.

Force Farce

The entire police force in a Hungarian town quit after winning more than $15 million on the lottery in 2009. The 15-strong squad in Budaörs resigned immediately after scooping the jackpot.

Short Journey

Six-year-old Heidi Kay Werstler tossed a message in a bottle into the sea at Ocean City, New Jersey, in 1985 and it washed ashore 24 years later at Duck, North Carolina—less than 300 mi (480 km) away.

Swing the Lizard

As a change from roaming the grassland at India's Corbett National Park, an Indian elephant named Madhuri picked up a passing monitor lizard and played with it for several days. With the lizard's tail firmly grasped in her trunk, she carried it with her wherever she went, swinging it around in the air over and over again, sometimes tossing it high and even dropping it before finally letting the dazed reptile go.

Money to Burn

A German snowboarder stranded in the Austrian Alps for six hours in February 2010 was rescued after attracting attention by setting fire to his money. Stuck 33 ft (10 m) above ground after the ski lift was switched off at dusk, Dominik Podolsky was finally spotted by cleaners as he burned the last of his euros.

Buried Alive

After spending hours digging a 10-ft-deep (3-m) tunnel at a beach on Tenerife in Spain's Canary Islands, a 23-year-old German tourist had to be rescued when the sand collapsed and buried him up to his head. He was trapped on the beach for nearly two hours before 15 firefighters were able to free him.

Bridge Picnic

More than 6,000 people sat down to breakfast on Sydney's famous Harbour Bridge in October 2009 after it was closed to traffic and carpeted with grass for a giant picnic.

Bacon Envelopes

U.S. company J & D's Foods, whose motto is "Everything should taste like bacon," have created "Mmmvelopes," envelopes that have a bacon flavor when you lick them.

Face Paint

Lucky Diamond Rich (*right*) is almost 100 percent covered with tattoos. Every inch of his skin is inked, including his eyelids and the insides of his ears. Lucky's incredibly dense face tattoos have developed over the last few years: He was last featured in *Ripley's Believe It or Not! Expect the Unexpected*, and his amazing transformation can clearly be seen (*above*). A circus and street performer from Adelaide, Australia, Lucky has alloy-capped teeth with which he can perform extreme feats of strength.

Double Yolks

Fiona Exon from Cumbria, England, beat odds of more than a trillion to one when she discovered that all six eggs she had bought in a single carton from her local grocery store had double yolks.

Lucky Seven

On March 31, 2010, the four-number state lottery in Pennsylvania came up 7-7-7-7 and had a $7.77 million payout!

Bearded Mother

Richard Lorenc of Kansas finally tracked down his birth mother in 2010—and discovered that she is a famous bearded lady who as a young girl worked in a circus sideshow. Vivian Wheeler boasts an 11-in-long (28-cm) beard, as a result of inheriting the condition hypertrichosis, also known as werewolf syndrome, which causes the growth of excessive facial hair from an early age.

Lung Stolen

Organizers offered $2,000 for the return of a left lung that was stolen from a traveling exhibition of human cadavers in Peru in 2009.

Kept Corpses

Jean Stevens of Bradford County, Pennsylvania, lived with the corpse of her dead husband for ten years and with the body of her dead twin sister for almost a year. After her family members died, Jean had their embalmed bodies dug up and stored at her house. She maintained the immaculately dressed corpses as best she could, spraying sister June with expensive perfume and keeping her on a couch in a spare room while husband James rested on a couch in the garage.

Frustrated Caller

A woman from Clarksville, Tennessee, was arrested after she kept calling 911 to complain that a man refused to marry her.

Confused Clergy

Two female clerics at the same church in Cambridgeshire, England, share the same three names—Rhiannon Elizabeth Jones. Both are also graduates of the same college.

Off Road

Lin Su from China drove his brand new Subaru SUV 100 ft (30 m) into the sea from Sanya beach, Hainan Province, in 2010, before getting out and leaving his vehicle in the waves. He announced that the car was no longer needed, and that he had abandoned it as an offering to the Chinese dragon water god, to ask for respite for recent severe flooding. The Subaru was eventually salvaged from the sea by the police.

Cash Stash

Four children aged between ten and 13 who found $20,000 stuffed in a brown envelope on their way to school in Frankfurt, Germany, shared it out among their friends in the playground. After teachers were alerted, police managed to recoup most of the cash.

Antique Gown

When three-month-old George Parfitt was baptized in Devon, England, he wore the same antique christening gown that had been used by 20 members of his family since it was made by his great-great-great-grandmother in 1884.

51

Cheating Death

GREAT BALL OF FIRE

Pilot Captain Brian Bews parachuted to safety seconds before his $30-million CF-18 fighter jet crashed and exploded in a devastating ball of fire at Lethbridge County Airport, Alberta, Canada. Having completed his practice routine for the 2010 Alberta International Air Show, he was returning to the airport when the plane suddenly nose-dived on approach. Just 100 ft (30 m) from the ground, he managed to escape using the plane's rocket-powered ejector seat. Moments later, the plane smashed into the ground and was engulfed in smoke and flames, but Captain Bews survived with only minor injuries.

CHEATED DEATH

Stunt pilot Dino Moline cheated death by a split second by deploying his built-in parachute after a wing of his plane fell off at an air show in Santa Fe, Argentina. After performing a series of daring, acrobatic maneuvers, Moline was flying upside down when he felt an explosion and saw the shadow of the detached wing pass the cockpit. As the plane spiraled out of control, he instantly activated its parachute, which slowed the aircraft's descent and allowed it to float gently to the ground where it caught fire. Moline escaped with only one small injury— a burned foot.

GLIDER CRASH

Former racing-car driver Mike Newman escaped unharmed except for three broken vertebrae after the glider he was piloting crashed at high speed into the runway in front of 15,000 spectators at an air show in West Sussex, England. After performing his routine, he prepared to land but a malfunction caused the glider to plunge almost vertically to the ground, striking its wing first. The nose section crumpled around him and the cockpit burst open, leaving him dangerously exposed. He lay stunned amid the wreckage for a minute before managing to stumble out onto the runway.

BELIEVE IT!

Sundae Lunch

A London ice-cream parlor offered a new twist on the traditional British Sunday roast, with each course being a frozen dessert. The "Sundae Lunch," designed by Italian mixologist Roberto Lobrano, comprised a starter of fresh pea sorbet with mint, followed by a main course of beef bouillon and horseradish sorbet topped with a Yorkshire pudding wafer. The final course was an apple-and-blackberry-crumble gelato.

Chocolate Coin

Chocolatiers Gary Mitchell, Jess Nolasco, and Rita Craig, from Purdy's Chocolates, Vancouver, Canada, spent more than eight hours making a 25-lb (11.3-kg) chocolate coin, measuring 24 in (60 cm) wide and 1½ in (4 cm) thick, and valued at $625.

Fast Food

"Humble" Bob Shoudt from Royersford, Pennsylvania, won first prize of $2,500 for eating 7 lb 14½ oz (3.58 kg) of French fries in ten minutes at the Curley's Fries Eating Championship at Morey's Piers, Wildwood, New Jersey, in May 2010.

Fat Dragon

Japanese-born pastry chef Naoko Sukegawa created a sculpture of a dragon made from margarine. The dragon, built over a steel and mesh frame, stood 29 in (74 cm) high, weighed 35 lb (16 kg), and took four months to make.

54

Mice Lunch

While making sandwiches for his family, a father from Oxfordshire, England, found an unwelcome ingredient in the bread he had bought from a local grocery store—a dead mouse baked into the half-eaten loaf. To make matters worse, the unfortunate rodent was missing its tail, leading Stephen Forse to wonder whether his family had already eaten it.

Sushi Roll

In November 2009, hundreds of students at the University of California, Berkeley, assembled a 330-ft-long (100-m) sushi roll. They used 200 lb (90 kg) of rice, 180 lb (82 kg) of fish, 80 lb (36 kg) of avocado and 80 lb (36 kg) of cucumber. To cater for vegetarians, the final 15 ft (4.5 m) contained tofu instead of seafood.

Status Symbols

Pineapples were status symbols in 17th-century Britain, and wealthy people would rent them by the day to place on their dinner table and impress their friends.

Super Potato

Amateur gardener Peter Glazebrook of Northampton, England, grew a potato that weighed 8 lb 4 oz (3.74 kg)—the weight of a newborn baby and 25 times more than the weight of an average potato. The supersized potato would make 66 bags of potato chips, 33 portions of fries, 80 roast potatoes, or 44 portions of mashed potato.

Vintage Cognac

A French entrepreneur bought a bottle of Cognac dating back to 1788—the year before the French Revolution—for nearly $37,000 at a Paris wine auction in December 2009.

Banana Bonanza

Banana peels make up more than half of the trash collected on Scotland's Ben Nevis mountain. During a September 2009 survey, more than 1,000 discarded banana skins were found on the summit plateau.

March of the Lava

Run! These scientists got a little too close when the eruption began in 1983.

The active volcano of Kilauea in Hawaii has been constantly erupting since 1983, and its unstoppable flow of burning lava has devastated hundreds of homes and businesses in its vicinity. Incredibly, it has also gradually extended Hawaii's coastline by an area the size of Washington, D.C.

In 1990, the entire town of Kaimù and part of the town of Kalapana were buried under 50 ft (15 m) of slow-moving lava from Kilauea. Despite the constant threat from the volcano, there are a few Kalapana residents who still choose to live alongside the lava.

As the lava builds in height, road signs are lifted out of the ground before the lava cools to solid rock.

The building finally succumbs to the heat.

Molten lava oozes toward the house.

Down the Drain

This giant chasm in Lake Berryessa, California, is the biggest drain hole in the world, at 30 ft (9 m) in diameter. When the lake reaches capacity, water tips over the lip of the drain and surges down a 700-ft-long (213-m) concrete pipe to exit through the Monticello Dam some 300 ft (91 m) below. Swimming or even boating near the hole is strongly discouraged; in 1997, a swimmer strayed too close and was sucked into the powerful drain. Water gushes through the "glory hole," as locals have named it, at a rate of 362,057 gal (1,370,534 l) every second—that's enough to fill 15,000 bathtubs. When the lake's level is low, local skateboarders and BMX bikers ride the giant exit pipe.

King Carbone

Former flower grower Giorgio Carbone spent nearly 50 years championing the independence of the Italian village of Seborga, which he claimed should be recognized as a separate nation because it had never been formally included in the 19th-century unification of Italy. Proclaiming himself His Tremendousness Giorgio I, he ruled over 360 subjects until his death in 2009. He gave the principality its own currency, stamps, flag and even a Latin motto—*Sub Umbra Sede* ("Sit in the Shade").

Inaccessible Inn

Built in the middle of the 17th century, the Old Forge pub on the Knoydart peninsula in Northern Scotland can be reached only by boat or by walking 18 mi (29 km) from the nearest road over hills that rise to 3,500 ft (1,067 m).

Acid Drip

Snottites are colonies of bacteria that hang from the ceilings of caves and are similar to stalactites. The bacteria derive their energy from volcanic sulfur compounds and drip sulfuric acid that is as corrosive as battery acid.

Dam Cops

Nevada's Hoover Dam has its own police department whose duties include protecting the dam and safeguarding the lives of visitors and employees.

Sewer Fat

In a huge underground cleanup of central London in 2010, more than 1,000 tons of putrid fat were removed from sewers—enough fat to fill nine double-decker buses.

Moon Lake

Lake Titan, on the north of Saturn's moon, is 39,000 sq mi (101,000 sq km), bigger than Lake Superior. The lake is most likely filled with liquid methane and ethane.

Limestone Forest

Water erosion has turned parts of Madagascar's Tsingy de Bemaraha National Park into forests of giant limestone spikes made of fossils and shellfish that died in the sea 200 million years ago.

Desert Snow

China's largest desert, the Taklamakan, covers approximately 125,000 sq mi (325,000 sq km) and, in January 2008, snow blanketed the entire area for the first time ever.

Jesus Image

While looking for holiday destinations on the mapping website Google Earth, Zach Evans from Southampton, England, spotted an outline of the face of Jesus Christ in satellite pictures of a field near Puspokladany, Hungary.

Hanging Coffins

The Bo people, an ethnic group from China's Sichuan Province that disappeared hundreds of years ago, hung the coffins of their dead on the sides of cliffs. The coffins were lowered on ropes from above to rest on precipices or wooden stakes. Some were hung as high as 425 ft (130 m) above ground, as the belief was that the higher the coffin was placed, the more propitious it was for the dead. The earliest hanging coffins found in the region date back 2,500 years.

Great Hedge

The Great Hedge of India was planted across the country by the British in the mid-19th century to prevent salt smuggling. The barrier of living impenetrable thorny hedge was 2,000 mi long (3,200 km) and was patrolled by up to 14,000 attendants.

Last Speaker

An ancient dialect called Bo, thought to date back 65,000 years, became extinct in 2010 after Boa Sr., the last person to speak it, died on a remote Indian island. At 85, Boa Sr. was the oldest member of the Great Andamanese Bo tribe before her death in Port Blair, the capital of Andaman and Nicobar Islands.

Burning River

The Cuyahoga River in Ohio was so polluted in the 20th century that it caught fire more than half a dozen times.

Volcano Video

In May 2009, U.S. scientists videotaped an undersea volcanic eruption off the coast of Samoa, 4,000 ft (1,220 m) beneath the surface—the first time a sea-floor eruption had been filmed.

Rabbit Island

It cost more than one million dollars to rid the tiny Scottish island of Canna of rats in 2006, and now, less than four years later, it has been overrun with thousands of rabbits—because there are no rats to keep their numbers down! The island's only restaurant has responded by adding a number of rabbit dishes to its menu.

Mail Boat

Since 1916, a boat has been delivering mail to dozens of homes on Lake Geneva, Wisconsin—and because it never stops, teenage carriers are hired to jump off the moving boat, put the mail in mailboxes on the dock, then scurry back on board, hopefully without falling into the lake.

Watery Grave

As drought conditions dried up a pond in Aligarh, Uttar Pradesh, India, in May 2009, 98 human skulls were found at the bottom.

Sparsely Populated

The state of Nevada covers an area about the size of the U.K. and Ireland combined, but has only 70 towns, whereas the British Isles has more than 40,000.

Shifting City

The Chilean earthquake of February 27, 2010, moved the city of Concepción about 10 ft (3 m) to the west. The quake was so powerful that it shortened the length of the day by 1.26 microseconds, and even Buenos Aires—840 mi (1,350 km) from Concepción—shifted by 1.5 in (3.8 cm).

Dual Rule

The U.S. city of Bristol straddles the borders of Virginia and Tennessee and has two governments, one for each side.

Huge Hailstone

A giant hailstone that fell in Vivian, South Dakota, on the night of July 23, 2010, measured 8 in (20 cm) in diameter, 18½ in (47 cm) in circumference, and weighed 1 lb 15 oz (900 g)! This and other ice missiles were so large that some punched holes into roofs big enough for householders to put their arm through, while other hailstones gouged holes in the ground more than an inch (2.5 cm) deep.

Bone Décor

The Sedlec Ossuary in Sedlec, Czech Republic, is a Roman Catholic chapel containing more than 40,000 human skeletons, the bones of which have been arranged to form the chapel's decorations and furnishings.

Tough Tree

A Sabal palm tree with a 6-in-wide (15-cm) hole through its trunk has survived several hurricanes in Estero, Florida.

Taking a Liberty

At 8.45 p.m. on the night of September 22, 2010, New York City photographer Jay Fine took this incredible photo of lightning striking the Statue of Liberty. He spent two hours braving the storm and took more than 80 shots before finally striking lucky. The iconic statue attracts more than 600 bolts of lightning each year.

Poop Light

In 2010, a park in Cambridge, Massachusetts, had a street light that was powered by dog poop. Created by artist Matthew Mazzotta, the "Park Spark" project encouraged dog walkers to collect their pets' poop in biodegradable bags and drop it into one of two 500-gal (1,900-l) steel tanks. Microbes in the waste gave off methane gas, which was fed through a second tank to the lamp and burned off.

School Mascot

The mascot of Yuma Union High School in Yuma, Arizona, is a criminal dressed in a prison uniform. It was adopted nearly a century ago after classes were held in a prison building when the original school burned down.

Railroad Room

The Washington Hotel in Tokyo, Japan, has created a special room for model railway enthusiasts to sleep in. It includes a grand model of the local area, complete with working railroads. Train lovers can bring their own models or, alternatively, the hotel will happily provide some.

Tunnel Vision

Over a period of four weeks, sculptors Dan Havel and Dean Ruck from Houston, Texas, transformed two connected properties to create a large, tunnel-like vortex, making it look as if the interior of the buildings had exploded. The outer skin of the two houses—made from planks of pine—was peeled off and used to create a 60-ft-long (18-m) spiral, which narrowed to a width of about 2 ft (60 cm) at the far end.

Cigarettte House

A house in Hangzhou, Zhejiang Province, China, is brightly decorated throughout with more than 30,000 empty cigarette packets. The occupant collected them over a period of six years and has even created seats and tables from the empty packs.

Mecca Clock

The Royal Mecca Clock, located on a skyscraper in Mecca, Saudi Arabia, has four amazing faces each measuring 151 ft (46 m) in diameter—that's more than six times larger than the faces of London's Big Ben clock. Over 90 million pieces of colored glass mosaic decorate the sides of the clock, which is visible from every part of the city. On special occasions, 16 bands of vertical lights shoot from the clock 6 mi (10 km) into the sky.

Home Wrecker

In February 2010, a man bulldozed his $350,000 Moscow, Ohio, home when a bank claimed it as collateral for outstanding debt.

Lost Language

The writing on the back of a letter discovered in 2008 by archeologists at a 17th-century dig site reveals a previously unknown language spoken by indigenous peoples in northern Peru. The letter, found under a pile of clay bricks in a collapsed church near Trujillo, shows a column of numbers written in Spanish and translated into a mysterious language that has been extinct for at least 400 years.

Vast Collection

The British Museum in London has 80,000 objects on display—but that is only one percent of its total collection.

Rotating House

A rotating house north of Sydney, Australia, guarantees Luke Everingham and his family a different view every time they wake up. The octagonal-shaped house sits on a turntable powered by a small electric motor and controlled by a computer, which allows it to move on demand, completing a full rotation in half an hour.

Whistle Blowers

Officials in Alor Setar, Malaysia, blow whistles loudly at litterbugs in the hope of shaming them into never littering again.

65

Buried Lake

At 155 mi (250 km) long and 31 mi (50 km) wide, Lake Vostok is about the same size as Lake Ontario—but lies beneath 2.5 mi (4 km) of Antarctic ice.

Ginkgo Stink

The ginkgo tree species, native to Asia, is so resilient that several trees survived the atomic bomb blast in Hiroshima, Japan. However, their smell is becoming a problem in Iowa City, U.S.A. When the tree eventually drops its seed shells, it produces a sticky mess that smells of rotten eggs, creating a very smelly city.

River Logjam

Over several centuries, a natural logjam in North America's Red River grew to a length of more than 160 mi (256 km). When people began clearing it in the early 1800s, it took 40 years to complete the task.

Lightning Storm

In just one hour on September 9, 2010, Hong Kong was hit by 13,102 lightning strikes. The violent electrical storm contained wind gusts of 62 mph (100 km/h) and caused power cuts that left people trapped in elevators.

Pink Lake

Lake Retba (the Rose Lake), situated 25 mi (40 km) north of Dakar in Senegal, has pink water, which can even turn purple in strong sunshine. The 1-sq-mi (3-sq-km) lake gets its unusual color from unique cyan bacteria in the water and also from its very high salt content.

Widespread Snow

On February 12, 2010, all of the states in the U.S.A. except Hawaii received some snow.

Asteroid Blast

A 33-ft-wide (10-m) asteroid exploded with the energy of three Hiroshima atom bombs in the atmosphere above Indonesia on October 8, 2009. The asteroid hit the atmosphere at about 45,000 mph (72,000 km/h), causing a blast that was estimated by NASA to be equivalent to 55,000 tons of TNT, and which was heard by monitoring stations 10,000 mi (16,000 km) away. There was no damage on the ground, however, because it occurred at least 9.3 mi (15 km) above the Earth's surface.

Life on Mars?

Huge plumes of methane—a gas that can indicate the presence of living organisms—have been found on the northern side of Mars. The methane may come from live organisms or from the decomposing remains of dead ones.

Hot Water

At the bottom of shallow bodies of very salty water, temperatures can reach 176°F (80°C) and stay that way 24 hours a day.

Unconquered Peak

Gangkhar Puensum, a mountain in Bhutan standing 24,836 ft (7,570 m) tall, is the highest unclimbed mountain on the planet.

Floating Stump

The Old Man of the Lake, a 30-ft-tall (9-m) tree stump, has floated around Crater Lake, Oregon, for more than 100 years. During that time, high winds and waves have caused it to move great distances—in one three-month period of observation in 1938 it traveled more than 62 mi (100 km).

Fog Nets

Communities in Chile's Atacama Desert use nets to catch the morning fog—the only accessible fresh water in the region. One of the driest places on Earth, it gets significant rainfall only two to four times a century, and in some parts of the desert no rain has ever been recorded.

Starling Flock

Thousands of starlings in the sky above Taunton in Somerset, England, formed the shape of one giant starling! These acrobatic birds have created many different patterns in the sky, including a rabbit, a rubber duck and a turtle.

Storm Hole

A Guatemala City clothing factory and an entire traffic intersection were swallowed by a cavernous sinkhole, which suddenly opened up during a tropical storm in 2010. The sinkhole was almost perfectly round and measured 65 ft (20 m) wide and 100 ft (30 m) deep.

Jet Power

The Dubai Fountain, located beside the Burj Khalifa skyscraper in Dubai, is almost 900 ft (275 m) long and can fire jets of water 500 ft (150 m) into the air.

Souvenir Snowball

For more than 30 years, Prena Thomas of Lakeland, Florida, has kept a snowball in her freezer—the souvenir of a rare Florida snowfall. When 2 in (5 cm) of snow fell on the normally balmy state on January 19, 1977, she was so surprised that she collected some of the snow and put it in her freezer.

Cave Man

After living in a 7-ft-wide (2.1-m) cave for 16 years, officials evicted Hilaire Purbrick of Brighton, England, in 2009 because his underground home lacked a second fire exit.

No Flow

When astronauts cry in space, their tears stay in a ball against their eyes until they are wiped away, because there is no gravity to make them fall naturally.

Violent Quake

On February 7, 1812, a massive earthquake struck near New Madrid, Missouri, and shook so violently that the Mississippi River flowed backward for several hours.

Windy Planet

Wind speeds of 4,350 mph (7,000 km/h) were measured in 2010 in the atmosphere of planet HD209458b, which orbits a star in the constellation Pegasus, some 150 light years from Earth. The planet has a temperature of about 1,800°F (1,000°C) on its hot side.

Space Smash

A 4.6-billion-year-old meteorite smashed through the windshield of a truck in Grimsby, Ontario, Canada, in September 2009. Minutes beforehand, local astronomers had witnessed a "brilliant fireball," 100 times brighter than a full moon, streaking across the night sky.

Fish Rain

For two days in February 2010, the remote desert town of Lajamanu in Australia's Northern Territory was bombarded with hundreds of small fish falling from rain clouds in the sky—even though it is 326 mi (525 km) from the nearest river.

Disappearing Island

An island that was at the center of a 30-year dispute between India and Bangladesh disappeared beneath rising seas in 2010. Measuring 2.2 mi (3.5 km) long and 1.9 mi (3 km) wide, uninhabited New Moore Island in the Bay of Bengal had been claimed by both countries—however, environmental experts said that global warming had finally resolved the matter of ownership.

Deadly Icicles

In the winter of 2009 to 2010, Russia's coldest in 30 years, five people were killed and over 150 injured by icicles falling from the rooftops of buildings in St. Petersburg.

Snowball Payment

For hundreds of years, Scotland's Clan MacIntyre delivered a single snowball in the summer to Clan Campbell as part of a long-standing debt.

Freeze that Fire!

When water was used to put out a burning building in Montreal, Quebec, Canada, in the late 19th century, the air temperature was so cold that the water quickly turned to ice.

St. James Street Fire, Montreal

Haunted House

Josh Bond of Cuchillo, New Mexico, put his 130-year-old haunted house up for sale on the Internet auction site eBay. The listing offered 1,250 sq ft (115 sq m) of space spread over three bedrooms, an antique wood-burning stove, and the spirits of the restless dead.

New Ocean

A 2005 volcanic eruption caused a 35-mi-long (56-km) rift, 20 ft (6 m) wide in places, to open up in the Ethiopian desert in just days. In 2010, geologists predicted that the rift would slowly become a new ocean, as Africa begins to split in two.

Cursing Festival

Every February, youngsters in the neighboring South Nepalese villages of Parsawa and Laxmipur hurl insults at each other and passersby in a ten-day cursing festival. On the final day of the festival, they set heaps of straw ablaze and celebrate the Hindu festival of Holi, which is marked by raucous "play" fights using powdered colored paints and water. Villagers say the best thing about the tradition is there are no bad feelings after the festival.

More Singapore

Thanks to numerous land reclamation projects, the island city-state of Singapore has 20 percent more land than it did four decades ago.

Cargo Cult

For more than 60 years, villagers on the island of Tanna, Vanuatu, have worshiped "John Frum," an American they believe will one day return with a bounty of cargo. Clan leaders first saw the mysterious figure in the late 1930s and he is said to have appeared before them again during World War II, dressed in white like a Navy seaman. In his honor, the islanders celebrate John Frum Day every February 15.

Crystal Clouds

Noctilucent clouds are formed by ice crystals 50 mi (80 km) above the Earth, on the very edge of space. They reflect sunlight at night, so that they glow.

Tree Dwellers

Members of the Korowai tribe of Papua New Guinea live in tree houses that are built as high as 150 ft (46 m) off the ground. They reach them by climbing vines or stairs carved into the trunks.

Starfish Graveyard

More than 10,000 starfish died on a beach in Norfolk, England, in December 2009 after being washed ashore during a storm. The creatures had gathered in the shallows to feed on mussels, but were swept on to the beach during high tide and quickly perished once they were out of water.

Shrinking Storm

Jupiter's giant storm, the Great Red Spot, shrank by more than 0.6 mi (1 km) per day between 1996 and 2006.

Passion Play

The village of Oberammergau, Bavaria, Germany, has held a Passion play, depicting the Crucifixion of Jesus, every ten years with few exceptions since 1633, when villagers swore an oath to perform the play every decade after their town was spared from the plague.

High Cloud

Morning Glory clouds, which appear regularly over Northern Australia each spring, stand 1 mile (1.6 km) high and can stretch for hundreds of miles. The clouds are often accompanied by sudden wind squalls and can move at speeds of up to 37 mph (60 km/h).

Festival of the Skulls

Every year worshipers in the Bolivian city of La Paz offer gifts of flowers, food and alcohol to the "snub noses"—decorated skulls of their relatives—to thank the dead for protecting the homes of the living. The "Day of the Skulls" festival is part of wider "Day of the Dead" rituals across Latin America, and traditionally entire skeletons were honored in this way.

71

All the Fun of the Fair

CHICAGO WORLD'S FAIR
MAY 27th
NOV. 1st

1833 A CENTURY OF PROGRESS 1933

Between 1933 and 1934, about 48 million people visited the Chicago World's Fair—a showcase of thousands of exhibits including the latest scientific, architectural and transport innovations.

The Century of Progress Exposition, as the Fair was known, was held to commemorate Chicago's 100th anniversary and to illustrate the amazing technological developments that had taken place worldwide in that time. It was staged on an area of 427 acres (173 ha) along the shoreline of Lake Michigan, and opened on May 27, 1933. It closed on November 12, but had proved so popular that it was re-opened the following May, and ran until the end of October 1934.

SKY RIDE, CHICAGO WORLD'S FAIR

36A29

HAVOLINE THERMOMETER *Century of Progress International Exposition* CHICAGO 1933

ROCKET TRAVEL

The most recognizable symbol of the Fair was the Sky Ride, an aerial tramway that visitors used to travel from one side of the Fair to the other. It had a span of 1,850 ft (564 m) and two towers 628 ft (191 m) tall. Visitors could travel to the top of the towers using high-speed elevators that ascended at a rate of 700 ft (213 m) per minute, and from the top, four different states were visible on a clear day. Suspended from the tramway 220 ft (67 m) above ground were rocket-shaped cars, each carrying 36 passengers across the Fair.

HIGH-RISE TEMPERATURE

Another principal landmark of the Fair was the 218-ft-high (67-m), 21-story thermometer that was sponsored by the motor oil manufacturer Havoline. The air temperature was shown by means of neon light tubes on the outside of the building.

Fair Facts

- The electric lighting for the 1934 Fair came from 250,000 incandescent bulbs and totaled 30,000,000,000 candlepower—enough electricity to supply the needs of a town of 10,000 people.

- More than six million people rode in the Sky Ride elevators in the first 5½ months of the Fair.

- If all the steel cable in the Sky Ride had been stretched out in a single cable, it would have been more than 100 mi (160 km) long.

- The fountain at the 1934 Fair shot water 45 ft (14 m) into the air, pouring out 68,000 gal (260,000 l) a minute.

- A restaurant seating 3,500 people was a replica of the Old Heidelberg Inn, Germany.

- On October 26, 1933, the 776-ft-long (238-m) German airship Graf Zeppelin visited the Fair.

- The 1933 Fair employed 350 painters to create a "carnival of color" by using 25 different exterior colors and 36 interior colors of more than 25,000 gal (113,500 l) of paint to cover 10,500,000 sq ft (975,500 sq m) of surface area.

Ripley's Odditorium

Also appearing at the Fair was the first-ever Ripley's Odditorium, which was one of the most popular crowd-pullers, attracting over two million visitors. Show-business agent Clint Finney had been assigned by Robert Ripley to find the best performers to appear at this Odditorium, and Finney managed the show in 1933 and 1934 with C.C. Pyle. With their help, Ripley scoured the world for unusual performers, his "human rarities and oddities." Ripley's many international contacts also sent him photographs and telegrams suggesting possible people to include.

A CENTURY OF PROGRESS
INTERNATIONAL EXPOSITION
1933

Serial No. 11303   1933
IDENTIFICATION CARD
(NOT A PASS)
S. B. Ricketts   2
EMPLOYEE OF CONCESSIONAIRE
International Oddities, Inc.
AT A CENTURY OF PROGRESS
PAY ROLL No.
EMPLOYEE'S SIGNATURE
S. B. Ricketts
ACCEPTED SUBJECT TO CONDITIONS ON PASS
ISSUED BY
A CENTURY OF PROGRESS
Lenox R. Lohr
GENERAL MANAGER
FORM 5 O 44

NOTICE TO KULI ALI BEI, FAKIR CEKANAVICIUS AND OTHERS

People with peculiar characteristics or peculiar physical built (freaks), are wanted for worlds Fair in Chicago, from June 1 to November 1, 1934. certain firm will pay a round trip passage fare living expenses such as meals, board etc. to such exponents that will be demonstrated at fair. The firm will cover all expenses and ages to guides who will accompany non English speaking exponents. It will also furnish all documentary needs and formalities for the entrance into the United

Postal Telegraph
THE INTERNATIONAL SYSTEM
Commercial Cables   All America Cables
Mackay   Radio
following message, subject to the terms on back hereof

New York   Aug. 21, 1933
Captain Goio
Imperial Hotel   Dubrovnik   Jugu Slavia
rrange to bring small man and father to America at onc
ll pay all expenses and reasonable salar
otos immediately

Postal Telegraph
THE INTERNATIONAL SYSTEM
Commercial Cables   All America Cables
Mackay   Radio

19 54 WIRELESS COLLECT VIA MACKAYRADIO=N MANILA 1048A MAR 7
1934
RIPLEY KINGSYN=
=NEWYORKNY (RIPLEY KINGS FEATURES SYNDICATE 235 EAST 45 ST)=
AINABLE TWELVE MALE FEMALE PRIEST MAGNUNUS FIRE WALKERS
IRITUALIST DAGGER CEREMONY PRECEDING WALK STOP OBTAINABLE UP
O FIFTY COMPLETE SETS BONTOC IGOROT HEADHUNTERS ARMS WAR
OSTUMES PARAPHERNALIA FOR RITUALS DANCES CORRECTLY EXECUTED
ountaineers ALLOTTED TRAVEL NO DIFFERENCE LANGUAGE
APPEARANCE STOP IF INTERESTED CABLE FUNDS=
LILIUS CABLE ADDRESS AEOLUS.
Telegraph 851P   al Telegraph

Official Post Card of
RIPLEY'S
"BELIEVE-IT-OR-NOT"
ODDITORIUM
A CENTURY OF PROGRESS

The name & address on this card was written upside down and backwards and at ease. Now see if you can read this just fill in the closed spaces, not the open ones.
WHATS 1/2 of 12, vg = XII
CUT WALS VII

POST CARD
CENTURY OF PROGRESS
CHICAGO 1933
1933 U.S. POSTAGE 1933

Robert L. Ripley
c/o New York American,
South Street,
New York City,
N.Y.

Believe It or Not
ODDITORIUM
ripley

INTERNATIONAL ODDITIES, INCORP...
666 LAKE SHORE DRIVE
CHICAGO, ILLINOIS

May 8, 1934.

ELIEVE-IT-OR-NOT" EXHIBITION
NTURY OF PROGRESS
E 1. TO OCTOBER 31, 1934.

Memo for Mr. Simpson:

In regard to the Chin... man that
you believe could be dressed in Korean reli... costume
and... a good attraction, beg to advise th... ere are
m... here wh... from... ot beli... would
 making a... rati... r

FROM
RIPLEY'S
"BELIEVE-IT-OR-NOT" ODDITORIUM
A CENTURY OF PROGRESS—1934
CHICAGO, ILLINOIS

W.A. Cunningh...
817-So-...
Louisvil...

Billy Cunningh...
817 So 4...
Louiville...

Ripley
Ripley
Believe It or Not Believe It or Not
ODDITORIUM

Dear Joe:

NO SWORD SW...
Too Coney Isla...

OBTAIN "PINK MAN" FROM
HAITI.   THIS IS GOOD,   DON'T U...
STORY ABOUT PILL.

CANT GET BORNEO BELLES
"   " CARVED FACE MEN   Matahan
BUT TRY ALEKO E. LILIUS   Steel
P.O. Box 3220 Manila.   Cable address
AEOLUS

OBTAIN WILLIAM D'ANDREA
88 - South Elm St
Waterbury, Conn.
CAN PLACE HIS FOOT IN HIS POCKET

HINDU SITTING ON NAILS -   Many of
em.   Try "Cooks" Company - Calcutta
e Manager of CLARKS HOTEL
Benares.

At Chicago Exhibit of Believe-It-Or-Nots

Thousands of Americans who have followed the famous
Believe-It-Or-Not Cartoons of Robert Ripley are seeing
the actual Believe-It-Or-Nots housed in the palatial Ripley "Odditorium" at the Chicago Century of Progress. Included
among the exhibits are (left) Singhlee, a Hindu who can grasp a
red-hot metal bar and put it to his mouth; (below left) Albert Nelson
and his one-man mechanical band of thirty instruments; and (below
right) Blystone, the rice writer.

RIPLEY'S
BELIEVE IT - NOT

E L BLYSTONE
of ARDARA, PA
WROTE 2871 LEGIBLE LETTER...
A SINGLE GRAIN OF RICE
PRIZE WIN...
NATIONAL Believe It or Not CONTES...

Ripley's Curiosities

More than two million visitors flocked to the Ripley's Odditorium to see sword-swallowers, fire-eaters, eye-poppers, and many other curiosities. The attraction proved so popular that Ripley's founder, Robert Ripley, went on to open many other Odditoriums across the U.S.A.

Head contortionist Martin Laurello discovered his unusual ability as a child and spent many years mastering his stunt of looking backward while walking forward, baffling scientists and amazing Odditorium audiences.

Habu Koller from Germany could lift more than 100 lb (45 kg) using a hole in his tongue. According to his Ripley backstory, Habu reportedly received the hole as punishment for refusing to bear arms in World War I.

Freda Pushnik from Pennsylvania was born with no arms or legs, but she was determined to master everyday tasks. Aged just ten years old, she wowed audiences at the 1933 World's Fair with her cheerful repartee and demonstrations of writing and sewing. Freda performed in Ripley's Odditoriums for six years, and went on to have a successful sideshow career before retiring from the stage in the 1950s.

Grace McDaniels complained about her early billing as "the ugliest woman in the world," but nevertheless was a popular sideshow draw for many years, later becoming known by her preferred moniker, "The Mule-Faced Woman." After fielding several marriage proposals, she settled down and had a son, Elmer (pictured here), who later became her manager.

Charles Romano, the "Rubber Arm Man," could twist and turn and throw his arms around in such a way that audiences were amazed that he could return his body to its normal shape and position.

Professor A. L. Morrell, the "Jack-Knife King," was billed as the world's greatest whittler. Assisted by his wife, he wowed audiences with his astonishing exhibit of carved objects displayed in a variety of small-necked bottles.

Egyptian Hadji Ali could drink up to 50 glasses of water in quick succession and then return it all to a receptacle in a steady stream, turning himself into a "human fountain." He also swallowed a range of other items before regurgitating them in any order requested.

Agnes Schmidt from Hamburg, Germany, was known as the "Rubber Skin Girl." Her skin stretched for 14 in (35 cm) and could be pierced in any place without pain or drawing blood.

Arthur Loos was known as the "Rubber-Skinned Man," because the skin of his neck would hang 18 in (45 cm) down onto his chest.

Captain Ringman Mack—seen here holding two genuine shrunken heads—was a European strongman who could pull cars and suspend heavy weights with hooks through his nipples without any sign of pain. He had performed in sideshows since the early 20th century.

With his unique ability to make his eyes pop out of his head, Leonard "Popeye" Perry from Richmond, Georgia, was an Odditorium sensation. He went on to work in other Ripley's Odditoriums for many years after the Chicago Fair.

Singlee, the "Fireproof Man," belonged to an Indian fire-worshiping sect. He said that fire was part of his religion and as long as he was faithful to his fire god, fire could not harm him.

Known as the "Anatomical Wonder," Anato Hayes could displace his entire abdomen, raising his intestines into his chest. Ladies in the audience were advised to "get a good firm grip on [their] escort's arm" before he appeared!

J. T. Saylors from Georgia had never demonstrated his talent for jaw-dislocation and pulling funny faces professionally, despite offers from show people and motion picture companies, until he appeared at the Odditorium in Chicago.

Kanichka, or "The Man with the Ostrich Stomach," swallowed billiard balls, goldfish, silver dollars, wristwatches, and doorknobs—and would then regurgitate them. As a finale, he would swallow electric lights, visible within his stomach when switched on. He was described as having an ostrich stomach because they swallow stones.

Lydia McPherson of Los Angeles was billed as having the longest red hair in the world, which stretched 7 ft 5 in (2.3 m) in length.

Sword-swallower Joseph Grendol had worked a season for the Ringling Circus before joining Ripley's Odditorium. He would swallow a 20-in (50-cm) bayonet attached to the butt of a rifle and then fire the gun while the bayonet was in his stomach!

A seasoned performer known variously as the "Human Pincushion" or the "Painless Wonder," Leo Kongee would drive pins and nails into his face, and even had a button sewn onto his tongue, and seemingly felt no pain.

Time Tunnel

Ramchandra Das of Bihar, India, spent 14 years cutting a tunnel 33 ft (10 m) long and 13 ft (4 m) wide through a mountain with only a hammer and chisel so that his neighbors could avoid an arduous 4½-mi (7-km) trek around the mountain to work and so that he could park his truck closer to home.

Hidden Home

Sharon Simpson created a luxurious tent home—complete with solar shower and satellite TV—on a busy traffic circle in the center of Derby, England. She lived there unnoticed for five months and moved out only when leaves falling off nearby bushes took away her privacy.

Underwater Meeting

In October 2009, the government of the low-lying islands of the Maldives in the Indian Ocean held an underwater meeting to highlight the dangers of global warming. Dressed in full scuba gear, President Nasheed and ten colleagues took part in the 30-minute meeting at a depth of 20 ft (6 m) off the coast, near the country's capital Malé. Most of the Maldives is barely 3 ft (1 m) above sea level, and scientists fear it could be uninhabitable in fewer than 100 years.

Piping Hot

The sidewalks of Klamath Falls, Oregon, are kept free from snow and ice—and therefore safe for pedestrians—by hot-water pipes that run underneath them.

Brocken Specter

Local climbers in the Polish Tatra Mountains believe that if they witness a Brocken Specter—their own giant shadow projected on thick cloud below them—then they are doomed to die on the mountain. The phenomenon is named after the Brocken Mountain in Germany.

Purple Snow

In March 2010, purple snow fell in Stavropol, southern Russia. The unusual coloration was the result of dust from Africa rising in a massive cyclone to layers of the upper atmosphere and then mixing with regular snow clouds over Russia.

Ice Man

Nicknamed the "Ice man of Ladakh," retired Indian engineer Chewang Norphel has tackled environmental problems by building more than a dozen new glaciers in the Himalayas. He constructs his own glaciers by diverting meltwater through pipes into artificial lakes. Shaded by the mountains and kept in place by dams, the water in the lakes remains frozen until springtime when it melts and feeds the rivers below, which in turn irrigate surrounding farmland. He decided to act after melting glaciers caused floods that destroyed homes and crops.

River Runs Red

The water rushing over Cameron Falls, Alberta, Canada, turned pinky red following a heavy storm. The phenomenon was caused by high levels of rain that washed a red sediment called argolite from 1,500-million-year-old rocks into the river.

New Castle

Since 1997, some 50 workers in central France have been building a new "medieval" castle using only the tools and materials that were available in the 13th century. The brainchild of local landowner Michel Guyot, the Château de Guédelon is being built from sandstone, and when it's finished in around 2022 will boast a main tower more than 90 ft (27 m) tall.

Time Travel

Russia has no fewer than nine different time zones—and the eastern region of Chukotka (just across the Bering Strait from Alaska) is nine hours ahead of Kaliningrad in the extreme west of the country. There were 11 time zones in Russia until two were scrapped in 2010.

Leaning Skyscraper

The 530-ft-high (160-m) Capital Gate building in Abu Dhabi leans at an angle of 18 degrees—four times more than Italy's famous Leaning Tower of Pisa. The new 35-story building achieves this angle by using staggered floor plates from the 12th floor up.

Towering Tent

A giant tent 490 ft (150 m) high opened in Astana, Kazakhstan, in 2010. Designed to withstand the nation's extreme variations in temperature, the Khan Shatyr Entertainment Center took four years to build. Made from three layers of transparent plastic, it stands on a 650-ft (200-m) concrete base and houses shops, restaurants, movie theaters and even an artificial beach and a running track.

Security Cage

After being burgled eight times in six months, 80-year-old Chinese grandmother Ling Wan turned her apartment in Changsha into a giant birdcage. She sealed up the stairs and built an iron cage around the apartment so that the only way in and out is via a ladder that is securely locked on her balcony.

Container Store

Shoppers visiting the flagship Freitag bag store in Zurich, Switzerland, certainly need a head for heights, as the building is made from a dizzying stack of used steel shipping containers. It consists of 17 containers of which nine form the 85-ft-high (26-m) tower. The recycling theme of the building mirrors the bags sold inside, which are made from such items as old truck tarpaulins, bicycle inner tubes, and car seat belts.

Capsule Hotels

Japan's capsule hotels have rooms that measure roughly 7 x 4 x 3 ft (2.1 x 1.2 x 0.9 m)—not much bigger than a coffin! They are stacked side by side on two levels, with steps providing access to the upper capsule. Some hotels have more than 700 capsules.

Light Tower

The Eiffel Tower in Paris, France, weighs less than a cylinder of air occupying the same dimensions. The force of the wind causes the top of the lightweight metal tower to sway up to 3 in (7.6 cm).

Sole Occupant

Owing to the recession, for three years Les Harrington was the only resident of a 2.4-acre (1-ha) luxury village in Essex, England, that boasted 58 cottages and apartments.

Luxury Igloo

In January 2010, Jimmy Grey built a luxury, four-room igloo in the yard of his home in Aquilla, Ohio. The igloo had 6-ft-high (1.8-m) ceilings and an entertainment room, complete with cable TV (which was plugged into an outlet in his garage) and surround-sound stereo.

Luminous Beams

A mysterious "rain" of vertical luminous beams appeared for nearly an hour in the night sky above Xiamen, China, in July 2010. At first there were just five beams, hanging low in the sky, but soon the number increased to 50. A local observatory confirmed that it was definitely not a meteor shower.

Hard Wood

Ironwood trees—including the black ironwood species that is native to the U.S.A.—have wood so dense that it won't float in water. It sinks instead.

Glass Elephant

Built on top of an old coalminer's washroom, the Glass Elephant in the Maximillianpark, Hamm, Germany—designed in 1984 by artist and architect Horst Rellecke—stands an amazing 115 ft (35 m) tall.

Mud Volcano

A mud volcano in Sidoarjo, East Java, Indonesia, spews enough scalding mud daily to fill 50 Olympic-size swimming pools. Since its first eruption in 2006, it has buried 12 villages.

Falling Ice

In 2008, a 6-lb (2.7-kg) chunk of ice fell from the sky, crashed through the roof of a home in York Township, Pennsylvania, and hit Mary Ann Foster, who was sleeping, on the head. It turned out to be atmospheric ice, formed when moisture in the atmosphere freezes into small ice balls, which then bump into each other and sometimes attach themselves together to create larger chunks.

Crackers

During the Chinese Lantern Festival celebrations in Taiwan, it's customary for onlookers to launch firecrackers at a shirtless man who represents the god of wealth. The more fireworks that hit their intended target, the more successful the firework thrower will become. This dangerous-looking ritual has been performed in the area for over 50 years.

Underground Home

Unable to afford a bigger house, retired Chinese miner Chen Xinnian tunneled out a one-bedroom apartment measuring 540-sq-ft (50-sq-m) beneath his existing home in Zhengzhou, Henan Province. The apartment is 20 ft (6 m) underground and is so cool that food does not need to be kept in a refrigerator.

River Ritual

More than ten million devotees from all over the country came to Haridwar, India, in February 2010 for the Kumbh Mela Festival, held here once every 12 years, to bathe in the River Ganges.

Royal Shrine

Mehrangarh Fort in Jodhpur, Rajasthan, India, has a shrine bearing carvings of the handprints of royal widows that committed *suttee*—a ceremony in which women were burned alive upon the funeral pyre of their husbands.

Lunar Pit

Photographs of the Moon taken from the Japanese Kaguya spacecraft revealed a giant pit about 427 ft (130 m) in diameter on the lunar surface—that's large enough to swallow an entire football field.

Flaming Festival

Each year the city of Toyohashi in Japan hosts an extreme fire festival. Fearless volunteers launch enormous homemade bamboo fireworks, known as *tezutsu hanabi*, which explode inches from their face. The 300-year-old festival sets off 12,000 fireworks and can draw more than 350 homemade cannons that spew fire up to 65 ft (20 m) into the sky.

Fire in the Hole

In the middle of a remote desert in Turkmenistan, the Darvaza crater is continually ablaze. The 200-ft-wide (60-m) chasm was created when a sinkhole collapsed under a gas-mining rig in 1971. The miners started a fire to burn off the gas, but it just kept coming and the crater has been burning ever since. If you can stand the heat, it is possible to walk right to the edge of the hole, which is 65 ft (20 m) deep.

The Twitchhiker

Paul Smith traveled around the world for free in 30 days relying solely on the goodwill of people using the social networking site Twitter. By accepting free accommodation and transport from his fellow tweeters, he managed to travel from his home in Newcastle upon Tyne, England, to Stewart Island, New Zealand, via Amsterdam, Paris, Frankfurt, New York, Washington, D.C., Chicago, San Francisco, Los Angeles and Auckland.

Deadly Storm

On April 30, 1888, a violent hailstorm dropped ice balls the size of oranges on the city of Moradabad in India, killing 230 people.

Toilet Tour

German guide Anna Haase runs a different kind of sightseeing tour—instead of showing visitors the traditional sights of Berlin, she takes them on a tour of the city's famous toilets. These range from a historic 19th-century toilet block to a Japanese automatic toilet that costs as much as a small car.

Boy Power

China has 32 million more boys under the age of 20 than it has girls.

Tar Lake

Covering an area of 100 acres (40 ha) and delving to about 250 ft (80 m) deep at the center, Pitch Lake on the island of Trinidad is filled with liquid asphalt, the result of oil being forced up through the faults on which the lake sits. Despite the highly toxic chemicals, the lake is home to bacterial life.

Sewage Symphony

A sewage plant near Berlin, Germany, is breaking down sludge more quickly by playing the music of Mozart to its microbes. The composer's classics are piped in to the plant around the clock via a series of speakers because the sonic patterns of the music help stimulate activity among the tiny organisms, speeding up the breakdown of waste.

Hamster Hotel

In 2009, a hotel in Nantes, France, offered guests the chance to live like a hamster for a day. Architects Frederic Tabary and Yann Falquerho designed the room to resemble the inside of a hamster's cage, and for $130 a night visitors could feast on hamster grain, get a workout by running in a giant hamster wheel, and sleep in piles of hay.

007 Tribute

For a 2009 New Year's Eve party, James Bond fanatics Simon and Angie Mullane spent four months and $4,500 transforming their Dorset, England, home into a 007 movie set. Guests were greeted at a homemade checkpoint manned by dummies dressed in authentic East German border guard uniforms bought on the Internet, while a Sean Connery mannequin dangled from a real hang glider suspended in the garden.

Tunnel Network

During the Vietnam War (1955–75), Viet Cong soldiers using only hand tools dug a single tunnel network all the way from Saigon to the Cambodian border—a distance of over 150 mi (240 km). They created an underground city with living areas, kitchens, weapons factories and field hospitals, installing large air vents (which were disguised as anthills or termite mounds), baffled vents to dissipate cooking smells, and lethal booby traps. Up to 10,000 people lived underground for years, getting married, giving birth, and coming out only at night to tend to their crops under cover of darkness.

Secret City

Believe it or not, hidden directly below the busy streets of Paris, France, there are countless secret tunnels and caverns, and millions of human bones.

The city expanded so quickly in the 18th century that cemeteries and mass graves were soon literally overflowing—it is said that the cellar walls of adjoining buildings would ooze with human remains, and disease was rife. To solve the problem, bodies were removed each night and buried in caves adjoining the Parisian sewers. These catacombs—or underground cemeteries—and the tunnels between them were recycled Roman stone quarries that stretched for 500 mi (805 km). It is thought that the bones of six million Parisians are piled up in the catacombs—over half the current live population. It is still possible to wander through the maze of passages that run 65 ft (20 m) below the city streets.

OSSEMENTS DU
CIMETIERE DES
INNOCENTS
DÉPOSÉS LE
2 JUILLET 1809

Away from the more organized areas of the catacombs, bones lie scattered in forgotten tunnels.

- French resistance troops used the catacombs as a base during World War II, as did occupying German forces. The tunnels also served as air-raid shelters for Parisians seeking refuge from enemy bombing.

- In 1787, the future King Charles X of France held a party in a large cavern deep in the catacombs.

- A gang of thieves was arrested in the catacombs in 1905 after attempting to steal skulls and bones to sell to medical students.

- A team of experts constantly surveys hundreds of miles of the catacombs to prevent any of the caves collapsing, which would potentially cause parts of the city, lying directly above them, to fall into the ground.

- An escaped orangutan perished in the Paris underground tunnels over 200 years ago. Its skeleton is still kept on public display.

THE GATEWAY TO THE CATACOMBS STATES: "ARRETE! C'EST ICI L'EMPIRE DE LA MORT" ("STOP! HERE IS THE EMPIRE OF DEATH.")

Right: This inscription reads: "In the memory of Philibert Aspairt lost in this quarry on November 3rd 1793 found eleven years later and buried at the same place on April 30th 1804."

BURIED ALIVE

In 1793, Philibert Aspairt descended into the catacombs under the hospital where he worked, hoping to steal wine from cellars belonging to monks. His body was found 11 years later, only yards from an exit.

A LA MÉMOIRE
DE PHILIBERT ASPAIRT
PERDU DANS CETTE
CARRIÈRE LE III NOV.
MDCCXCIII RETROUVÉ
ONZE ANS APRÈS ET
INHUMÉ EN LA MÊME PLACE
LE XXX AVRIL MDCCCIV

Ice House

The Cleveland Harbor West Pierhead Lighthouse on the shores of Lake Erie, Ohio, looked more like a fairytale castle in December 2010 when it became completely covered in layers of ice. High winds caused waves to crash over the lighthouse, where the water then froze in the bitterly cold temperatures.

Reduced Alphabet

Rotokas, a language spoken on the island of Bougainville, Papua New Guinea, has only 12 letters in its entire alphabet—they are A, E, G, I, K, O, P, R, S, T, U and V.

Lonely Lighthouse

The Stannard Rock lighthouse, Michigan, is the only structure on a large rock 23 mi (37 km) off the coast of Lake Superior. It was staffed for eight decades, until it was finally automated in 1962.

Phone Access

Only about one-third of India's population has access to modern sanitation—but nearly half of the population has a cell phone!

Hot Ash

Volcanic avalanches of hot ash, rock fragments and gas—known as pyroclastic flows—can move at 150 mph (240 km/h) and are capable of knocking down and burning everything in their path.

Narrow House

A three-story house in Brighton, East Sussex, England, is just 6 ft (1.8 m) wide. Owners Iain and Rachel Boyle bought the former donkey-cart shed for just $12,000 in 1998, but have turned it into such a stylish home—complete with a mezzanine bedroom—that they now rent it out.

One-way Traffic

Between 2004 and 2009, nearly 10,000 North Koreans defected to South Korea—while only two people went in the other direction!

Judge Numbers

India has 11 judges for every million people, while the U.S.A. has 110 per million—ten times as many.

Ooh-la-Law!

In 2010, French politicians finally sought to repeal a 1799 law that banned women in Paris from wearing pants except when riding horses or bicycles.

New Ring

In 2009, U.S. astronomers discovered a new ring around Saturn that is so large it could hold a billion Earths. The ring is made up of debris from Saturn's distant moon Phoebe.

Flood Terror

In January 2011, torrential rain in the state of Victoria, Australia, killed over 22,000 sheep and 300,000 poultry and led to the formation of an inland lake of floodwater more than 50 mi (80 km) long. Farther north in Queensland, the floods submerged an area of land the size of France and Germany combined.

Weeping Glacier

A human face, appearing to cry, appeared in a glacier in Svalbard, Norway, in 2009. As the ice cap melted, the water poured into the sea, eroding the ice and creating the mysterious shape.

Crazy Kink

A 7.1-magnitude earthquake near Canterbury, New Zealand, in September 2010 caused rail tracks in the region to buckle alarmingly. A train engineer managed to stop his two engines just 100 ft (30 m) short of this crazy kink. Repairs involved removing the crippled rails and replacing them with new rails that measured about 6½ ft (2 m) shorter than the originals.

Ring of Fire

Three-quarters of the world's active and dormant volcanoes exist within the 25,000-mi (40,000-km) Ring of Fire, situated along the edges of the Pacific Ocean. Among them is Alaska's Mount Redoubt, which erupted in March 2009, sending a plume of smoke nearly 10 mi (16 km) into the air.

Shooting Spores

Pilobolis fungi live in animal dung and are less than ½ in (1 cm) tall, but they shoot packets of spores up to 6 ft (1.8 m) in the air to reproduce.

Meteorite Crater

Max Rocca, an amateur geologist from Buenos Aires, Argentina, found an ancient meteorite crater 31 mi (50 km) across in the Colombian rainforest—by examining satellite pictures. His interest was aroused after he detected a near-perfect semicircular curve in the Vichada River.

Multiple Eclipse

Solar eclipses are a major phenomenon here on Earth, but the planet Jupiter, because it has 50 confirmed moons, can have multiple eclipses happening simultaneously.

School Climb

Erping Village Elementary School in Sichuan Province, China, is built on a platform nearly 10,000 ft (3,050 m) up a remote mountainside. Until 2010, when a new steel stairway was built on the cliff, students could get to school only by climbing a series of rickety, homemade wooden ladders. The school's two teachers had to escort the children up and down the ladders because the journey was so dangerous and exhausting.

Nuclear Reactions

The Sun's core has enough hydrogen to continue fueling its nuclear reactions for another five billion years.

Young Star

On November 7, 2008, 14-year-old amateur astronomer Caroline Moore of Warwick, New York, discovered a supernova—and the exploding star she found (dubbed SN 2008ha) was about 1,000 times dimmer than a typical supernova.

Black Hole

NASA has found a gigantic black hole 100 million times the mass of the Sun, feeding off gas, dust and stars at the center of a galaxy, 50 million light-years away.

Toxic Lake

Argentina's Lake Diamante, shaped like a diamond, is filled with thriving bacteria despite being oxygen depleted, hyper-saline, spectacularly toxic, and bombarded with ultraviolet radiation.

Dry Run

The U.S. side of the mighty Niagara Falls was nearly as dry as a desert for five months in 1969. Engineers stopped the waterfall for the first time in 12,000 years by building a temporary 600-ft-wide (180-m) dam from 27,800 tons of rock and diverting the flow of the Niagara River over the larger Horseshoe Falls on the Canadian side. The work was carried out to remove a large quantity of loose rock from the base of the U.S. side of the Falls, which, if left in place, might eventually prevent the waterfall from flowing at all. To delay the gradual erosion of the U.S. side, faults were also mechanically strengthened. When the task was finished and the dam was blown up, 60,000 gal (227,000 l) of water once again thundered over the U.S. side of the Falls every second.

Sandstorm

A vast sandstorm engulfed the town of Golmud in central China in May 2010 as it roared in from the Gobi Desert at a rate of 70 ft (20 m) a minute. Such storms are increasingly common in this area in springtime and, although often short-lived, they can cause electrical blackouts and induce breathing difficulties in residents.

Monster Star

Scientists from the University of Sheffield, England, have discovered a new star that weighs 265 times the mass of our Sun and is almost 10 million times brighter. The monster star—named R136a1—is believed to be around a million years old and is so bright that if it were located where our Sun is, it would completely fry the Earth within minutes.

Painted Peak

Using water jugs to splash an eco-friendly whitewash onto the rocks, a team of workers in Peru have painted the 15,600-ft-high (4,756-m) Chalon Sombrero mountain white. The peak in the Andes was once home to a sprawling glacier and it is hoped that the newly painted mountain will reflect away sunlight and help cool down the slopes to trigger a re-growth of its ice.

Meteorite Attack

The same house in Gornji Lajici, Bosnia, was hit by meteorites six times in three years between 2007 and 2010. The repeated bombardment of white-hot rocks forced owner Radivoje Lajic to reinforce the roof with a steel girder. He says the chances of being hit by a meteorite once are so small that to be hit six times must mean that he is being targeted by aliens.

Glowing Urine

A glowing trail spotted in the night sky above North America in September 2009 was caused by a falling block of astronaut urine. It came from the Space Shuttle Discovery which, unable to unload human waste while it was docked to the International Space Station, had then been forced to dump nearly two weeks' worth of waste in one drop.

In the Dark

A power outage in 2009 left the town of Quipeio, Angola (population 1,000), in the dark for more than two months.

Toxic Island

Owing to the risk of toxic volcanic gases on Miyakejima Island, Japan, residents carry gas masks with them at all times—and sometimes even sleep with them.

Lightning Hotspot

An area near the village of Kifuka, in the Democratic Republic of the Congo, has the greatest number of lightning strikes per square kilometer in the world—about 158 a year.

Black Gold

Beverly Hills High School in California has oil wells beneath its grounds, which earn the school hundreds of thousands of dollars in revenue every year.

95

Burj Khalifa

The Burj Khalifa, which opened in January 2010, is the tallest structure ever built. At 2,717 ft (828 m) tall, it is more than twice the height of the Empire State Building—the equivalent of 180 giraffes standing on each other's heads. Each of the 160 floors took just three days to build, with the complete tower taking 5½ years to finish, at a cost of $1.5 billion.

Bio Blitz

On a single day in August 2009, a team of 125 scientists and volunteers found more than 1,100 species of life—plants, lichens, mushrooms, bees, bugs, butterflies, worms and bats—in just 2 sq mi (5 sq km) of Yellowstone National Park, including several species that were not known to exist there.

Blown Away

When Cyclone Olivia hit Australia's Barrow Island in 1996, it created a wind gust of 253 mph (407 km/h).

Changing Places

The moons Janus and Epimetheus are in the same orbit around Saturn, with one a little farther out and slower than the other. The faster moon catches up its neighbor every four years and the two moons swap places and the cycle begins again.

New Cloud

Meteorologists believe they have discovered a new type of cloud. The Cloud Appreciation Society has named it asperatus, after the Latin word for "rough," on account of its rough and choppy underside. If the cloud type becomes officially recognized, it will be the first new cloud type since 1951.

Rocky Rain

On the distant planet COROT-7b, which is nearly twice the size of Earth, it rains rocks! Scientists from Washington University in St. Louis, Missouri, found that the planet's atmosphere is made up of vaporized rock, and when a weather front moves in, pebbles condense out of the air and rain down on the surface.

Constant Eruption

Stromboli, off the coast of Italy, aka the "Lighthouse of the Mediterranean," has been erupting for over 20,000 years. The 3,038-ft-high (926-m) volcano emits smoke and lava fragments about every 20 to 40 minutes.

Sun Block

When Tambora, a volcano on the island of Sumbawa, Indonesia, erupted in 1815, the 200 million tons of sulfur dioxide gas that were ejected into the atmosphere reduced the amount of sunlight reaching the ground. This caused temperatures to drop dramatically all over the world, resulting in crop failures throughout Europe, and, in 1816, North America's "year without a summer," snow fell in June and New England experienced severe frosts even as late in the year as August.

Single Bloom

The *Tahina spectabilis* palm tree of Madagascar grows for decades up to a height of more than 50 ft (15 m) before it finally flowers for a single time, then dies.

Rapid Growth

Just a week after it first appeared in a Mexican cornfield in 1943, the volcano Parícutin had reached a height of five stories, and a year later it stood 1,102 ft (336 m) tall.

Deadly River

The 1783 Laki eruption in Iceland sent enough lava spewing from a 15-mi-long (25-km) crack to fill two deep river valleys and cover an area of more than 190 sq mi (500 sq km). The lava river, which was 100 ft (30 m) deep, engulfed villages and released poisonous gases that killed many of those who managed to escape its flow.

Undersea Blast

There are at least 1,500 active volcanoes on the surface of the Earth and an estimated 10,000 volcanoes beneath the ocean. When an underwater volcano off the coast of Iceland erupted in 1963, it did so with such force that it punched through the sea and formed the 1-sq-mi (2.7-sq-km) Surtsey Island.

Pub Crawl

Rather than demolish the 124-year-old Birdcage Tavern to make way for a new road tunnel in Auckland, New Zealand, the country's transport authority decided to move the landmark hostelry 130 ft (40 m) up a hill. After the walls were reinforced by inserting carbon-fiber rods, the three-story building was jacked onto concrete rails lubricated with Teflon and liquid silicon, then painstakingly pushed up the hill by hydraulic ramps. The move took two days.

Time for Change

A giant astronomical clock at Wells Cathedral in Somerset, England, was painstakingly wound by hand for more than 600 years—and from 1919 to 2010 it was operated by five generations of the Fisher family. From 1987, Paul Fisher spent an hour, three times a week, turning the three 550-lb (250-kg) weights about 800 times. The weights were winched up on a pulley system and powered the clock as they descended over the next two days.

Gold Machine

The Emirates Palace Hotel in Abu Dhabi, U.A.E., has a vending machine that dispenses gold bars—with prices updated to correspond to the world markets every 10 minutes.

Gladiator School

The University of Regensburg, Germany, has a summer camp in which students live and train like Roman gladiators.

Beer Crate House

Architect Jörn Bihain used 43,000 plastic beer crates to create what he named the "Pavilion of Temporary Happiness," in the grounds of the Atomium building in Brussels, Belgium, in 2008. The vast temporary structure commemorated 50 years since the Atomium was erected at the 1958 Brussels World Fair.

BRUXELLES
A LA CARTE
LA BELGIQUE
EN RÉSEAUX
PRENDRE LE TEMPS
DE COMPRENDRE

Pocket-size Pad

Quay House in Conwy, Wales, is one of the smallest houses in the world, at just 6 ft (1.8 m) wide and 10 ft (3 m) long. The fisherman's cottage squeezes a fireplace, bench, tap, small bed, table and washstand into about 120 sq ft (11 sq m) of space—smaller than most people's garages. Quay House was occupied until 1900, and the last owner, Robert Jones, stood 6 ft 3 in (1.9 m) tall!

The Smallest House IN GREAT BRITAIN
Y TY LLEIAF YM MHRYDAIN FAWR

Happy Harry

Harry Hallowes, an Irish tramp who squatted for more than 20 years in one of London's most expensive suburbs, was awarded a plot of land that could be worth up to $6 million. He was given squatters' rights to a patch of land 120 x 60 ft (36 x 18 m) on Hampstead Heath, where he has lived in a tiny shack since 1986.

Tower Highway

The 16-story Gate Tower Building in Osaka, Japan, has a highway running through its middle between the fifth and seventh floors. An exit of the Hanshin Expressway passes through as a bridge, held up by supports next to the building. The office block's elevator moves through the vacant floors in the building without stopping between floor four and floor eight.

4,200 Clocks

The Pentagon, headquarters for the U.S. Department of Defense, has 4,200 wall clocks. Over 200,000 telephone calls are made from the Pentagon every day through phones connected by 100,000 mi (160,000 km) of cable, and although there are 17½ mi (28 km) of corridors, it takes only seven minutes to walk between any two points in the building.

Rat Free

A Japanese shipwreck in 1780 inadvertently introduced rats to Rat Island, Alaska, and the island was heavily infested until 2009, when it finally became free of rats again—229 years later.

Creepy Crawly Carpet

They might look like strange extraterrestrial beings, but these creatures, photographed in Germany, are called harvestmen.

Although they look like spiders, harvestmen are actually another type of arachnid, only recently discovered in Europe. Different types of harvestmen often mass together in groups of tens of thousands, moving as one to resemble a single large organism. This seething carpet of tangled legs, which can each span 6 in (15 cm), is thought to deter predators—it also multiplies the effect of the unpleasant odor that harvestmen secrete when under threat.

Kamikaze Carpenters

A species of carpenter ant found in Borneo has a gruesome way to defend its colony. Designated soldier ants wait until a predator is close by and then sacrifice themselves by exploding glands that run along their body. These glands contain a sticky poisonous glue that ensnares the would-be invader, but also kills the carpenter ant in the process.

Jack's Journey

A whippet-terrier cross called Jack was reunited with his owners in Sheffield, England, after a marathon 31-hour trek that took him across the M1—one of Britain's busiest expressways—four major roads, and miles of treacherous moorland. The dog, who got separated from his owners on a walk, was especially brave considering he suffers from a fear of traffic, and walks with a limp after being knocked down by a truck in 2005.

Painful Ritual

To prove they are real men, teenage members of the Setere-Mawe people of Brazil subject themselves to being stung repeatedly by bullet ants, the sting of which is so painful it has been compared to a gunshot wound. For the initiation, boys wear a pair of gloves each laced with hundreds of live bullet ants, stingers pointing inward, for ten minutes—and they must go through this agonizing ritual 20 times.

Plunging Parrots

A mystery illness caused hundreds of lorikeets to fall out of the sky over Darwin, Northern Territory, Australia, in 2010. The birds appeared groggy and listless, as if they were suffering from a bad hangover, but recovered over a period of a few weeks.

Living Larders

Some members of honeypot ant colonies eat until they are unable to walk. They then become living food storage containers, regurgitating food for their nest mates as needed.

Adaptable Lungs

Elephant seals collapse their lungs before they dive for food and can stay underwater for up to two hours.

Population Boom

Under ideal conditions, a population of five pregnant female German cockroaches could grow to 45 million—in just a year.

Wasp Stings

A 53-year-old woman from Attleboro, Massachusetts, survived being stung more than 500 times after falling onto a wasp nest outside her home. Firefighters used a carbon dioxide chemical fire extinguisher to blast the aggressive insects off the woman's body.

Faithful Fowl

Of the thousands of pairs of mating swans studied over 40 years at the Wildfowl and Wetlands Trust in Slimbridge, England, only two have ever "divorced" and found themselves new partners.

Air Miles

Arctic terns migrate about 43,000 mi (70,000 km) each year, which, during their lifetime of 30-plus years, works out at a distance equal to three round trips from the Earth to the Moon.

Potty Plant

The mountain treeshrew of Malaysia has a handy place to go to the bathroom. There is a particular type of pitcher plant shaped conveniently like a treeshrew-sized toilet bowl that attracts the small creatures with its sweet nectar. And while the shrew feeds on the pitcher's nectar, the plant has been found to extract food of its own from the shrew droppings.

Bee-stung Lips

The 2010 Clovermead bee beard competition was abuzz with excitement as competitors were loaded with some of the millions of bees kept on the Clovermead farm in Ontario, Canada. A queen bee was attached to each competitor's neck, her smell attracting entire bee colonies. The champion beard belonged to Tibor Szabo, who wore a bee mask that covered his face. He was congratulated by a particularly courageous spectator.

ERMEAD

One Big Eye

Although sea urchins don't have actual eyes, they see by using the entire surface of their body as one big eye. They have light-sensitive molecules, mainly in their tube feet and around their spines, and use these to avoid predators or find dark corners to hide in. Therefore, the sea urchins with the most densely packed spines are the ones with the best vision.

Ram Raid

A ram smashed through the glass patio door of a house in Lancashire, England, and ran amok, butting the stove door, knocking over a TV, smashing up furniture, and wrecking carpets. It is believed the animal, which had fled from a nearby field and was agitated because of the breeding season, charged at the patio door after seeing his own reflection in the glass.

Greyhound Wedding

Inseparable greyhounds Pete and Zoe were married in a canine ceremony at an animal shelter in Cambridgeshire, England. The bride wore a specially made dress and afterward she and her spouse devoured a three-tier liver cake. Staff thought a wedding would be a good way to seal the dogs' love for each other and to ensure they would be adopted together.

Open Wide

This fearsome deep-sea creature sports what appear to be humanlike teeth at the center of its tentacles. An unusual species of squid, the Promachoteuthis sulcus was discovered at a depth of 6,560 ft (2,000 m) in the South Atlantic Ocean. In reality it is far less terrifying than it appears—what look like teeth are fleshy lips around its beak, and this specimen is actually only 1 in (2.5 cm) long.

Herd for Heights

These Alpine ibexes think nothing of climbing the near-vertical face of the Cingino Dam in the Italian Alps to lick minerals from the stones. Alpine ibex have incredible agility and balance, which enable them to cling to the rough rock of the 160-ft-high (49-m) dam with their hooves.

Hero Hugo

A cat saved a neighbor's life by rescuing him from his burning home. Andrew Williams was asleep when the fire broke out in his bungalow in Berkshire, England, and he would almost certainly have died but for his neighbor's cat Hugo coming in through a catflap and waking him by clawing at his face. Hugo and his brother Harvey are regular visitors to the home of cat-lover Mr. Williams.

Death Dance

Male Australian redback spiders, which weigh only one percent as much as females, must dance for well over an hour when approaching a female, otherwise they will be eaten before they can finish mating.

Fisherman's Luck?

While fishing 80 ft (25 m) above the water from a cargo ship off the coast of Queensland, Australia, Filipino engineer Algerico Salise was stung by a tentacle from a thimble-sized irukandji jellyfish. The potentially fatal sting happened when the engineer's face was splashed with seawater that contained the jellyfish as he reeled in a fish. Urgent hospital treatment saved his life.

Bird Deodorant

Scientists in New Zealand are seeking a deodorant for some of the country's smelly birds in a bid to make them less attractive to predators. Unlike their overseas counterparts, birds native to New Zealand did not evolve alongside traditional land mammals, and they emit a strong smell when preening themselves to produce the wax needed to protect their feathers. The kiwi emits a mushroom-like scent, while the kakapo parrot smells like a musty violin case—and these odors attract newly introduced foreign predators.

Lost Gator

In 2010, a 5-ft-long (1.5-m) freshwater alligator was found swimming with whales 20 mi (32 km) out to sea in the North Atlantic off the coast of Georgia. It is thought the reptile had been washed out to sea from the mouth of the Altamaha River during heavy rains.

False Legs

Meadow, a calf born in New Mexico who lost her two back hooves to frostbite, was able to walk again after being fitted with a pair of prosthetic legs by veterinarians at Colorado State University.

Thieving Spiders

Rather than build their own webs, dewdrop spiders steal food or eat the leftovers from the webs of larger spiders.

Bifocal Bugs

The principal eyes of the larvae of the sunburst diving beetle have bifocal lenses. The bifocals have been found in four of the larvae's 12 eyes and allow it to switch its vision from up-close to distance— all the better for seeing and catching its favorite prey, mosquito larvae.

Shark Rider

Attacked by a 14-ft-long (4.3-m) tiger shark off the coast of Hawaii, 68-year-old surfer Jim Rawlinson grabbed its fin, pulled himself onto its back so that he was straddling the shark, and then rode it for about ten seconds. Sliding off the beast's back and watching it swim off, Jim returned to what remained of his board (after the shark had bitten a chunk out of it) and fearlessly surfed for another 45 minutes before returning to the beach uninjured.

Boating Otter

Wolfgang Gettmann of Dusseldorf, Germany, has a pet otter that accompanies him on kayaking trips.

Natural Haircut

A manatee living off the coast of Florida receives a natural haircut from dozens of tiny blue gill fish, which crowd around the gentle sea mammal and eat algae, parasites and dead skin off its body.

Turtle Surprise

A monster grouper fish that died after being washed up on a beach in Townsville, Queensland, Australia, was found to have a whole sea turtle inside its stomach. The green turtle had a shell measuring 16 in (40 cm), while the fish, estimated to be 25 years old, weighed a mighty 330 lb (150 kg). Although the cause of the turtle's death was probably the grouper, veterinarians said it was unlikely that the turtle caused the grouper's death.

Draining Experience

Three weeks after disappearing from Susan Garr's home in Salt Lake City, Utah, Millie, a four-year-old Australian shepherd mix, was found stuck in a storm drain. Rescue crews freed the dog, whose weight had dropped from 35 lb (16 kg) to 22 lb (10 kg) during her ordeal.

Stunt Baboon

Moco, a baboon at China's Changzhou Yancheng Wild Animal Park, is such a talented gymnast and daredevil that he has joined a circus. He specializes in the flying rings but can also perform stunts involving the horizontal bars, parallel bars, balance beam, fire hoops and even bike riding!

Spot the Caterpillar

Underground Fish

Stygichthys typhlops, an extremely rare blind fish that lives underground in Brazil, was recently rediscovered almost 50 years after the only known specimen was collected. Biologists believe that the fish may be a living relict that has survived deep below ground while its relatives above ground became extinct.

Lucky by Name...

Lucky, a cat belonging to Keri Hostetler of New York City, survived a 26-story fall from the ledge of her owner's apartment building.

Giant Squid

In July 2009, a 19½-ft-long (6-m) giant squid was caught in the Gulf of Mexico—the first live giant gulf squid captured for more than 50 years.

Doggy Stroller

Jenny, a pug owned by Ellen Zessin of Portland, Oregon, loves to stand on her hind legs and push her soft toy pugs around the garden in a baby stroller.

Long Lives

Splish and Splash, two goldfish won at a funfair in Gloucestershire, England, by Hayley and Matthew Wright in 1977, were amazingly still alive 33 years later.

Bee Careful

Ellie, a Labrador Retriever owned by Robert and Sandra Coe of Santee, California, survived after eating a beehive containing pesticides and thousands of dead bees. The inquisitive dog has also eaten wooden toy train tracks and laptop computer keys.

Believe it or not, there's a hungry caterpillar standing on this leaf! The Baron caterpillar— *Euthalia aconthea gurda*—of Southeast Asia is almost invisible against the background of this mango tree leaf in Kuala Lumpur, Malaysia.

Helpful Marking

In case anyone has any doubt as to what sort of animal she is, Polly, a tabby kitten owned by Garry and Joan Marsh of Staffordshire, England, has the word "cat" clearly spelled out in her fur on her left side.

Four Wings

A guin—a rare hybrid between a chicken and a guinea fowl—was born in Worcestershire, England, with four wings. Although the strange chick had two extra wings at the front, it was unable to fly. Lyn Newman had introduced two guinea fowl into her coop to act as lookouts, unaware that they could in fact breed with her hens.

Hen-pecked

A cockerel and his three hens gained revenge for a series of attacks by killing a young fox that broke into their pen in Essex, England. A table in the corner of the coop had been kicked over, knocking the fox out, allowing Dude the cockerel and hens Izzy, Pongo and Pecky to peck the intruder to death.

Master of Disguise

The blue-striped fangblenny, a reef fish found off the coasts of Australia and Indonesia, can change its color at will to mimic other fish so it can get close enough to take a bite.

Swallowed Soccer Ball

Bracken, a two-year-old Labrador Retriever owned by John Grant of East Dunbartonshire, Scotland, needed emergency surgery after swallowing a whole toy soccer ball. The deflated ball—measuring 5 in (12 cm) long—had become lodged next to his heart, causing him to cough incessantly.

Antarctic Escape

In 2005, a lucky gentoo penguin narrowly escaped a pod of hungry killer whales off the coast of Antarctica when it jumped from the water into an inflatable boat full of tourists that happened to be floating nearby. The penguin then swam away, but quickly returned to the boat to escape the lingering whales for a second time.

Bat Line

More than 130 orphaned bats were wrapped in dust cloths and hung on clotheslines while they recovered after being rescued from the devastating floods that hit Queensland, Australia, in January 2011. Vulnerable after coming to the ground to feed, the baby bats were picked up by the Australian Bat Clinic and then bottle-fed and housed in the cloths to keep warm.

Bat Cave

Bracken Cave, near San Antonio, Texas, is home to 20 million bats that feed on more than 100 tons of insects every night.

Panda Puzzle

Giant pandas possess the genes needed to digest meat, but none of the genes required to digest their only significant food source—bamboo.

Beaver Attack

A large beaver weighing around 42 lb (19 kg) hospitalized fisherman Russ McTindal after launching an unprovoked attack on him. The animal swam across Georgia's Chattahoochee River and launched at him, gnawing at his arm while Russ tried fending it off by hitting it with his fishing rod.

Camel Freed

Fire crews shoveled mud for several hours to free a 1,500-lb (680-kg) camel that had fallen into an 8-ft-deep (2.4-m) sinkhole in Oregon City, Oregon.

Terrible Tusks

Babirusas, the "deer pigs" of the Indonesian archipelago, have a set of tusks that push straight through their nose and can grow long enough to curve back around and poke a hole in their forehead.

Parrot Alarm

Burglars who broke into a house in London's Docklands in July 2010 were scared off when owner Gennadi Kurkul's green Lory parrot, Kuzya, let out a screech that could be heard several streets away.

Crash Landing

A couple on a whale-watching trip off Cape Town, South Africa, got a closer view than they expected when a 40-ton, 33-ft-long (10-m), southern right whale suddenly jumped on to their yacht.

A species with notoriously bad eyesight, the whale navigates by sound, and as the boat had its engine off, this whale probably hadn't realized it was there.

After snapping the mast on impact, the whale thrashed around before sliding back into the water.

INTREPID

Unlucky Puppy

Smokey, a 12-week-old Chihuahua puppy from London, Kentucky, survived a freak accident at a garden party that left him with a barbecue fork stuck in his head. Despite having the 3-in-long (8-cm) fork prongs lodged in his brain for three days, veterinarians were eventually able to operate and save Smokey's life, and he was soon back at home with his owners.

Run Over Twice

A Utah railway company worker rescued a stray dog that had been run over by a freight train twice on the same day—April 4, 2010. Although hit by the train's snowplow, the small dog survived and was nursed back to health by Fred Krause and his family.

Vegetarian Spider

Unlike other spiders, *Bagheera kiplingi*, discovered recently in acacia trees in the forests of Central America, is vegetarian. It is almost exclusively herbivorous, only nibbling on ant larvae for an occasional change of diet. The males are also the only spiders that are known to help the females look after their eggs and young.

Sixth Sense

A lost cat found her way to an animal rescue center in Fife, Scotland, despite having a can of cat food stuck on her head! The cat was thought to have been scavenging for food when she came across the discarded can. Unable to see where she was going, she somehow managed to avoid being hit by a car and wandered into the Scottish SPCA unit in Dunfermline where the tin headgear was removed.

Domesticated Deer

Since being abandoned by her mother five years ago, Dillie the deer has shared the Canal Fulton, Ohio, home of the Butera family, where she has learned to turn lights on and off and fetch one of her favorite meals, ice cream, from the refrigerator.

Car Wash

To raise funds, three African elephants at the Wildlife Safari Park in Winston, Oregon, were taught to wash visitors' cars. For $20 a time, the elephants scrubbed the cars with sponges and rinsed the soap off with their trunks.

High-rise Heifer

A cow was rescued from the 13th floor of an apartment block in Chelyabinsk, Russia, in 2009. No one knows how it got there, but when fire crews arrived they found it trying to get into an elevator. They decided to bring it down the stairs instead.

Sex Change

A cockerel in Tuscany, Italy, changed sex after a fox raid on his enclosure killed all his hens. Within days of the raid, the bird that was previously a rooster suddenly started laying eggs and trying to hatch them.

Paws for Thought

Hope, a cat owned by Nicole Kane from County Carlow, Ireland, has 24 digits—six on each paw.

Determined Diner

Believe it or not, this incredible photograph shows a python attempting to haul a wallaroo out of a watering hole in Kimberly, Western Australia, in order to eat it. The wallaroo is a marsupial related to the kangaroo and can reach a length of 6½ ft (2 m), while the predator is an olive python, examples of which can stretch over 13 ft (4 m)—making it one of the biggest snakes to be found in Australia.

Chimp Chefs

Chimpanzees in the mountain forests of Guinea, Africa, have been observed fashioning their own cutlery to eat food more comfortably. They have been seen using pieces of stone and wood to chop up their food into bite-size portions. This is the first time such behavior has been witnessed in a nonhuman species.

Ticket Seller

A Chinese zoo recruited a baboon to work as a ticket seller. Tianjin Zoo in Tianjin, northeast China, said the baboon, named Chun Chun, accepted money from visitors, handed them their tickets, and gave them their change—but still had to work with a human supervisor because he would only accept 100-yuan banknotes as they are red, his favorite color.

Pig Voter

Pauline Grant took her pig Blossom to her local polling station in East Sussex, England, after the animal was sent a letter by the council asking it to vote at the 2010 general election. Owing to an administrative error, the pig receives several junk letters a month, plus repeated demands for overdue bills.

Joyriding Bear

A bear climbed into an empty car outside a house near Denver, Colorado, honked the horn, and knocked the gear shift on the automatic transmission into neutral, sending the vehicle rolling backward 125 ft (38 m) down the driveway into a thicket. The bear was still inside the car when deputies arrived on the scene. They suggested the bear had been attracted by a peanut butter sandwich left on the back seat.

Guardian Angel

Eleven-year-old Austin Forman of Boston Bar, British Columbia, Canada, was saved from a cougar attack by his 18-month-old Golden Retriever, Angel, who leaped in front of the cougar and blocked its path, giving Austin time to escape. Angel survived, too, despite receiving puncture wounds around her head and neck.

Frozen Journey

In January 2010, a dog was rescued by the crew of a Polish ship after being found huddled on an ice floe 15 mi (24 km) out in the Baltic Sea. The shivering dog had floated at least 75 mi (120 km) down the Vistula River and out into the sea as temperatures dipped to below −4°F (−20°C).

Hunter Hit

In January 2010, a 53-year-old hunter in Los Banos, California, was shot and injured by his own dog when it stepped on the trigger of his loaded gun.

Full House

A 60-year-old woman shared her home in a suburb of Stockholm, Sweden, with her mother, her sister, her son—and 191 cats.

Spider Fossil

Scientists discovered a well-preserved, 165-million-year-old spider fossil in Inner Mongolia, China. It closely resembles a family of modern arachnids.

Artistic Dog

Paintings by Sam, a pet dog owned by Mary Stadelbacher of Eastern Shore, Maryland, sell for up to $1,700. Sam has created more than 20 different works of art, each made by holding a tailor-made paintbrush in his mouth.

Irwin Legacy

A new, rare species of Australian tree snail has been named Crikey steveirwini in honor of the country's famous wildlife advocate, Steve Irwin, who was tragically killed by a stingray barb in 2006.

One Ear

Rabbit breeder Franz-Xaver Noemmer from Egglham, Germany, holds his pet white rabbit born in February 2010 with only one ear.

Heat Alert

A chocolate Labrador trapped in a car in Macungie, Pennsylvania, on a 90°F (32°C) day in July 2010 honked the horn until he was rescued. Max's owner had gone shopping and forgot that the dog was still in the car, but when she heard the sound of the horn she went outside and saw Max sitting in the driver's seat, honking the horn.

Gallant Granny

A 60-year-old grandmother fought off an attack from a 5-ft-long (1.5-m) shark by repeatedly punching and kicking it after it had ripped off chunks of her flesh. Paddy Trumbull suffered deep bite wounds and lost a huge amount of blood in the incident, which occurred while she was snorkeling off the coast of Queensland, Australia.

Four Ears

A four-eared kitten was found living at a gas station in Vladivostok, Russia, in 2010. Named Luntik, his second, smaller pair of ears do not have any canals, however, so his hearing is no better than that of the average cat.

Smoking Viper

Po the viper enjoys two cigarettes a day after picking up on his owner's 20-a-day habit. When Sho Lau of Taipei, Taiwan, casually threw a cigarette butt away, the snake went for it and seemed to enjoy having it in his mouth, subsequently becoming hooked on nicotine.

Diving Dachshund

Sergei Gorbunov, a professional diver from Vladivostok, Russia, has taught his pet Dachshund Boniface to scuba dive in a specially built wetsuit, complete with helmet.

Ankle Biters

A police officer who was escorting a teenager home following a traffic violation was hospitalized after being attacked by a gang of angry Chihuahuas. The five dogs ran from the boy's home in Fremont, California, and rushed the officer, leaving him with a number of injuries, including bites to his ankle.

Rooster Arrested

A rooster was taken into police custody in Benton, Illinois, after it confronted a woman and her child in an aggressive manner. It was the latest in a series of incidents involving the bird, which had been bothering local residents and preventing them from going about their business.

Fish Hospital

Patit Paban Halder runs a hospital for pet fish at his home in Chandannagore, West Bengal, India. The fish doctor does his rounds of the 32 aquariums, takes blood samples, checks the patients for fungus and bacteria, and even gives them tiny injections.

Swallowed Glass

A German Pointer dog had to undergo emergency surgery after downing a shot of Jägermeister liqueur—and the glass—at a party in Australia. Billy made a full recovery following a three-hour operation to remove the glass from his stomach.

Crab Crawl

The 100 million red crabs living on Christmas Island in the Pacific Ocean walk from the inland forest to the island's shoreline and back in an annual breeding migration. Roads are closed and special tunnels dug as the entire island is turned into a creeping crimson carpet.

Pretty Boy

Despite his bug eyes, crooked mouth, and distinctive teeth, Ug, a partially blind two-year-old Pointer cross, proved a big hit with the ladies. April Parker from Doncaster, England, paid £200 ($320) for him—and renamed him Doug—after her two teenaged daughters fell in love with him on an animal sanctuary's website.

Escape Bid

A Tokyo Zoo worker dressed as an orangutan pretends to make a bid for freedom from his enclosure as part of the zoo's animal escape drill. Staff practice confronting the escapee, as well as surrounding him with nets, before pretending to shoot him with a tranquilizer dart.

Ace Ape

Following a stint as a painter, where her works fetched up to $3,000, Nonja, an orangutan at Schoenbrunn Zoo, Vienna, Austria, turned her hand to photography. Keepers gave her a digital camera, which issued a fruit treat whenever a picture was taken, and set up a Facebook page for her on which thousands of fans viewed images of her food and her companion, and of the ape herself climbing her rope.

Eight Lives Left

Sandy LaPierre's pet cat Smoka was found alive—after being buried deep in rubble for 26 days. Sandy had assumed that the cat had perished in the fire that destroyed her apartment in Franklin, Ohio, but almost a month later when demolition crews moved in to tear down what remained of the building, they found Smoka's head sticking out from under 16 ft (5 m) of debris.

Breast-fed Calf

After a calf's mother died when it was just three days old, Chouthi Bai of Kilchu, Rajasthan, India, saved the young animal's life by breast-feeding it three or four times a day. As well as giving the calf her own milk, Bai supplemented its diet with chapatis and water. Many people in India consider the cow to be a sacred animal.

Monkey Smuggler

When customs officials at Mexico City International Airport noticed a passenger with a mysterious bulge in his clothing, they discovered that he had 16 live monkeys hidden inside his sweater.

Shrinking Sheep

A breed of Scottish sheep has shrunk in body size by five percent over the last 24 years—because of climate change. The legs of the Soay sheep have got steadily shorter and their body weight has decreased as milder winters help smaller sheep to survive.

Permanently Pregnant

European brown hares are capable of being pregnant twice at the same time—and can therefore potentially be permanently pregnant. Researchers in Berlin, Germany, fertilized female hares in late pregnancy and found they became pregnant again about four days before delivery, a phenomenon known as superconception. Simultaneous pregnancies mean the hares can give birth to up to a third more offspring each reproductive season.

Parachuting Pooches

As part of their training, U.S. Army police dogs make parachute jumps, plummeting 12,500 ft (3,800 m) from a military helicopter at speeds of 120 mph (193 km/h).

Bear-faced Cheek

A 125-lb (57-kg) black bear walked through the automatic doors of a Hayward, Wisconsin, grocery store in October 2009. He climbed 12 ft (3.6 m) onto a shelf in the beer cooler, and sat there for an hour before being tranquilized by wildlife authorities.

Lucky Lamb

A lamb in Shangdong Province, China, gets around well and is steady on his feet despite being born with only two legs. Sheep farmer Cui Jinxin would normally have killed the lamb at birth, but she was so moved by his determination to survive that she spared him and kept him as a pet.

Ripley's Help Ripley

When the My Heart's Desire animal rescue group in Louisiana found this abandoned poodle in a ditch, he was in such an unbelievable condition that they named him Ripley, after Ripley's Believe It or Not! According to shelter co-director Tracy Lapeyrouse, "You would have never believed there was a dog under there. He didn't even look like a dog. He looked like the elephant man. All you could see was his snout." Ripley's fur was so overgrown and twisted that he couldn't see or even get up and walk.

When Ripley's Believe It or Not! heard about Ripley's predicament, they stepped in to help, making a donation to the animal rescue center and pledging to help his new owners cover Ripley's food and grooming expenses. At the shelter, Ripley was shorn of 2 lb 8 oz (1.2 kg) of thick, matted hair, given a wash and a feed, and was soon looking like a dog again, ready for adoption.

Before

After

Pretty in Pink

This rare, bright-pink grasshopper was found in the garden of a house in Havant, England. Grasshoppers are normally green and this one's colorful pigmentation is bad news, as it makes the insect more vulnerable to attack from predators.

Swollen Tongue

Penny, an 18-year-old dog from Paisley, Scotland, nearly suffocated after a freak accident caused her tongue to swell to four times its normal size. She was eating her favorite treat of pig's heart when membrane from the pig's aorta wound itself around the base of her tongue, cutting off the blood supply to the tongue and causing it to swell up. As she tried to paw her tongue free, blood began gushing from her mouth. Luckily, veterinarian Dermot Mullen managed to separate the pig's aorta from her tongue.

Dog on Wheels

Tillman, a five-year-old bulldog owned by Ron Davis of Oxnard, California, can skateboard 325 ft (100 m) in under 20 seconds. The 60-lb (27-kg) dog began skateboarding at just nine months and is now so good that he can do turns and tricks. Tillman can also surf and snowboard. "He's an adrenaline junkie," says Davis.

Mini Horse

Einstein, a horse born in April 2010 in Barnstead, New Hampshire, weighed just 6 lb (2.7 kg) and stood only 14 in (35 cm) tall at birth.

Yoga Bear

Santra, a female brown bear at Ahtari Zoo, Finland, performs a 15-minute yoga routine every morning. Visitors watch in amazement as she calmly stretches both legs before balancing on her bottom and pulling her legs up around her ears.

Too Small

An owl chick had an incredible escape at Paignton Zoo, Devon, England, after it fell from its nest and landed right next to an adult lioness. The tawny owls nest in a tree in the lion enclosure, and this one got lucky because the lioness, Indu, presumably decided it was too small to eat.

Chewed Toe

Kiko the Jack Russell terrier saved his owner's life by eating his big toe. After Jerry Douthett of Rockford, Michigan, passed out one day, Kiko sensed an infection festering in his master's right big toe and chewed most of it off. Douthett woke up to find lots of blood and rushed to a nearby hospital where doctors diagnosed him with diabetes, with a dangerously high blood-sugar level. A bone infection meant the toe needed to be amputated.

World Tour

Together with his South African owner Joanne Lefson, Oscar the dog visited five continents and 29 countries in 2009. During their nine-month world tour, Oscar walked on the Great Wall of China, posed beneath the Statue of Liberty, and took in such sights as the Eiffel Tower and the Taj Mahal.

Colorful Cat

Natasha Gregory from Swindon, Wiltshire, England, dyed the white fur of her cat pink with food coloring so that it matched her own pink hair.

Pigs Can Fly

Scarlet, a Hungarian mangalitza pig, loves to bounce around on a trampoline at her home in Shropshire, England. Gwen Howell discovered her pet's hidden talent after leaving her on the family's trampoline in the garden, and soon the pig was spending 45 minutes a day on it.

Swooping Hawk

Canada Post temporarily suspended mail service to 150 homes in a suburb of Calgary, Alberta, in 2010 because a hawk repeatedly swooped down from the sky and attacked the postman. The bird was so aggressive it even broke a bike helmet the mail carrier was wearing for protection.

Seagull Sniper

A seagull was seen flying around the seaside town of Scarborough, England, for more than a month with a crossbow bolt through its head. Local animal rescue officers tried to catch and treat the bird, but to no avail. The victim of a mystery sniper, the seagull was able to survive because the bolt miraculously missed its brain.

Fearsome Furry Family

In the wild, predators Baloo, Shere Khan and Leo would be mortal enemies, but at the Noah's Ark animal center in Georgia, the 1,000-lb (454-kg) American black bear, 350-lb (159-kg) Bengal tiger, and 350-lb (159-kg) African lion live, eat, and sleep together in the same custom-built cabin. The three gentle giants, all male, were rescued as a group of cubs in 2001 and their amazing relationship has developed as they've grown up together.

Bird Slippers

A baby African Crowned Crane was able to walk properly after keepers at a wildlife park in Cornwall, England, fitted its feet with a pair of tiny bright green slippers. The hand-reared chick had been born with a slight defect that left it with curled toes, but the slippers helped to straighten them out.

Happy Reunion

Twelve-year-old Brierley Howard was reunited with her pet Labrador dog Iggy in 2010—nearly five years after he vanished. Amazingly, Iggy turned up 130 mi (209 km) away from the family home in Lancashire, England.

Rare Reptile

A two-headed, albino hognose snake was unveiled at a Venice Beach, California, sideshow in June 2010. Todd Ray paid $20,000 for the bizarre serpent—called Lenny and Squiggy—which he saw on an online reptile message board. Each of the snake's heads is fed twice a week.

Bewildered Bear

An inquisitive black bear in Vermont had a milk can stuck on its head for more than six hours in 2010. After the bear had been seen running around aimlessly, bumping into trees and boulders, rescuers successfully cut the can from the animal's head.

Bravery Medal

In 2010, a nine-year-old black Labrador dog named Treo was given Britain's Dickin medal—the highest military honor an animal can receive—for his work sniffing out explosives in Afghanistan. The medal has been awarded to more than 60 animals since its inception in 1943, including 32 carrier pigeons, three horses and a cat.

Fox's Revenge

A wounded fox turned the tables on a hunter in the Grodno region of Belarus by accidentally putting its paw on the trigger of the hunter's rifle and shooting him. The hunter, who had been trying to finish the animal off with the butt of his rifle, was taken to a hospital with a leg wound while the fox made its escape.

High Hound

Giant George, a blue Great Dane owned by David Nasser of Tucson, Arizona, stands 43 in (1.1 m) tall from paw to shoulder and weighs 245 lb (111 kg). He eats around 110 lb (50 kg) of food each month and is so tall that some children mistake him for a horse!

Muscle Hound

No, this is not trick photography, and this dog has not been pumping iron. Her oversized muscles are perfectly natural, albeit very unusual. Wendy, from Canada, is a "Bully" whippet, a mutation of the breed that causes muscles to grow to double their normal size, meaning Wendy is twice as heavy as a regular whippet.

Close-ups

Dr. Richard Kirby of the University of Plymouth, England, has taken high-magnification photographs of sea angels (*Clione limacina*), microscopic plankton that live in the ocean around the U.K. Despite their size, they anchor the entire marine food chain by providing fish with food and the world with oxygen, and they also play a key role in the global carbon cycle.

Ice Dive

The dagger-shaped bill of the common kingfisher is so sharp that the bird can dive straight through a thin layer of ice to catch fish.

Zucchini Attack

When a 200-lb (91-kg) bear tried to force its way into a house near Frenchtown, Montana, in September 2010, a woman sent the animal fleeing by pelting it with a large zucchini. As the bear stuck its head through the doorway, the woman grabbed a 14-inch-long (35-cm) zucchini from the kitchen counter and hurled the vegetable at the bear, hitting it on the top of its head and causing it to run off.

Food Sharing

Bonobos—a sister species of chimpanzees—share things just like humans. A scientific study of bonobos in the Democratic Republic of the Congo showed that they voluntarily shared their food with other members of their group, making them the only species known to do this apart from humans.

Cat Nap

A house fire in Port Townsend, Washington State, was started by a cat that managed to depress a toaster lever while sleeping on top of the toaster oven. The cat, which slept there to avoid the family's dog, escaped unharmed.

Clean Kitten

A kitten had an incredible escape after climbing into a washing machine and going through a full wash cycle. Liz Fear's seven-month-old Burmese cat Suki was soaked, rinsed, and then spun dry after climbing in with a load full of dirty clothes at the family home in Melbourne, Australia. Despite her horrible ordeal, Suki was later given a clean bill of health.

Wine Buffs

Baboons invaded the vineyards in South Africa's Franschhoek Valley in early 2010 and ate thousands of bottles' worth of grapes right from the vines.

Monster Bug

Giant isopods are a cousin of the humble pill bug and often measure up to 15 in (38 cm) long. They live 1,000–7,000 ft (300–2,100 m) deep in the ocean and can weigh almost 4 lb (1.8 kg). In April 2010, oil workers in the Gulf of Mexico discovered a giant isopod double this size, measuring 2½ ft (76 cm) long!

131

Human Mimic

A pet dog in Zhumadian, China, prefers to walk upright on her back legs—just like a human. Owner Zhou Guanshun taught Lu Lu to walk on two legs at the age of four months by holding one of her front paws—and she hasn't stopped since! Even when she rests, Lu Lu chooses to squat on her back legs while keeping her body upright and her front legs off the ground.

Shell Slice

When veterinarians at Brazil's Anhembi Morumbi University discovered that a pregnant tortoise was unable to deliver her eggs naturally, they cut away a small square section of her shell with an electric circular saw and safely retrieved the eggs. They then replaced the piece of shell and left the tortoise to recover.

Purr-fect Day

In an unofficial ceremony, postman Uwe Mitzscherlich, from Possendorf, Germany, "married" his cat Cecilia in May 2010 after being told that the animal did not have long to live. As marrying an animal is illegal in Germany, Uwe paid an actress $395 to officiate at the ceremony.

Royal Lineage

Queen Elizabeth II has owned more than 30 Corgis, nearly all descended from her first dog, Susan, who died in 1959, and was a gift from her parents on her 18th birthday.

Cliff Plunge

Oscar, a five-year-old Cocker Spaniel owned by Rupert and Emma Brown, survived despite running over the edge of a 120-ft-high (37-m) cliff in Dorset, England. He emerged from his death-defying leap with nothing worse than a slight limp after being rescued from the rocks below by a canoeist who had witnessed the accident.

Eggs-hausted

A chicken belonging to Chris Schauerman of Honeoye Falls, New York State, laid a 5-oz (140-g) egg (two-and-a-half times normal size), along with five normal eggs—but the stress was so great that the bird died.

Splash of Color

A beluga whale at the Qingdao Polar Ocean World in China paints pictures that sell for hundreds of dollars. Xiao Qiang paints with the brush in his mouth while his keeper holds the paper. Belugas are able to manipulate a brush because they have more soft tissue around their mouth than other whales, and the turning of the head to paint is a natural movement that they perform in the wild when cleaning sand from their food.

Wire Walk

At a zoo in Fuzhou, Fujian Province, China, visitors flock in their hundreds to see a goat walking a tightrope while being ridden by a small monkey!

Swooping Swan

A motorcyclist in Worcestershire, England, suffered a broken collarbone after being knocked off his bike by a low-flying swan.

Mosquito Killer

In a contest organized by an insect trap company, Huang Yuyen, a pig farmer from Taiwan, killed and caught more than four million mosquitoes in a month. Her haul weighed in at just over 3 lb 5 oz (1.5 kg).

Rabbit Whisperer

Cliff Penrose, of St. Austell, Cornwall, England, has treated hundreds of rabbits with behavioral problems by hypnotizing them. By massaging certain parts of a rabbit's body, particularly the belly, he is able to relax the animal in a matter of seconds. He then "bows" to the rabbit by lowering his head so that it does not feel threatened before shutting its eyelids, leaving it in a trance. He says the rabbit emerges from the trance a happier, more relaxed pet.

Selective Breeding

Researchers at Yale University are working to bring back to life a species of giant Galapagos tortoise that became extinct hundreds of years ago. The selective breeding program, based on the DNA of the tortoises' great-great-great-grandchildren, will take over a century to complete owing to the reptiles' long lifespan and the fact that they don't reproduce until they are between 20 and 30 years old.

Turtle Eggs

In 2006, scientists in Utah discovered a 75-million-year-old fossil of a pregnant turtle, with a clutch of eggs inside.

Regurgitates Fish

A performer with the Great Moscow Circus swallows and regurgitates a live fish. Local authorities banned her act when the circus visited Australia in 2010 for being cruel to the fish.

Sewer Snake

In 2005, a 10-ft-long (3-m) python lived in a neighborhood sewer system in Manchester, England, for three months—moving from toilet to toilet before it was eventually caught.

Replica Romance

Timmy, a 60-year-old tortoise who lives in a sanctuary in Cornwall, England, has fallen in love with a plastic toy tortoise. He never hit it off with other tortoises, but since Tanya the replica was introduced into his enclosure, he has started nuzzling and kissing her and fetching food for her.

Thieving Octopus

Victor Huang was diving off the coast of Wellington, New Zealand, in April 2010 when an octopus suddenly lunged forward and grabbed his bright blue digital camera. The octopus quickly swam off with its booty but, after a five-minute chase, Huang used his speargun to extract the camera from its grasp.

Musical Fish

Diane Rains from Hudson, Wisconsin, owns a goldfish that can play musical instruments, including the glockenspiel and handbells, in perfect time to music playing outside its tank. Jor Jor has been trained to play single notes, chords and four-part harmonies, using its mouth to tug on a string attached to each instrument.

Old Hen

A hen in China is 22 years old—the equivalent of around 400 years in human age. Hens normally live for only seven years, but the bird owned by Yang Shaofu of Yunnan Province has reached three times that age, during which time she has laid more than 5,000 eggs.

Climbing Fish

The climbing perch of Africa and Southeast Asia is a fish that can breathe air and use its spiky gill covers and pectoral fins to "walk" on dry land from one body of water to another. It can live out of water for several days and will actually drown if it is held underwater.

Drink Tears

Three species of worker bee drink human tears. Either singly or in groups of up to seven, the bees were observed in Thailand landing on people's lower eyelashes and sipping lachrymation. It is thought the insects have adapted to drink tears as a means of gaining extra protein.

1

2

3

Frogs in their Throats

Humans might be divided on eating frog's legs, but eating frogs remains very popular in the natural world.

(1) Tad and Karen Bacon from Maryland discovered this giant bullfrog snacking on another frog after taking a dip in their swimming pool. Bullfrogs can grow to over 12 in (30 cm) long. (2) Luis Fernando Espin from Ecuador came upon an Amazonian whipsnake slowly devouring a large tree frog. The frog has toxic chemicals in its skin but that didn't prevent the snake from eventually swallowing it whole. (3) A burrowing owl in Florida makes short work of a large frog—legs included.

Fishing Dog

A dog in China's Hubei Province has become a local celebrity after taking up fishing. Mr. Lin's dog, Ding Ding, had always loved swimming in Donghu Lake, but in 2009 he suddenly started catching live fish. His owner says the dog locates the fish by watching bubbles coming from the water.

Busy Beavers

A beaver dam in Wood Buffalo National Park, Northern Alberta, Canada, is more than 2,800 ft (850 m) long. The construction, which has been worked on by several generations of beavers since the 1970s, is so big that it can be seen on NASA satellite photographs taken from outer space.

Clever Horse

Lukas, a 17-year-old thoroughbred horse owned by Karen Murdock of Chino Hills, California, has mastered 35 feats of intelligence—including counting, spelling and shape sorting. He can spell his own name, Karen's name and that of Karen's husband Doug. Lukas has also learned to nod his head for "yes" and shake it for "no," curtsy and pretend to be lame.

Rodent Infestation

Police who raided an apartment in Aachen, Germany, discovered that it was overrun by 300 guinea pigs—and in some rooms the pile of droppings was 4 in (10 cm) high.

Hero Buddy

Buddy the German Shepherd saved his owner's home by guiding emergency service personnel to the blazing building. The dog was in the Caswell Lakes, Alaska, workshop of his owner, Ben Heinrichs, when a stray spark started a fire. Buddy then ran out, found an Alaskan Trooper at a crossroads and, by running in front of the patrol car, steered him through a series of back roads to the scene of the fire.

Bee Line

A swarm of 20,000 bees attached themselves to colorful socks and underpants that were hanging on a woman's clothesline in Victoria, Australia.

Burpless Sheep

Australian scientists are working on a program to breed sheep that don't burp, in a bid to reduce greenhouse gas emissions. The agriculture sector in Australia produces about 16 percent of the country's total emissions, and two-thirds of that figure comes from livestock, chiefly the result of methane being released from the guts of grazing sheep and cattle.

Balancing Act

A pig in Xincai County, Henan Province, China, can walk despite being born with only its two front legs. Owner Wang Xihai started training the two-legged piglet to walk when it was just a few days old by lifting it up by its tail, and after a month it was able to walk upside down without help. Named by villagers Zhu Jianqiang ("strong-willed pig"), it can balance and move well on its front trotters even though it weighs over 110 lb (50 kg).

The lion approaches the white Toyota and tries the door handle with its teeth.

Curiosity gets the better of the cat and the lion opens the unlocked door.

Any Chance of a Ride?

The occupants are momentarily frozen in fear before they drive off, the lion looking after them.

A couple visiting Lion Safari Park, Johannesburg, South Africa, had the fright of their lives when a 300-lb (136-kg) lion opened the rear door of their car with its teeth. As they drove off, the lion chased the car to the park gates, where a game warden managed to shoo it back into the enclosure.

Pigeon Spy

A white pigeon that landed in the Indian state of Punjab, close to the border with Pakistan, was taken to a police station where it was held under armed guard and accused of spying. It had a ring around its foot and a Pakistani phone number and address stamped on its body in red ink, but the message it was suspected of carrying was never found.

Secret Growl

Scientists at San Diego Zoo, California, have discovered that, in addition to the familiar trumpeting call, elephants communicate in a secret language that is largely inaudible to humans. They say two-thirds of the elephants' growling sound is at a frequency too low to be picked up by human ears.

Tortoise Masks

Following a fire at Poestlingberg Zoo in Linz, Austria, fire crews saved the lives of six giant tortoises by strapping oxygen masks onto their heads. Although the masks were designed for humans, they fitted the 140-lb (63.5-kg) tortoises and prevented them dying from smoke inhalation.

Pink Hippo

British wildlife photographers Will and Matt Burrard-Lucas were picnicking on the banks of the Mara River in Kenya's Masai Mara game reserve in 2010 when they spotted a pink hippo emerge from the water onto the opposite bank! The animal's rare coloring is a result of leucism, a condition in which pigmentation cells fail to develop properly, causing pale skin color.

Lone Wolverine

Buddy, California's last wolverine, was discovered roaming the Tahoe National Forest in 2008—almost 90 years after the species was declared extinct in the state. He was seen marking his territory to attract a mate—even though the nearest other wolverines are thought to be more than 800 miles (1,290 km) and two states away.

Bear Steals Teddy

A black bear broke into a house in Laconia, New Hampshire, in 2010 and stole a teddy bear! The burglar bear ate a selection of fruit, and drank from the Parkinson family fishbowl, before making off with the stuffed toy after the sound of the garage door being raised scared it.

Tug-of-War

A thirsty baby elephant that ventured to the edge of a waterhole in South Africa's Kruger National Park got the fright of its life when a lurking crocodile suddenly grabbed it by the trunk. As the croc tried to drag its prey into the water, the baby's distress calls alerted the rest of the herd and they managed to scare off the reptile by trumpeting loudly and stamping their feet.

Toadally Cool

You've heard of leather made from cows, and even alligators and kangaroos, but what about toads? Marino Leather Exports, from Cairns, Australia, has been making bags, purses and hats from giant cane toads since 1994. There are now more than 60 items in the range, some using the entire toad, which can grow to a length of 15 in (38 cm)—and that's not counting the legs.

No Hurry

At its average speed of 0.03 mph (0.05 km/h), a garden snail would take 34,519 days to slide around the world—that's nearly 95 years.

Giant Amphibians

The giant salamanders of China and Japan can grow to more than 5 ft (1.5 m) in length and live for as long as 50 years.

Yap Nav

Taxi driver Andrzej Szymcakowi from Lodz, Poland, decided to switch off his GPS after realizing that Bobo, his Yorkshire Terrier, is better at giving him directions. Bobo, who has traveled in the cab since he was a puppy, knows all the routes. He yaps and raises his right paw to indicate a right turn, lifts his left paw for a left turn, and barks and wags his tail for straight on.

Croc House

Shaun Foggett from Oxford, England, shares his semi-detached house with his fiancée, their three children and 24 crocodiles and alligators. He spends $12,000 a year feeding the reptiles.

Clever Collie

Whereas most dogs can recognize about 15 commands, Betsy, a seven-year-old Border Collie in Austria, can recognize more than 340 words. She can also fetch an object after seeing a picture of it.

Gambling Rabbit

Daisy the pet white rabbit has become a regular at the Prince of Wales pub in Malvern, England, where he enjoys a drink of cider while playing the fruit slot machine. His owner says the rabbit loves the flashing lights.

Slippery Surface

A highway in northern Greece was closed for two hours in May 2010 after millions of frogs emerging from a nearby lake caused three drivers to skid off the road.

MATCH	PAUL'S PICK	RESULT	
Germany vs. Australia	Germany	Germany 4	Australia 0
Germany vs. Serbia	Serbia	Serbia 1	Germany 0
Germany vs. Ghana	Germany	Germany 1	Ghana 0
Germany vs. England	Germany	Germany 4	England 1
Germany vs. Argentina	Germany	Germany 4	Argentina 0
Germany vs. Spain	Spain	Spain 1	Germany 0
Germany vs. Uruguay	Germany	Germany 3	Uruguay 2
Netherlands vs. Spain	Spain	Spain 1	Netherlands 0

Psychic Octopus

Paul the Psychic Octopus became a worldwide celebrity after correctly predicting all of the German national soccer team's results at the 2010 World Cup. Before each match, two plastic boxes, one with a German flag and one with the flag of their opponents, were lowered into his tank at the Oberhausen Sea Life Center in Germany. Each box contained a tasty mussel, and the box that Paul opened first was judged to be the predicted winner. After correctly forecasting five German victories, he upset the nation by choosing Spain to win their semifinal clash. Spain duly defeated Germany, and Paul maintained his 100 percent record by predicting that Spain would beat the Netherlands in the final.

Insect Velcro

A species of South American ant—*Azteca andreae*—has its own Velcro-like device that enables it to hold on to about 6,000 times its body weight— the equivalent of a domestic cat holding on to a humpback whale. The ant's claws are shaped like hooks and fit neatly into fibrous loops on the undersides of the leaves where it lives, enabling it to trap much bigger insects as prey.

Big Stink

An infestation of stinkbugs hit Brooklyn, New York City, in January 2010. The small brown flying beetles, which are native to the Far East, emit a smell like rotting cheese when they are squashed or even vacuumed.

Watch Bird

Lorenzo the parrot was arrested in Colombia for trying to tip off a local drug cartel while police officers carried out an undercover raid. Police suspicions were confirmed when Lorenzo spent the whole of his first morning in custody squawking: "Run, run, you are going to get caught."

Quicker by Pigeon

A carrier pigeon proved faster than a rural broadband connection in an English race to determine which was more efficient at sending a video from East Yorkshire to Lincolnshire. Rory the pigeon made the journey carrying the five-minute video loaded onto a computer memory card in 80 minutes, reaching his destination while the computer was still uploading the video.

Tiny Frog

A new species of frog found in Borneo measures a tiny 0.4 in (10.2 mm) long as an adult—that's about the size of a fingertip. The micro species *Microhyla nepenthicola*, which was named after a plant that is also found on the island, had been documented before, but scientists had wrongly assumed it was a juvenile of another species of frog instead of an adult in its own right.

Alien Monster?

Tomas Rak uses macro photography to make tiny, harmless British jumping spiders look like alien monsters from a horror movie. He scours the country in search of the spiders, which measure just 1/4 in (6 mm) long, but can jump six times their own height. Tomas sometimes waits for up to three weeks to get the right shot.

Pet Wash

Animal owners in Japan can wash their cats and dogs in specially designed washing machines at pet supermarkets. The machines, which are claimed to be entirely safe, give the animals a shampoo, a rinse, and a dry in a half-hour cycle for around $10.

Bionic Cat

A cat that lost both of his back paws in an accident can run and jump again after being fitted with two bionic legs. The mechanical implants were drilled into Oscar's ankles by British veterinarian Noel Fitzpatrick, and then treated with a substance that allows bone and skin to grow around them. To give Oscar full movement, fake paws were then fitted on "see-saw" joints at the ends of the prosthetics.

Romantic Stork

A stork named Rodan flies 8,080 mi (13,000 km) each year from South Africa to Brodski Varos, Croatia, to visit his handicapped mate, Malena, who is unable to fly. They have chicks each year and Rodan teaches them to fly. He then takes them with him to South Africa for the winter and returns with them to Malena in the spring.

Ink Intact

Even though it died around 155 million years ago, scientists were still able to extract ink from the fossilized remains of a squid-like creature discovered in a rock in Wiltshire, England. The odds of finding a squid's delicate ink sac intact after so many centuries are put at a billion to one.

UNBELIEVABLE FEATS

Great Escapes

At 32 years old, Akash Awasthi is already one of the most daring escapologists in India, risking life and limb to escape from a burning haystack, a locked box deep underwater, and a coffin placed in the path of a speeding truck.

He has also ridden a motorbike through the packed city streets of Trivandrum, Kerala, while blindfolded. He is following in the footsteps of his father, Anand Awasthi, one of the most famous magicians in the country.

Akash fights his way out of the burning haystack, which becomes an inferno within seconds.

Akash is hoisted into the air by a 120-ft (37-m) crane.

146

Famous Escapes

1. Matt the Knife (U.S.A.) took just 11 seconds to free himself from **handcuffs while underwater**.

2. Dorothy Dietrich (U.S.A.) **escaped from a straitjacket while suspended** from a burning rope hundreds of feet in the air.

3. Dean Gunnarson (Canada) **escaped from a straitjacket while hanging upside down** from a trapeze 726 ft (221 m) above the gorge of the Hoover Dam.

4. David Merlini (Hungary) **escaped from a shark-filled pool** while in a straitjacket, weights and restraints.

5. Zdenek Bradac (Czech Republic) **escaped from a pair of real police handcuffs** in 1.6 seconds.

6. David Straitjacket (U.K.) **escaped from a straitjacket while on stilts** in 1 minute 38 seconds.

7. David Blaine (U.S.A.) took 15 minutes to **free himself from shackles and a gyroscope** that had been spinning him around 50 ft (15 m) above Times Square, New York, for 52 hours.

Akash emerges from the flames, unchained, moments before the haystack is completely engulfed. He is tended to by volunteers.

Solo Sailor

At age 16, Jessica Watson of Queensland, Australia, finished a 210-day, 23,000-nautical-mile (42,600-km), solo, nonstop and unassisted voyage around the world. In her 34-ft-long (10-m) yacht *Ella's Pink Lady*, she battled 39-ft (12-m) swells and a ripped sail, and ate 576 chocolate bars.

Jail Jaunt

In June 2009, 194 French inmates made a 1,430-mi (2,300-km) bicycle trip through the country in a prisoners' Tour de France.

Head-to-Head

Croatian tennis player Goran Ivanisevic needed stitches when he tried to head the ball over the net at the 1998 Canadian Open, only to bang heads with his doubles partner Mark Philippoussis, who had tried to do the same thing. Philippoussis got away with only a bruised forehead.

Dodgeball Tournament

In October 2009, more than 235 teams in three divisions competed in a dodgeball tournament in Richmond, Virginia, involving more than 4,000 players.

Novice at 90

Ninety-year-old Mary Tattersall from West Yorkshire, England, hit a hole-in-one at a golf course near Bradford in 2010. She had been playing golf for only two years.

World Cup Miss

Spain's international goalkeeper Santiago Cañizares missed the 2002 soccer World Cup after dropping a bottle of aftershave onto his right foot, severing one of his tendons.

Board Marathon

A team of ten wakeboarders (a cross between waterskiing and surfing) completed 1,448 laps of a Cincinnati, Ohio, cable wakeboard park in 24 hours in June 2010. They traveled just over 506 mi (814 km)—roughly the distance from Cincinnati to Atlanta, Georgia.

Delayed Game

Twenty-one years after a 1989 New Jersey high-school hockey championship game between Delbarton and St. Joseph's was canceled because of a measles outbreak, the players—now in their late thirties—finally took to the ice to play the deciding game for charity.

Mighty Mouth

A man in Lagos, Nigeria, lifts a bar carrying 110 lb (50 kg) of iron weights with his mouth!

Bike Climb

In November 2010, Colombian cyclist Javier Zapata rode up the 649 steps of the Piedra del Peñol monolithic formation in Guatapé, Colombia, in just 43 minutes. Zapata is no stranger to epic climbs. In 2003, he rode his bike up the 1,318 stairs of Mexico City's Torre Mayor, the tallest building in Latin America.

One-legged Wrestler

Michigan-based Zach "Tenacious Z" Gowen, who lost his leg at age eight, made his debut at 19 as a one-legged professional wrestler.

Thrown Away

Jesus Leonardo of Wanaque, New Jersey, earns about $45,000 a year examining discarded horse-racing tickets for winning stubs accidentally thrown away.

Master Jockey

Since 1974, Canadian jockey Russell Baze has won more than 11,000 horse races. In the space of just two days—October 17 and 18, 2007—he won no fewer than 11 races.

Insect Aside

Spotting that an insect had landed on his ball at the 1950 U.S. Open Golf Championship, Lloyd Mangrum of the U.S.A. instinctively picked up the ball and flicked the insect away. However, he was penalized two strokes for his misdemeanor, which ended up costing him the title.

Blind Catch

Sheila Penfold, a legally blind grandmother from London, England, caught a catfish that weighed in at a whopping 214 lb (97 kg) and measured 8 ft 2 in (2.5 m) long on Spain's Ebro River in January 2010. It took Mrs. Penfold, who stands just 5 ft 3 in (1.6 m) tall, 30 minutes to reel in the monster.

Bill paddled his board into the water at 7.24 a.m. on a Saturday morning—he didn't stop surfing until 9.26 a.m. on Sunday!

The super-surfer's fingers appear severely wrinkled as a result of being submerged in the water for 26 hours straight.

Surf's Up!

Surfer extraordinaire Bill Laity of San Clemente, California, surfed for 26 hours straight at the state's Huntington Beach in November 2010, during which time he caught 147 waves.

Bill emerges from the seawater following his surfing extravaganza with bloodshot eyes and dusted in salt.

Sky Walker

Californian Dean Potter walked across a highline 100 ft (30 m) long and more than 1,000 ft (305 m) above the ground in Yosemite National Park in 2009. He walked barefoot, and unattached. Dean has many years of experience on the highline—if he does slip off, he grabs the line with his arms or legs.

Flying Fish

One of the favorites to win the 2010 Missouri River 340—a grueling 340-mi (550-km) canoe and kayak race—Brad Pennington from Houston, Texas, was forced to quit just hours into the event after a 30-lb (13.6-kg) Asian silver carp leaped out of the water and hit him in the head. He described the blow as like being hit with a brick, and was left with a pounding headache.

Tug of War

Fishing on the Victoria Nile River in Uganda, Tim Smith from Enniskillen, Northern Ireland, landed a 249-lb (113-kg) Nile perch, which at 6 ft (1.8 m) long, was taller than him. He battled for 45 minutes to reel in the monster—and then had to pry his catch from the jaws of a crocodile that launched itself at his tiny boat in a desperate bid to snatch the fish.

Soccer Saints

An executive box at the Hamburg stadium of German soccer club St. Pauli is decorated like a Gothic chapel, complete with stained glass windows, candles, an altar to football, and depictions of the team's players as saints.

Frozen Toe

The U.S.'s Rulon Gardner, the 2000 Olympic Greco-Roman wrestling gold medalist, lost a toe to frostbite in 2002 and kept it in a jar in his refrigerator for years, apparently to remind him of his mortality.

Free Throws

Perry Dissmore, a pastor from Hartford, Illinois, made 1,968 successful basketball free throws in one hour in September 2010—an average of one throw every 1.8 seconds.

Matador Fled

Matador Christian Hernandez quit his job mid-bullfight in Mexico City—by running away from the charging bull, jumping over a wall, and fleeing the stadium to a chorus of boos.

Loyal Fan

Nesan Sinnadurai, a U.S.-based fan of English soccer club Arsenal, has flown more than 6,000,000 mi (9,600,000 km) supporting the club since 1967. Every other weekend during the soccer season, the Sri Lankan I.T. consultant makes the 9,000-mi (14,500-km) round trip from Columbus, Georgia, to London to watch his favorite team.

Blind Abseiler

Blind extreme sports enthusiast Dean Dunbar abseiled down the 658-ft-high (200-m) Eas a' Chual Aluinn waterfall in Scotland. He has also competed in power boating, mountain biking, sea kayaking, and hill running events, bungee jumped from a helicopter, and been hurled through the air as a human catapult.

Super Sprinter

Irish sprinter Jason Smyth can run the 100 meters in 10.32 seconds—even though he is legally blind. He suffers from Stargardt's disease, a disorder that has reduced his vision to about ten percent of that of a fully sighted person, but can run so fast that he competed against able-bodied athletes at the 2010 European Championships.

Too Much Yelling

Manchester United goalkeeper Alex Stepney dislocated his jaw while shouting at his defenders during a 1975 soccer match against Birmingham City.

Bowling Star

Retired high-school principal Allen Meyer of Toronto, Canada, was still bowling twice a week in a league that he ran at the age of 106.

Foul Ball

After years of attending Philadelphia Phillies baseball games, Steve Monforto made a great grab to catch his first foul ball. He high-fived his three-year-old daughter Emily and handed her the prize ball… which she then threw back over the railing! The family still went home with a ball after Phillies officials saw what happened and took a ball up to him. What's more, spectators threw back every foul ball caught for the remainder of the game so that Emily didn't feel bad for losing her dad the special ball.

Extreme Hole

The "Extreme 19th" hole at the Legend Golf and Safari Resort in Limpopo, South Africa, has a tee-off on a mountain that is accessible only by helicopter—and sits 1,300 ft (400 m) above a green designed in the shape of the continent of Africa. In 2008, Ireland's Padraig Harrington became the first golfer to make a par-3 at this hole.

Double Faults

In her first-round ladies' singles match at Wimbledon in 1957, Brazilian tennis player Miss M. de Amorim began by serving 17 consecutive double faults.

Airbed Race

At the annual Glen Nevis River Race in Scotland, competitors on inflatable airbeds don helmets and lifejackets to navigate a treacherous 1½-mi (2.4-km) course along the Glen Nevis River, tackling white-water torrents, rapids and even a 30-ft (9-m) waterfall.

Solo Row

In her 19-ft-long (5.8-m) rowboat *Liv*, Katie Spotz, 22, from Mentor, Ohio, rowed solo 2,817 mi (4,533 km) across the Atlantic Ocean from Dakar, Senegal, to Georgetown, Guyana, in just over 70 days. Previously she has swum the entire 325-mi (520-km) length of the Allegheny River, run 150 mi (240 km) across the Mojave and Colorado deserts, and cycled 3,300 mi (5,310 km) across the U.S. from Seattle, Washington, to Washington, D.C.

Welly Wanging

Under the British rules of "welly wanging" (or gumboot throwing), competitors take a maximum run-up of 42 paces before hurling a size 9, non-steel toecap gum boot through the air as far as possible. Finland's Jouni Viljanen has hurled a gum boot more than 208 ft (64 m).

Anvil Blast

In the U.S. sport of competitive anvil shooting, participants use black gunpowder to launch 100-lb (45-kg) anvils up to 200 ft (60 m) into the air. One anvil is placed upside down on the ground, the brick-shaped cavity in its underside is filled with gunpowder, and then a second anvil is placed on top of it. A fuse is lit—and the anvil-shooter runs as fast as he can.

Fiery Bull

In a festival dating back to the 16th century, a Bull of Fire runs through the streets of Medinaceli, Spain. The bull's body is covered in mud to protect it from burns and it wears an iron frame on its horns that bears two torches. The bull is chased through the streets until the torches go out.

Milk Man

New Yorker Ashrita Furman once walked more than 80 mi (130 km) around a track in Queens, New York, with a full milk bottle on his head.

Beach Towel

A beach towel covering a whopping 24,110 sq ft (2,240 sq m) of beach was unveiled near Las Palmas on the Canary Islands. A team of 25 people spent 15 days making the towel, and more than 50 people were needed to roll it out on the beach.

Human Dominos

Thousands of people in Ordos, Inner Mongolia, China, formed a human domino chain. Arranged in lines, the 10,267 participants slowly fell backward onto each other in sequence from a sitting position like a line of toppling dominos.

Wheelchair Crossing

Setting off from his home in Lynn, Massachusetts, Matt Eddy crossed the U.S.A. by wheelchair in just over four months. Matt has been confined to a wheelchair since the age of ten and suffers from Duchenne Muscular Dystrophy, as a result of which he is strong enough only to move two fingers and requires a ventilator to breathe. Traveling on the quieter back roads to reach his destination of Long Beach, California, he averaged at least 25 mi (40 km) a day.

Lunge Runner

Jamasen Rodriguez of Modesto, California, is an expert in lunge running, where instead of running, the athlete lunges to his knees, alternating left and right with each step. In August 2010, he completed a lunge mile in 25 minutes 21 seconds, taking 1,370 lunges.

Heavy Suit

U.S. Air Force Staff Sergeant Owen Duff ran a mile (1.6 km) in 9 minutes 22 seconds at Kirkuk Regional Air Base, Iraq, in 2010 while wearing an 80-lb (36-kg) bomb suit.

Balancing Act

One man rode a bicycle 165 ft (50 m) along a tightrope suspended 26 ft (8 m) above a tiger enclosure while another hung below him on a ladder at China's Changzhou Yancheng Zoo in March 2010. The pair, who were part of a stunt that involved a three-year-old girl walking the rope behind them, narrowly avoided tragedy when one of the zoo's Siberian tigers leaped high off the ground and grabbed at the ladder, nearly causing the men to fall into the enclosure.

OLYMPICS!

Famous Olympians

Lieutenant George S. Patton (U.S.A.)
A leading general during World War II, he finished fifth in the modern pentathlon at the 1912 Olympics.

Johnny Weissmuller (U.S.A.)
He won three gold medals in freestyle swimming at the 1924 Olympics, plus a bronze in the men's water polo, and two more swimming golds in 1928—feats that helped him earn a lucrative Hollywood career playing Tarzan.

Harold Sakata (U.S.A.)
He won a weightlifting silver in 1948 before going on to play the evil, super strong Oddjob in the James Bond movie *Goldfinger*.

Philip Noel-Baker (G.B.)
He won silver in the 1,500 meters at the 1920 Olympics—and in 1959 was awarded the Nobel Peace Prize.

Crown Prince (later King) Constantine (Greece)
He won a sailing gold medal at the 1960 Olympics.

Zara Phillips (G.B.)
A grandchild of Queen Elizabeth II, she won silver at the 2012 London Olympics as part of the equestrian team.

Remarkable Torch Relays

Tokyo 1964
This torch relay featured the most torchbearers ever used—101,866—comprising a carrier, two reserve runners, and up to 20 accompanying people for every kilometer of its land journey.

Grenoble 1968
In the later stages of the relay, a diver swam across the French port of Marseilles holding the torch's flame out of the water.

Mexico City 1968
The relay retraced the steps of Christopher Columbus to the New World and featured one of his direct descendants, Cristóbal Colón de Carbajal, as the last runner on Spanish soil before the torch made its way across the Atlantic Ocean.

Montreal 1976
The Canadians organized the transmission of the flame by satellite between Athens and Ottawa by transforming it into a radio signal that was sent by satellite to Canada, where it triggered a laser beam to relight the flame on Canadian soil.

Lillehammer 1994
The flame was transferred between two parachute jumpers—in midair—and then made an impressive entry at the opening ceremony of the Games when it was carried by a ski jumper during his actual jump!

Olympic Oddities

Not Allowed Harvard University refused to give student James B. Connolly eight weeks' leave of absence in order to compete in the 1896 Olympics in Greece. So he resigned from the university, paid for the voyage himself—and went on to win the triple jump.

Wrong Anthem At the medal ceremony for the 1964 Tokyo Olympics marathon, won by Abebe Bikila of Ethiopia, the stadium band did not know the Ethiopian national anthem, so they played the Japanese one instead.

First Gold India has 17 percent of the world's population, but the country did not win its first individual Olympic title until 2008 when Abhinav Bindra won the 10-meter air rifle shooting event.

Bully-off As a reward for winning gold in the women's field hockey tournament at the 1980 Moscow Olympics, every member of the Zimbabwe team was presented with a live ox on their return home.

Walk, Don't Run The three leading competitors in the women's 20-km walk at the 2000 Sydney Olympics were all disqualified for running in the final kilometer, leaving China's Wang Liping to claim an unlikely gold medal.

No Gold Long-Jumper Robert LeGendre, from Washington, D.C., set a new world record of 25 ft 5½ in (7.76 m) at the 1924 Olympics—but he didn't win a gold medal because he was competing in the pentathlon.

Olympic Heroes

Dislocated Arm Konrad von Wangenheim helped Germany's equestrian team to win gold at the 1936 Olympics despite riding with a broken collarbone and his left arm in a sling.

Incredible Double At the 1924 Paris Olympics, Finland's Paavo Nurmi won the men's 1,500 meters final and then just over an hour later he won the 5,000 meters final, setting Olympic records in both events.

Changing Hands Hungarian pistol shooter Károly Takács lost his right hand in 1938 when a grenade that he was holding exploded. So he taught himself to shoot left-handed and won a gold medal at the 1948 London Olympics, successfully defending his title four years later in Helsinki.

Heroic Horsewoman Despite being paralyzed below the knees after contracting polio, Denmark's Lis Hartel, who had to be helped on and off her horse, won silver medals in the individual dressage event at both the 1952 and 1956 Olympics.

Wooden Leg U.S. gymnast George Eyser won six medals in one day at the 1904 Olympics in St. Louis—three of them gold—despite having a wooden leg. His left leg had been amputated after he was run over by a train. He even won gold in the long horse vault, which he jumped without a springboard.

Olympic Howlers

Calendar Chaos After spending over 16 days at sea, the U.S. team arrived in Athens for the first modern Olympic Games in 1896 believing that they still had 12 days to prepare for the competition. In fact, the Games started the very next day—the Americans had forgotten that Greece still used the Julian calendar and was therefore 12 days in advance.

Joined Picnic Exhausted by the heat of the 1912 Olympic marathon in Stockholm, Sweden, Japan's Shizo Kanaguri stumbled into the yard of a family who were enjoying a picnic and stayed with them rather than rejoining the race.

Lost Medal After winning a rowing gold medal at the 1956 Olympics, 18-year-old Russian Vyacheslav Ivanov quickly lost it. He threw the medal into the air in celebration, but it landed in the lake. He dived in but was unable to find it.

Missing Gloves Moments before he was due to fight at the 1992 Barcelona Olympics, Iranian boxer Ali Kazemi was disqualified because he had forgotten his gloves.

Hot Stuff To prepare himself for the heat of Rome, where he won the 50-km walk at the 1960 Olympics, Britain's Don Thompson kept the heat on at all times in his bathroom for 18 months—and ran up a gas bill of over £9,000 ($14,300). He returned home from his triumph to find that the gas had been cut off.

Lost in Translation American athlete Loren Murchison was left at the start of the 1920 Olympic men's 100 meters final in Antwerp, Belgium, because he didn't understand French. When the starter said *prêt* ("get set"), Murchison thought that the crouching runners had been told to stand up and was doing so when the starting gun went off.

Shot in Foot U.S. Lieutenant Sidney Hinds won gold in the free rifle team event at the 1924 Olympics in Paris, shooting a perfect 50—despite having been accidentally shot in the foot partway through the competition when the Belgian rifleman positioned next to him threw his loaded weapon to the ground during an argument with an official.

Unusual Olympic Events

Vertical Rope Climb (1896, 1904, 1906, 1924, 1932)

So hard was this event that in 1896 only two of the climbers made it to the top, prompting officials to send the rope back for alterations.

Men's Sailor's 100 Meter Freestyle (1896)

This event was open only to sailors in the Greek Royal Navy. Only three competitors took place in the event. And the winner was from... Greece!

Long Jump for Horses (1900)

A horse named Extra Dry won at the Paris Olympics with a jump of 20 ft ¼ in (6.1 m)—that's shorter than the men's record in 1901.

200 Meter Obstacle Swimming Race (1900)

Held in Paris' River Seine, competitors had to climb over a pole, clamber over a row of boats, and then swim under another row of boats.

Pistol Dueling (1906)

Participants shot over 20 and 30 meters at mannequins that wore fancy frock coats with bull's-eyes embroidered on the chest.

Underwater Swimming Race (1900)

Not the most thrilling visual spectacle, this race was held over 60 meters with competitors being awarded points for each meter swum and time spent underwater.

Pigeon Shooting (1900)

Paris 1900 featured the only Olympic event in history at which animals were deliberately harmed—300 live pigeons. Belgium's Leon de Lunden won gold, bagging himself 21 birds.

Tug of War (1900, 1904, 1908, 1912, 1920)

The Ancient Greeks staged the first tug in 500 BC, but in modern Olympic rules, a team of eight had to pull the opposition 6 ft (1.8 m) to win. London 1908 saw the sport at its most intense, when the United States was beaten in just a few short seconds by Great Britain. The unhappy losers accused the British team—all policemen—of wearing illegal spiked boots, so they were offered a rematch, with the British in their socks. They still lost.

Cold Climb

In February 2010, Andreas Spak from Norway, Christian Pondella from California, and Canadian Will Gadd became the first adventurers to scale the Vøringfossen waterfall in Norway, one of the highest in Europe. In warmer weather, the water surges at 40 ft (12 m) per second, but winter temperatures of 5°F (−15°C) transformed the torrent into a 650-ft (198-m) ice skyscraper.

Surf Club

The Palestinian territory's Gaza Strip has its own surf club, which was founded after a Jewish surfer donated a dozen surfboards to the community.

Fast Match

In October 2009, Jo-Wilfried Tsonga of France and Spain's Fernando Verdasco played a tennis match on board a train traveling at 268 mph (431 km/h). The mini-tennis court was laid out in one of Shanghai's high-speed Maglev trains, so that the players were traveling faster than their serves.

Round-the-World

In 2010, 34-year-old Vin Cox from Cornwall, England, cycled 18,225 mi (29,330 km) around the world in just 163 days. Starting and finishing his journey in London, he took 12 plane and boat transfers, crossed six continents— Europe, (northern) Africa, Asia, Australia, South America, and North America—and cycled through 17 countries.

Big Haul

In August 2010, Jeff Kolodzinski caught 2,160 fish—mostly small bluegills and perch—from Lake Minnetonka, Minnesota, in a 24-hour period.

Liberty Walk

French high-wire walker Didier Pasquette crossed a 150-ft-long (46-m) wire tied between two replicas of the Statue of Liberty on top of the 23-story Liberty Building in Buffalo, New York State, in September 2010. The feat took him about three minutes, and he stopped twice during his walk to wave to the crowds on the ground some 230 ft (70 m) below.

Back Handsprings

At Valmeyer, Illinois, 13-year-old Chelsey Kipping did 32 consecutive back handsprings. She has been doing gymnastics since age four and practices for at least nine hours a week.

Africa Trek

French adventurers Alexandre and Sonia Poussin spent three years walking 8,700 mi (14,000 km) from Cape of Good Hope, South Africa, to Israel, living solely on the hospitality of people they met along the way.

Trapeze Veteran

In his early seventies, Tony Steele still performed as a trapeze artist with the Gamma Phi Circus of Illinois State University, the oldest collegiate circus in the U.S.A.

Karate Kid

Varsha Vinod from Alappuzha, India, became a karate black belt in May 2009—the highest grade in the martial art—at the age of just five. She had been training since she was two and already had more than 15 *katas*, or karate disciplines, to her name.

Manhole Museum

Stefano Bottoni has collected manhole covers from across the world—including from Holland, Finland, Cuba, the Czech Republic, Austria and Romania—for exhibition at his International Manhole Museum in Farrara, Italy.

Ball Control

Twenty-five-year-old schoolteacher Rohit Timilsina of Kathmandu, Nepal, managed to hold 21 standard tennis balls on the palm of his hand for more than 14 seconds in 2008. It took him three years of practice to achieve the feat.

Cat Statues

Winnie Ferring has a collection of more than 1,000 cat statues arranged on every available space inside and outside her home in Lansing, Iowa. She has been collecting them for more than 50 years, and each piece is numbered and documented.

Underwater Juggler

With a single breath, Merlin Cadogan from Devon, England, was able to juggle three objects underwater for 1 minute 20 seconds.

Spinning Yo-Yos

At the 2010 London Toy Fair, Ben McPhee from Australia kept 16 yo-yos spinning simultaneously. He had yo-yos hanging off hooks, his fingers, and even his ears and teeth.

Extra Load

In 2009, British former soldier Kez Dunkley ran the 26.2-mi (42-km) Leicester Marathon in 5 hours 53 minutes with an 84-lb (38-kg) tumble-drier strapped to his back. The previous year he had run the race with a bag of cement on his back.

Harley Jump

California stunt rider Seth Enslow jumped 183 ft 8 in (56 m) on a Harley-Davidson motorcycle near Australia's Sydney Harbour in March 2010. Three years earlier, the bike ace had performed a 200-ft (60-m) jump over a Convair 880 passenger jet airplane.

Young Climber

At just five years old, Sail Chapman of East Yorkshire, England, achieved his ambition of scaling all 214 peaks listed in Alfred Wainwright's famous Lake District guidebooks. He began walking the Cumbrian hills with his family at the age of two and completed the Wainwright peaks when he reached the top of his namesake fell, Sale, which stands at 2,536 ft (773 m).

Tough Granny

Pint-sized Sakinat Khanapiyeva, a 76-year-old grandmother from Dagestan, Russia, can tear through phone books, lift a 52-lb (23.5-kg) dumbbell while standing on a bed of nails, and break iron horseshoes. She first realized how strong she was at the age of ten when she moved a 660-lb (300-kg) box of grain—equal to the weight of four grown men.

Seven Out

In 2009, in his first game as a pitcher for the St. Louis Cardinals, John Smoltz struck out seven hitters in a row—something he had never managed to do in 708 trips to the mound with his previous team, the Atlanta Braves.

Flying Kayak

Miles Daisher of Twin Falls, Idaho, paddles a kayak—across the sky at an altitude of 13,000 ft (4,000 m). The daredevil has invented a new sport, skyaking, a combination of skydiving and kayaking. Sitting in his kayak he jumps from a plane, pulls the chute at about 5,000 ft (1,525 m), and descends at nearly 100 mph (160 km/h), reducing to half that speed as he finally swoops to land spectacularly on water.

Stilt Stunt

In 1891, Sylvain Dornon from Landes, France, walked from Paris to Moscow, Russia, on stilts! He completed the 1,830-mi (2,945-km) journey in 58 days, averaging more than 30 mi (50 km) each day. Earlier in the 19th century, stilts were a fairly common means of getting around marshy terrain in parts of France, especially among shepherds, but, by 1891, Dornon was considered very strange indeed.

Hot Hood

The Russian Extreme Games in Moscow were an opportunity for some of the most daring and crazy stuntmen in Russia to compete against each other in such dangerous events as riding BMX bikes with flaming tires, setting themselves on fire, and riding on the hood of a vehicle as it crashed through an inferno.

Wheelchair Wheelie

Nineteen-year-old Michael Miller of Ellington, Wisconsin, performed a 10-mi (16-km) wheelie in a wheelchair. Michael, who was born with spina bifida, completed 40 laps of a high-school track on two wheels in just under four hours. He performed his first wheelchair wheelie when he was just four years old.

Text Exchange

Nick Andes and Doug Klinger, two friends from central Pennsylvania, exchanged a thumb-numbing 217,033 texts during March 2009. At the end of the month, Andes received an unexpected itemized bill for $26,000—for the 142,000 texts he had sent and the 75,000 he had received from Klinger.

Tea Potty

Over a period of 25 years, Sue Blazye from Kent, England, has built up a collection of more than 6,000 teapots— and they take up so much room that she has converted her home (called Teapot Island) into a museum. Her favorite teapot is in the shape of Princess Diana's head, and was made when Diana got engaged to Prince Charles.

Mayor Moore

Hilmar Moore has served as the mayor of Richmond, Texas, for more than 60 years. He was first appointed in 1949 and has been re-elected every two years since, although the last time he had an opponent was 1996.

Bat Breaker

At the Riverwalk Stadium, Montgomery, Alabama—home of the Montgomery Biscuits Minor League baseball team—Steve Carrier broke 30 baseball bats over his leg in less than a minute. The 6-ft-4-in (1.9-m), 290-lb (131-kg) Carrier, from Dallas, Texas, also bends steel with his teeth.

Happy Hugger

In Las Vegas, Nevada, on Valentine's weekend 2010, 51-year-old Jeff Ondash (a.k.a. Teddy McHuggin) of Canfield, Ohio, gave out 7,777 hugs in just 24 hours—the equivalent of more than five hugs a minute.

RIPLEY'S ASK

Why did you first start balloon flying?

I first became interested in balloon flight as a child—I wondered at a balloon, and how it floated upon the air. Then I thought "If I just get enough of these, couldn't I go into the sky?" As an adult, I left behind the idea that such a thing isn't possible and awakened a dream that had grown quiet.

What inspired you to cross the channel?

The English Channel is a challenge that has called to aviators for generations. There is romance in flying over the famous White Cliffs of Dover and the Lighthouse at Dunkirk.

What was it like when you were in the sky?

A quiet dream. I was 1,000 ft (305 m) above the water and I could hear only the waves. When you're in the air, you move perfectly with the wind, not knowing where you'll land.

Was it a bumpy landing?

The landing was smooth, but after the landing, as I worked to release the helium and take my balloons down, the winds kicked up!

What are your balloon ambitions?

I would like to launch out of California, within sight of the ocean, and then fly inland, above the Sierra Nevada mountains, into the heart of America.

Into the Skies

Aerial adventurer and qualified pilot Jonathan R. Trappe from North Carolina made history in May 2010 by traveling 76 mi (122 km) across the English Channel attached to a bunch of 55 helium balloons. Drifting from Ashford, England, toward France, Jonathan reached speeds of 35 mph (56 km/h) and heights of 7,000 ft (2,135 m). Three hours 22 minutes after taking off, and after a flight adjustment to avoid Belgium, he landed safely in a cabbage field near Dunkirk, France.

Nose-to-Nose

In March 2010, Robert Officer and John Milhiser from the Serious Lunch comedy group touched noses together for 10 hours 34 minutes, with no breaks or interruptions. Robert and John's record-breaking task included a trip on the New York subway and bathroom breaks together before appearing live on the Jimmy Fallon show.

Saddle Sore

Riding 49cc mini-bikes that averaged just 20 mph (32 km/h), Ryan Galbraith and Chris Stinson traveled the 445 mi (716 km) from Denver, Colorado, to Sturgis, South Dakota, in 25 hours 29 minutes in 2009.

Senior Student

Hazel Soares of San Leandro, California, received her college diploma in May 2010—at age 94! "It's taken me quite a long time because I've had a busy life," said the mother-of-six, who has more than 40 grandchildren and great-grandchildren.

Rabbit Jumping

As well as pioneering show jumping, where horses clear obstacles, Sweden established the sport of rabbit jumping, in which domestic rabbits are trained to jump miniature fences without touching them.

Backward Running

Germany's Achim Aretz ran 6 mi (10 km) backward in 41 minutes 26 seconds at the third Retrorunning World Championships in Kapfenberg, Austria, on August 8, 2010.

Ruff Justice

In Athens, Georgia, a woman scared off a would-be burglar by acting like a dog. She got on the floor and began scratching at the door when the intruder tried turning the door knob—he then ran away.

Everest Landing

British skydivers Leo Dickinson and Ralph Mitchell and Indian Air Force officer Ramesh Tripathi successfully landed their parachutes at an altitude of 16,800 ft (5,120 m) on Mount Everest in September 2009. After jumping out of a helicopter at 20,500 ft (6,250 m), they had just five seconds of free fall in which to open their chutes. The trio had to home in on Gorak Shep—a narrow, sand-covered lakebed and the only safe landing spot for miles. "It was pretty hairy," said 62-year-old Dickinson. "If you missed that or overshot it, you were either going to die or end up with something important broken."

First Female

In 2010, Kelly Kulick of the U.S.A. became the first woman to qualify for the Professional Bowlers' Association's Tournament of Champions—and she went on to beat an all-male field of 62 to claim the title.

Pole Balance

David Cain of Liberty Township, Ohio, can balance a 58-ft-long (17.7-m) fiberglass pole on his chin for more than 21 seconds. It took him two years to master the skill.

Sports Survivors

These heroic athletes and fans have the scars to show how sport can be dangerous. Incredibly, all have survived and, believe it or not, returned to the arena for more.

Let's work it out together.

HOCKEY HORROR

Buffalo Sabres' goaltender Clint Malarchuk narrowly escaped death after a collision caused a player's skate to cut the carotid artery in his neck during a 1989 hockey match against the St. Louis Blues. If the skate had hit Malarchuk ⅛ in (3 mm) higher, he would have been dead within two minutes. The injury was so horrific that 11 fans fainted and two had heart attacks, while three players vomited on the ice. Malarchuk needed 300 stitches to fix the wound, but was back playing in goal ten days later.

DANGEROUS RING

Celebrating a goal for Swiss team Servette in 2004, recently married Portuguese soccer player Paulo Diogo jumped on the stadium fence and caught his wedding ring on the top. When he jumped off, he left the ring and half his finger behind. To add insult to injury, the referee showed him a yellow card for time wasting as the doctors searched for the missing finger! Although doctors were unable to reattach the digit, Diogo quickly resumed his career.

MOST DANGEROUS SPORTS IN THE U.S.A.
(Injuries per year)

1. Basketball 512,213
2. Cycling 485,669
3. Football 418,260
4. Soccer 174,686
5. Baseball 155,898
6. Skateboarding 112,544
7. Trampolining 108,029
8. Softball 106,884
9. Swimming/diving 82,354
10. Horseback riding 73,576

UNLUCKY BREAK

Brazilian-born Croatian soccer player Eduardo suffered a horrific broken leg when playing for his club team, Arsenal, in England's Premier League in 2008. A tackle by Birmingham City's Martin Taylor left Eduardo's anklebone sticking through his sock and kept him out of the game for almost a year.

DIVING BELLE

Seventeen-year-old Columbus, Ohio, diver Chelsea Davis smashed the bridge of her nose on the diving board while competing at the 2005 World Swimming Championships in Montreal, Canada. She was lifted on to a stretcher, her face covered in blood, but she never lost consciousness and was soon back competing.

FACEBALL BAT

When baseball player Kelly Shoppach of the Cleveland Indians let the bat slip at a game against the Texas Rangers in Arlington, Texas, in 2006, this unfortunate fan failed to notice Shoppach's bat flying straight toward his face. In 2009, Shoppach claimed another victim when he struck a female fan in the face with a foul ball during a game against the Kansas City Royals.

175

Ice Bath

Wearing only swimming trunks, Jin Songhao and Chen Kecai immersed themselves in ice up to their necks for 120 minutes and 118 minutes, respectively, high up on Tianmen Mountain in China's Hunan Province in January 2011. Jin was even able to write Chinese calligraphy during his ordeal.

California Wingwalk

Traveling at speeds of 100 mph (160 km/h), often in the face of strong winds, Ashley Battles of Tulsa, Oklahoma, stood on the wing of a biplane for more than four hours in June 2010. Her wingwalk took place over San Francisco, California, giving her fabulous views of the Golden Gate Bridge and Alcatraz.

陈可财

长沙南湖医院
2011
天門山传奇
冰凍活人挑战极限

长沙南湖医院
2011
天門山传奇
冰凍活人挑战极限

金松浩

Shark Incentive

Spain's David Calvo solved two Rubik's Cube puzzles one-handed simultaneously in just 76 seconds while inside a tank with six sharks at the Terra Natura Park in Benidorm, Spain.

Tightrope Walk

Chinese tightrope walker Adili Wuxor spent more than five hours a day for 60 days gingerly walking across a 1.3-in-thick (3.3-cm) steel wire strung across Beijing's Bird's Nest stadium at a height of more than 200 ft (60 m) above the ground. He walked about 12 mi (19 km) a day, so that he covered around 700 mi (1,130 km) in total.

Gorilla Run

More than 1,000 people dressed in gorilla suits to take part in the 2009 Denver Gorilla Run, a 3½-mile (5.6-km) charity run/walk through the streets of the city to help raise funds for mountain gorilla conservation.

Poker Session

Professional poker player Phil Laak of Los Angeles, California, played poker for more than 115 hours from June 2 to June 7, 2010, at the Bellagio Hotel in Las Vegas, Nevada. He finished $6,766 up.

Hang Tough

Strapped into special gravity boots and hanging upside down from a frame, Zdenek Bradac from the Czech Republic juggled three balls for 2 minutes 13 seconds, during which time he made 438 consecutive catches.

Speedy Mower

Don Wales drove a lawn mower at a speed of more than 87 mph (140 km/h) at Pendine Sands in Wales, in May 2010. His grandfather, Sir Malcolm Campbell, broke the world land speed record, in a car, at the same venue in 1924.

Stiletto Sprinters

Running along a 263-ft (80-m) course at Circular Quay in Sydney, New South Wales, Australia, a relay team of four women from Canberra—Brittney McGlone, Laura Juliff, Casey Hodges and Jessica Penny—completed the four legs in 1 minute 4 seconds—while wearing 3-in-high (7.5-cm) stiletto heels.

Bulky Wear

Croatia's Kruno Budiselic managed to wear 245 T-shirts—ranging in size from medium to extra large—at the same time. The extra clothing added around 150 lb (68 kg) to his overall weight.

Bathtub Voyage

Rob Dowling of Dublin, Ireland, sailed 500 mi (800 km) down the Amazon River in a motorized bathtub in 2006. The 5-ft-7-in (1.72-m) fiberglass tub was supported by six 36-gal (136-l) steel drums and propelled by a 15-horsepower motor. He had intended to sail from Iquitos in Peru to the Atlantic—2,465 mi (3,967 km)—but his journey ended after just over 500 mi (800 km) when Brazilian authorities told him he didn't have a licence for the bathtub!

Switch Hitters

It took 134 years for the Arizona Diamondbacks' Felipe Lopez to become the first baseball player in history to switch-hit homers from both sides of the plate on Opening Day. It took just one inning, in the same 2009 game, for Tony Clark to become the second.

King Gnome

Andy and Connie Kautza of Wausau, Wisconsin, built a concrete garden gnome that stands 15 ft (4.5 m) tall and weighs more than 3,500 lb (1,590 kg).

Chopper Leap

Defying potentially dangerous turbulence, U.S. daredevil motorcyclist Travis Pastrana successfully backflipped a dirt bike over a helicopter that was hovering off the ground in front of Australia's Sydney Harbour Bridge, clearing the revolving chopper blades by about 13 ft (4 m).

Paper Round

Ted Ingram has been delivering newspapers in Dorset, England, for nearly 70 years. He started his job in 1942 and estimates that he has since delivered more than half a million papers.

Human Wheelbarrow

In Helsinki, Finland, Adrian Rodrigues Buenrostro from Mexico and Sergiy Vetrogonov from Ukraine finished a 131-ft (40-m) human wheelbarrow race in just 17 seconds.

Mass Waltz

More than 1,500 couples—from children to pensioners—danced a waltz in the main square of Tuzla, Bosnia, in 2010. Organizers estimated that as many as 25,000 people danced in the surrounding streets, but the square had to be sealed off so that the couples had room to move.

Free Haircuts

Working round the clock, a team of ten stylists from Pump Salon completed 618 free haircuts in 24 hours in Cincinnati, Ohio, in September 2010.

Car Wash

Students from Bloomington High School South, Indiana, cleaned 1,207 cars in 10 hours in a marathon car-wash.

Still Life

S.C. Naganandaswamy of Karnataka, India, can float in 20 ft (6 m) of water for 22 hours continuously without moving any limbs.

Human Sparkler

Dr. Peter Terren of Bunbury, Western Australia, shot more than 200,000 volts of electricity down his body to create a spectacular version of Rodin's *The Thinker*. He turned himself into a human sparkler for 15 seconds by using a homemade Tesla coil, which transforms a feed of domestic electricity into a supercharged bolt of power. He was saved from electrocution by wrapping his torso, arms and legs in builders' insulating foil—the electricity traveled through the foil and out to the earth from his foot. He also wore a tin-foil cap and a wire-mesh mask, and taped steel wool to the bottom of his left shoe to create the shower of sparks from his foot.

Mirror Image

U.S. golfer Phil Mickelson is right-handed in everything but golf. He plays left-handed after mirroring his father's right-handed swing as a child.

One Hand

At 6 ft 10 in (2.1 m) tall, Kevin Laue of Pleasanton, California, received a scholarship to play basketball for Manhattan College despite having only one hand.

Every Ground

In February 2010, Scott Poleykett from Kent, England, completed a 50,000-mi (80,000-km) journey to visit every soccer ground, professional and amateur, in England and Wales. In the course of his ten-year mission, he took photographs of 2,547 soccer fields.

Sand Skis

Germany's Henrik May prefers to ski on sand rather than snow—and in the Namibian Desert he reached a speed of 57.24 mph (92.12 km/h) while skiing down a 246-ft-high (75-m) dune. He has developed a special type of wax that enables the skis he uses to slide over sand.

Tattoo Tribute

Colombian soccer fan Felipe Alvarez has had his upper body tattooed to resemble a jersey of his favorite team, Atletico Nacional. The tattoo is in honor of Andrés Escobar, the Colombian player who was shot dead as a result of scoring an own goal, which lost his side the match, while playing against the U.S.A. at the 1994 World Cup. Seen here with Atletico player Victor Aristizábal, Alvarez now has Escobar's number 2 permanently marked on his back.

Tennis Marathon

At the 2010 Wimbledon Tennis Championships, John Isner of the U.S.A. beat France's Nicolas Mahut in a match that lasted more than 11 hours over three days. The match began at 6.18 p.m. on Tuesday, June 22 and finished at 4.49 p.m. on Thursday, June 24, Isner eventually winning 6-4, 3-6, 6-7, 7-6, 70-68 in a final set that lasted 8 hours 11 minutes.

Flying Shot

In 2010, Tyler Toney, a student from Texas A&M University, made a basketball shot he threw from a low-flying airplane!

Atlantic Crossing

A four-man crew led by Scotsman Leven Brown overcame 40-ft (12-m) waves, two capsizes and an outbreak of food poisoning to row 3,500 mi (5,600 km) across the Atlantic from New York to the Isles of Scilly, which lie off the southwest coast of England, in 43 days in 2010. They were following the route of a Norwegian crew who had made the same crossing in 55 days back in 1896.

Wrestling Champs

In 2010, Blair Academy of Blairstown, New Jersey, won its 30th consecutive National Prep School Wrestling Championship.

Veteran Coach

Soccer coach Ivor Powell finally hung up his boots at age 93. A former Welsh international forward, he went on to train more than 9,000 players during his 53-year coaching career.

Monkey Guards

Organizers at the 2010 Commonwealth Games in New Delhi, India, hired monkeys to work as guards at the athletes' village. They hoped that the special team of 40 gray langur monkeys would chase off the packs of smaller rhesus monkeys that had been breaking into buildings and stealing from the competitors' quarters.

Leap of Faith

Escape artist and evangelist Anthony Martin performed a daring skydive from an airplane flying at 13,500 ft (4,115 m) over Illinois—wearing handcuffs that were locked to a chain around his neck and linked to leather cuffs fastened above each elbow.

To add to the stunt's death-defying nature, the safety device attached to his parachute that automatically deploys the chute at 700 ft (215 m) was turned off. Without this backup, he had just 45 seconds, while spinning to Earth at 180 mph (290 km/h), to free himself from the handcuffs and chains and to reach back to pull the release handle and activate the canopy.

Falling in a sitting-back position, Anthony seemed to struggle with the lock for about 25 seconds before working himself free and safely deploying the chute.

The 45-year-old from Sheboygan, Wisconsin, has been picking locks since he was a child and made his first authenticated escape at age 12, when he managed to work his way out of a regulation police straitjacket. He jokes that he comes from the "School of Hard Locks."

Since childhood he has broken out of a locked box thrown from an airplane, escaped from being buried alive beneath 2,000 lb (907 kg) of sand, and freed himself from a heavily secured coffin submerged underwater. He has even requested permission to break out of Fort Knox—where most of the U.S. gold bullion reserves are stored—but the U.S. Government refused to allow the escape bid.

Underpants Man

Gary Craig from Newcastle, England, also known as the Geordie Pantsman, took 25 minutes to clamber into an incredible 211 pairs of underpants in an unusual charity challenge in April 2010. Gary initially planned to wear 200 underpants, but an Australian rival had achieved this landmark only a few days before, so Gary was forced to set his sights higher and find bigger pairs of pants. This caused problems, as the smaller the underpants the greater the pressure, making it a painful physical challenge.

Beer House

In Schleiden, Germany, Sven Goebel spent three months building a five-room apartment made entirely from 300,000 beer mats. It featured a table, chairs and a fireplace—all made of beer mats. After spending up to eight hours a day, seven days a week, on construction, he then had to knock down the finished building to prove that it had been held together only with static, not adhesive.

Free-fall Solution

After jumping from an airplane at an altitude of 14,000 ft (4,300 m), Ludwig Fichte of Dresden, Germany, flew through the air while sitting in a rubber dinghy and solving a Rubik's Cube puzzle. It took him 31.5 seconds during a free-fall descent of 5,900 ft (1,800 m) to solve the cube, at which point he deployed his parachute.

Stamp Collector

Postman Alan Roy from Dorset, England, spent 70 years painstakingly peeling off two million stamps from envelopes. He soaked each envelope in water and then carefully removed the stamp with tweezers. His collection is so big it fills up 40 packing crates that stack as high as a house.

Old Scout

Reg Hayes, 95, of Oxford, England, retired in 2010 after 87 years as a Boy Scout. He joined the 2nd Oxford Wolf Cub pack in 1923 and moved up to the SS Mary and John 2nd Oxford Scouts in 1930, where he stayed for the next 80 years.

Cucumber Man

Frank Dimmock, 87, from Oxfordshire, England, grew a cucumber 41¼ in (104.8 cm) long in 2010. Known as the "Cucumber Man," he has been growing vegetables since before World War II when he became an apprentice to a gardener.

Pi Chart

Using only a single standard desktop computer costing less than $3,000, French software engineer Fabrice Bellard calculated pi to nearly 2.7 trillion decimal places. The complex calculation took him 131 days.

Plane Pull

In Jilin, China, in 2010, martial-arts expert Dong Changsheng took less than a minute to pull a half-ton airplane for 16 ft (5 m)—by a rope hooked to his eyelids! He had previously pulled a car with his eyelids but this was his first attempt with a plane.

Giant Clock

The family clock-making firm Smith of Derby, England, built a huge mechanical clock 42 ft 8 in (13 m) in diameter with a minute hand 25 ft 7 in (7.8 m) long. The 11-ton clock took a year to design and build and was delivered to its final home—in Ganzhou, China—in 2010 for installation in the 371-ft-high (113-m) Harmony Tower.

Golf Balls

When Chris Morrison from Dunfermline, Scotland, noticed a strange rattling sound coming from the stomach of his black Labrador, Oscar, he took the five-year-old dog to a veterinarian—who removed 13 golf balls from the animal's stomach. One of the balls had been in Oscar's stomach so long that it had turned black and was decomposing.

Commentator's Nightmare

The finish of an August 2010 race at Monmouth Park, New Jersey, was fought out between horses named Mywifeknowseverything and Thewifedoesn'tknow. The two horses were completely unconnected, and had separate trainers and owners.

Human Fly

Jem Stansfield climbed the side of a 30-ft (9-m) wall of a school in Brighton, England, using nothing more than suction from two vacuum cleaners. The 168-lb (76-kg) aeronautics graduate adapted the household appliances' motors into giant suckerpads, which were strong enough to support him and enabled him to cling to the wall.

Flying Lanterns

More than 10,000 twinkling white paper lanterns were released simultaneously into the night sky from a beach in Jakarta, Indonesia, in December 2009. The flying lantern is a Chinese tradition. It is basically a paper bag containing a block of paraffin with a wick suspended by wire across the opening. When the wick is lit, the air inside warms like a hot-air balloon and the lantern lifts off into the sky.

Rubber Bands

Eleven-year-old Allison Coach of Chesterfield Township, Michigan, created a chain of 22,140 rubber bands that stretched nearly 7,000 ft (2,130 m)—or 1.3 mi (2 km)—long.

Champion Plowgirl

Thirteen-year-old schoolgirl Elly Deacon beat experienced farmers for first place in a plowing competition in Hertfordshire, England. Elly, who had driven a tractor for the first time only four days before the event, impressed judges with her straight and smooth plow marks on a 53,000-sq-ft (4,900-sq-m) patch of land, while at the wheel of the six-ton tractor.

Turbo Terry

Terry Burrows from Essex, England, cleaned three windows, each measuring 45 sq in (290 sq cm), and wiped the sills in just 9.14 seconds during a window-cleaning competition in Blackpool, Lancashire. "Turbo Terry" actually finished the task in 8.14 seconds, but was handed a one-second time penalty for leaving two water marks on the glass.

Rain Dance

More than 230 dancers took to the wet streets of Bath in Somerset, England, with umbrellas in May 2010 to perform a five-minute version of Gene Kelly's classic "Singin' in the Rain."

Sand Burial

As part of the 2010 Clogherhead Prawn Festival in County Louth, Ireland, 524 people simultaneously buried themselves up to their necks on a sandy beach.

Cake Tower

Chef Gilles Stassart and architect Jean Bocabeille designed a cake for display in Paris, France, in July 2010 that was nearly 26 ft (7.8 m) tall— that's as high as a two-story house. The "Tower without Hunger" was made from 1,385 lb (628 kg) of flour, 1,120 lb (508 kg) of sugar, 350 eggs, and 40 lb (18 kg) of butter. The towering cake was meant to last four days outdoors but sweltering temperatures made it soft and unstable and it had to be taken down after just 24 hours.

Slow Progress

Lottie the tortoise disappeared from her home in Essex, England, in 2008—and was found safe and well nearly two years later, having traveled just 1½ mi (2.4 km).

Emerald Hunter

Jamie Hill of North Carolina has dug up nearly 18,000 carats of emeralds in his home state since 1998.

Poker Face

Bai Deng from Shandong, China, can hurl a regular playing card so hard and with such accuracy that he can slice a cucumber in two. It's not as impossible as it might seem, given that in 2002 U.S. magician Rick Smith Jr. threw a playing card a distance of 216 ft 4 in (66 m) at a speed of over 90 mph (145 km/h).

Major Mite

Clarence C. "Major Mite" Howerton was born in February 1913, and was billed by the press in the 1930s as the smallest man in the world. He stood only 28 in (71 cm) tall and weighed just 20 lb (9 kg). He was so small that he once traveled from New York to Chicago to find a tailor who would make a tuxedo for his diminutive size. He wore custom-made shoes just 2.5 in (6 cm) long.

The Ringling Brothers and Barnum & Bailey Circus signed up Major Mite in 1923, when he was ten years old, and he starred in its sideshow for more than 25 years. As well as being a big draw on the sideshow circuit, Major Mite featured in several Our Gang comedy shorts and played a trumpet-playing munchkin in the 1939 film *The Wizard of Oz*.

After a life in show business, he died in Oregon at the age of 62.

At only 28 in (71 cm) tall when fully grown, Major Mite was no bigger than the average toddler.

Tiny Major Mite being held aloft by his friend, giant Jack Earle.

Major Mite performed with many extreme individuals, such as 700-lb (318-kg) Ruth Pontico.

Reports suggest that Major Mite had a rebellious streak, sometimes dressing in children's clothes and then shocking the public by smoking, shouting— or posing on a motorbike.

What Knife?

Julia Popova of Moscow, Russia, was attacked by a mugger in February 2010 but walked home not aware that she had been stabbed and that the knife was still impaled in her neck.

Skeleton Growth

A person's skeleton continues to grow until around age 25, when the collarbone finally finishes developing.

Miss Plastic

A 2009 beauty contest in Budapest, Hungary, was open only to women who had undergone cosmetic surgery. "Miss Plastic" featured contestants who had enhanced their bodies with everything from new breasts and liposuction to hair transplants.

Secret Bullet

Vasily Simonov of Togliatti, Russia, has lived with a bullet in his lung for 70 years. As a child in 1941, he was playing with a rifle cartridge when he decided to take out the bullet and shove it up his nose. After trying in vain to remove it, he then breathed it in. He forgot all about it and the lodged bullet never caused him any problems, only coming to light during an MRI scan in 2009. Even then, doctors decided it was best to leave the bullet where it was.

Big Baby

At age two, Fan Sijia of Yuncheng City, Shanxi Province, China, was 3 ft 7 in (1.1 m) tall and weighed 100 lb (45 kg)—about four times the average weight for a girl her age.

Strong Boy

Kyle Kane, a 12-year-old schoolboy from the West Midlands, England, lifted a 308-lb (140-kg) weight—more than twice his own body weight—at a junior bodybuilding event in 2010.

Kept "Dying"

Motorcyclist Steven Nixon from Derbyshire, England, suffered a massive heart attack after being in a collision with a car—but he pulled through even though he had technically "died" 28 times over the next few hours when his heart repeatedly stopped beating.

Body Sale

In 2010, anatomist Gunther von Hagens launched a mail-order service for his Plastinarium museum in the German town of Guben, selling human and animal body parts that had been preserved with a special plastic solution. Items for sale included a smoker's lung ($4,440), a chunk of human head ($2,000), a slice of a human hand ($228), and a cross-section of giraffe neck (price unspecified).

Human Skeleton

Billed as the "Skeleton Dude" at Coney Island's Dreamland Circus in 1917, Eddie Masher of Brooklyn, New York, stood 5 ft 7 in (1.7 m) tall, but he declared he weighed just 38 lb (17 kg). Other records have put him at 48 lb (22 kg) or as much as 67 lb (30 kg), but even those weights were astonishingly light for an adult man. He was so skinny that tailors struggled to make a suit that would fit him. He died in 1962 at 70 years old—a good age for a skeleton!

EDDIE MASHER, Skeleton Dude, Height 5 ft. 7 in. Weight 38 lbs.

Constantly Seasick

Jane Houghton from Cheshire, England, went on a week-long Mediterranean cruise—and still feels permanently seasick more than nine years later. She suffers from the rare Mal de Debarquement Syndrome, which causes people to feel as though they are constantly bobbing about on a rough sea. She feels so nauseous and wobbly that she has even had to stop buying clothes with stripes or busy patterns because she is unable to focus to iron them.

Busy Brain

The number of neurons in your brain—100 billion—is about the same as the number of stars in our galaxy.

Matching Horns

A Chinese grandmother who grew a 2.4-in (6-cm) horn on the left side of her forehead in 2009 began to develop a similar growth on the right side of her forehead a year later. Zhang Ruifang from Linlou has cutaneous horns—growths made of keratin, the same substance that makes up fingernails. Most cutaneous horns are just a tiny fraction of an inch long, but occasionally they can extend a number of inches from the skin.

Weight Loss

In January 2010, former postman Paul Mason of Suffolk, England, weighed 980 lb (444.5 kg)—but then he instantly lost 294 lb (133.5 kg) after undergoing gastric bypass surgery. The operation involved having part of his stomach stapled off so that all the food he eats goes into a small pouch, vastly restricting the amount he can consume. At his heaviest he ate 20,000 calories a day—eight times the amount needed by an average man.

Coal-powered Bike

Sylvester H. Roper of Roxbury, Massachusetts, built a steam-powered velocipede in the 1860s that drove like a motorcycle but was instead fueled by coal.

Teenage Toddler

Although she is old enough to drive a car, Brooke Greenberg of Reisterstown, Maryland, weighs just 16 lb (7.2 kg), is 30 in (75 cm) tall, and rides around in a stroller pushed by her mother. The teenager has the body and behavior of a tiny toddler, thought to be the result of a mutation in the genes that control her aging and development, and which has apparently left her frozen in time.

Chute Terror

Skydiver Paul Lewis survived after falling 3,000 ft (900 m) onto the roof of a hangar at Tilstock Airfield, Shropshire, England, in August 2009. His main parachute failed to open at 3,000 ft (900 m) and although his reserve chute opened at 2,000 ft (600 m), a problem caused him to spiral out of control from 1,000 ft (300 m) with the canopy only partially opened. Luckily, the parachute became snagged on the hangar roof, preventing him from plunging to the ground and to almost certain death.

Bionic Bottom

After suffering massive internal injuries in a motorcycle crash, a man from South Yorkshire, England, now presses a remote control to open his bowels and go to the toilet. Surgeons rebuilt his bottom by taking a muscle from above his knee, wrapping it around his sphincter, and then attaching electrodes to the nerves. He can operate the electrodes using a handset that he carries in his pocket and switches to on or off to control his bowel movements.

Twisted Tiger

Double contortionists Hassani Mohammed (right) and Lazarus Mwangi of Cirque Mother Africa bend over backward to entertain the audience at a show in Hamilton, New Zealand.

Tooth Test

Scientists can determine the ages of people born after 1943 to within 18 months by examining the amount of radioactive carbon in their teeth, caused by above-ground nuclear weapons testing in the 1950s and 1960s.

Iron Man

In 1848, a man working on the Vermont railway survived having an iron rod blasted right through his face and out of the top of his skull. Phineas Gage had been using explosives to clear space for the tracks by packing gunpowder into holes in rock with a heavy iron rod when a spark ignited the powder and the rod shot through his head.

Unbelievably, Gage survived this horrific accident and remained physically able for the rest of his life, although damage to his brain significantly altered his character. His injury became famous in medical circles, and contributed to an understanding of how the brain works. Gage returned to work as a coach driver and died in 1860, 12 years after his accident.

Identified as Gage in 2009, this photo shows him with the same 13-lb (6-kg) temping iron that pierced his brain, which he kept as a gruesome souvenir. He lost the sight in his left eye when the rod passed behind it.

Hair Insured

American football player Troy Polamalu, a defender with the Pittsburgh Steelers, has had his hair insured for $1 million by Lloyd's of London. His 3-ft-long (90-cm) black curls are so famous that he has not cut them since 2000. Although he wears a helmet while playing, his hair is still at risk—in 2006 he was tackled by his ponytail by Larry Johnson of the Kansas City Chiefs after intercepting a pass.

Magnetic Disruption

Placing a magnet on your head can temporarily turn a right-handed person into a left-hander. By positioning a powerful magnet on the left posterior parietal cortex—a region of the brain that deals with planning and working out the relationship between three-dimensional objects—researchers at the University of California, Berkeley, found that normally right-handed volunteers started to use their left hand more frequently for tasks such as picking up a pencil or calling an elevator. This is because the magnet disrupted and confused the volunteers' brains.

Epic Climb

Three U.S. war veterans climbed 19,341-ft (5,895-m) Mount Kilimanjaro in Tanzania in 2010—despite having only one good leg between them. Amputees Dan Nevins, 37, of Jacksonville, Florida, who lost his legs in Iraq; Neil Duncan, 26, of Denver, Colorado, who lost both legs in a roadside bomb attack in Afghanistan; and Kirk Bauer, 62, of Ellicott City, Maryland, who lost a leg in Vietnam in 1969, made the climb on their prosthetic legs in just six days.

Human Heads

When airport workers in Little Rock, Arkansas, noticed a package that was not labeled properly, they checked the contents and found a shipment of 60 human heads. Further investigation revealed the heads were on their way to a company in Fort Worth, Texas, to be used by neurosurgeons for the study of ear, nose and throat procedures.

Face Booked

In 2010, Chang Du from Lishuguo, China, went public with an offer to sell advertising space on his oversized chin. After a small pimple in his mouth swelled massively over a period of five years, Chang made the bizarre proposal in order to raise funds to reduce his chin back to normal size. He confirmed that an $8,000 offer would be enough to secure the space on his face.

197

Heads of State

Chinese micro-artist Jin Y. Hua has painted the face of every President of the U.S.A. from George Washington to George W. Bush—that's 42 portraits—on a single human hair less than ½ in (1.3 cm) long and just 0.0035 in (0.09 mm) thick. Jin uses a brush made from a single rabbit hair to apply the paint.

Lyndon B. Johnson 1963–1969

Ronald Reagan 1981–1989

Thomas Jefferson 1801–1809

George Washington 1789–1797

John Adams 1797–1801

Thomas Jefferson 1801–1809

James Madison 1809–1817

James Monroe 1817–1825

John Quincy Adams 1825–1829

Andrew Jackson 1829–1837

Martin Van Buren 1837–1841

William Henry Harrison 1841

John Tyler 1841–1845

James K. Polk 1845–1849

Zachary Taylor 1849–1850

Millard Fillmore 1850–1853

Franklin Pierce 1853–1857

James Buchanan 1857–1861

Abraham Lincoln 1861–1865

Andrew Johnson 1865–1869

Ulysses S. Grant 1869–1877

Rutherford B. Hayes 1877–1881

James A. Garfield 1881

Chester A. Arthur 1881–1885

Grover Cleveland 1885–1889 & 1893–1897

Benjamin Harrison 1889–1893

William McKinley 1897–1901

Theodore Roosevelt 1901–1909

William Howard Taft 1909–1913

Woodrow Wilson 1913–1921

Warren G. Harding 1921–1923

Calvin Coolidge 1923–1929

Herbert Hoover 1929–1933

Franklin D. Roosevelt 1933–1945

Harry S. Truman 1945–1953

Dwight D. Eisenhower 1953–1961

John F. Kennedy 1961–1963

Lyndon B. Johnson 1963–1969

Richard Nixon 1969–1974

Gerald Ford 1974–1977

Jimmy Carter 1977–1981

Ronald Reagan 1981–1989

George H. W. Bush 1989–1993

Bill Clinton 1993–2001

George W. Bush 2001–2009

John F. Kennedy 1961–1963

Richard Nixon 1969–1974

Beautiful Bite

To enhance their beauty, women in the Mentawai Islands of Indonesia have their teeth filed into sharp points. The unusual rite of passage, in which the teeth are chiseled into shape with no anesthetic, conforms to local opinions of beauty rather than any practical purpose. Observers have commented that Mentawai women seem to feel no pain during the process, and that they willingly undergo the ritual.

Worm's-eye View

After John Matthews of Bellevue, Iowa, noticed two spots obscuring the vision in his left eye, doctors diagnosed the cause—a worm had got into his eye. The worm—thought to be either a hookworm or a raccoon roundworm—was then killed by medics who shot a laser into his left eyeball. "I could see it from behind," he said, "moving, trying to dodge the laser."

Free Leg

Needing a $60,000 bionic leg so that he could walk again, David Huckvale of Leicestershire, England, happened to go to his local pub on the same day as surgeon Alistair Gibson, who specializes in fitting the computer-controlled limbs. When the two got talking, Mr. Gibson mentioned he had a spare leg and could fit it for free!

Changing Beard

Sameer Mehta, a businessman from Gujarat, India, makes weekly trips to the barber and has had more than 60 styles of short beard in the last four years. These have included a heart-shaped beard and another trimmed in the design of his country's flag.

Rare Phenomenon

A woman who had been pronounced dead hours earlier at a hospital in Cali, Colombia, following a series of unsuccessful resuscitation attempts, suddenly started breathing again in a funeral home as workers began to apply formaldehyde to her body. Doctors later diagnosed her condition as a case of Lazarus Syndrome, an extremely rare phenomenon in which the body's circulation spontaneously restarts after failed resuscitations.

26 Digits

Heramb Ashok Kumthekar from Goa, India, has six fingers on each hand and seven toes on each foot, giving him a total of 26 digits. He is proud of his condition, called polydactylism, even though he has insufficient nerve endings to feel all his fingers and toes.

Super Schoolgirl

At just 16 years old, schoolgirl Marvadene Anderson stood 6 ft 11 in (2.1 m) tall, making the New Jersey school basketball star 5 in (12.5 cm) taller than her idol, Michael Jordan. Height must run in the family, because the Jamaican-born teenager's older sister, Kimberly, is 6 ft 4 in (1.9 m) tall.

Bullet in Head

After being shot at point-blank range by a German soldier in 1944, Ivan Nikulin of Chita, Russia, lived happily with a bullet lodged in his head for nearly 70 years.

Nose Leech

Tyrannobdella rex, a new species of leech with savage, sawlike teeth, was first discovered in the nose of a nine-year-old Peruvian girl. Named after the most ferocious dinosaur in history, the 2-in (5-cm) bloodsucker came to light after the girl, who regularly swam in tropical rivers and lakes, complained of feeling a sliding sensation in one of her nostrils.

Body Piercing

In April 2010, Ed Bruns of Gillette, Wyoming, had more than 1,500 16-gauge needles inserted into his arms, back, and legs by a body-piercing artist in less than 4½ hours.

Tattoo Proposal

When San Diego, California, tattoo artist Joe Wittenberg decided to propose to his girlfriend, he inked the words "Rachel, will you marry me?" on his own leg.

Dissecting Dad

To help teach anatomy to his students, Dr. Mahantesh Ramannavar dissected the body of his father, Dr. Basavanneppa Ramannavar, which had been embalmed for exactly two years. His father had specified in his will that his body should be donated to the university in Belgaum, India, where his son worked and that his son should perform the dissection, which was shown live on Indian TV.

Serial Sleeper

Claire Allen from Cambridge, England, falls asleep 100 times a day. Her condition—an extreme form of narcolepsy—causes her to fall into a trancelike state where she is unable to see or move. Each episode lasts between 30 seconds and five minutes and is triggered by emotions such as surprise and anger, and especially surfaces when she laughs.

Join the Dots

Inspired by the idea of getting her birthmarks numbered, Colleen A.F. Venable from New York City has a connect-the-dots tattoo that creates the shape of a giraffe on her left leg.

Hiccup Cure

After hiccupping an estimated 20 million times over a period of three years, Chris Sands of Lincolnshire, England, finally stopped in 2009 following brain surgery. It is thought that a tumor on his brain stem had been pushing on nerves, causing him to hiccup every two seconds, 24 hours a day.

Turning the Screw

After an operation to remove a tumor left a gaping hole in his leg, 14-year-old Simeon Fairburn from Brisbane, Australia, saved the limb by turning surgical screws on a leg brace four times every day for over two years to stretch the bone by 1 ft (30 cm). He initially faced amputation, but after wearing the brace and undergoing 20 operations, he still has a chance of achieving his dream and becoming a basketball player.

Skewered Neck

Twelve-year-old Garret Mullikin from Houston, Texas, survived after a 9-in-long (23-cm) stick skewered his neck. Falling off a dirt bike, he hit the ground and the piece of tree branch, as thick as a broom handle, plunged into his neck and down into his chest, through his lung, and past vital arteries and his heart. Doctors said that if the stick had been pulled out before he was in hospital, he could have bled to death.

Diamond Tattoo

South African jeweler Yair Shimansky designed a temporary tattoo made of 612 diamonds and carrying a price tag of $924,000. It took more than eight hours to encrust the ornate floral design on the skin of a model using a special water-based adhesive.

Dental Dirt

This is what your used dental floss looks like when magnified more than 500 times. Dental plaque, formed from bacteria and saliva, is clearly visible on the tiny floss fibers. Photographer Steve Gschmeissner from Bedford, England, used an electron microscope capable of magnifying objects more than 500,000 times to show everyday household items in a completely new light.

Guardian Angel

Angel Alvarez survived despite being shot 23 times by New York City police officers during a disturbance in August 2010. Although he was shot in the arms, legs, abdomen and jaw, all the bullets somehow missed his vital organs.

Deadly Device

U.S. Army Private Channing Moss survived a direct body hit from an anti-vehicular rocket in Afghanistan. Luckily, the explosive head failed to detonate, but he was impaled by the rocket shaft.

Tiny Tot

A premature baby boy born at the University of Goettingen Hospital, Germany, in 2009 survived despite weighing less than 10 oz (283 g) at birth. The tiny tot weighed just 9.7 oz (275 g)—which is 75 g (2.6 oz) below the weight doctors consider the minimum birth weight for a baby to survive.

Canadian Citizen

On December 31, 2008, a Ugandan woman gave birth on an airplane flying over Nova Scotia, Canada. Her newborn daughter was granted Canadian citizenship.

Reading Mystery

On July 31, 2001, Canadian mystery writer Howard Engel awoke from a stroke and discovered he could no longer read—but could still write. He was diagnosed as having alexia sine agraphia, which meant that newspapers and even his own books appeared to be written in indecipherable oriental script.

Supersized Son

At age three, Xiao Hao of Guangzhou, China, weighs a massive 140 lb (63.5 kg)—as much as an adult man. He dwarfs his mom and has been banned by some nurseries as a hazard to other children.

Extreme Survival

Jonathan Metz of West Hartford, Connecticut, saved his own life by partially sawing off his left arm after it had become trapped in his furnace boiler and started to turn gangrenous. Taking a blade from his toolbox, he began sawing through the arm to prevent the infection spreading to the rest of his body. To stem the flow of blood, he used first his shirt and then a telephone cord as a tourniquet. After more than two days—during which his only drink was rust-colored boiler water scooped into his mouth with a flip-flop he had been wearing—he was rescued and taken to hospital where doctors completed the amputation.

Rare Quads

In December 2009, Lisa Kelly of Middlesbrough, England, gave birth to a set of quadruplets made up of two sets of identical twins—a ten-million-to-one chance!

Vulture Tonic

In southern Africa, vultures' brains have become so popular as a traditional medicine that it has contributed to seven of the region's nine vulture species becoming endangered.

Knife Horror

Xiao Wei, a 16-year-old from Jilin, China, had a knife stabbed through his head that went in one side and out the other—but he survived after a two-hour operation to remove the blade.

Lucky Bounce

An 18-month-old boy escaped without a scratch after falling 80 ft (24.4m) from his seventh-floor apartment in Paris, France, bouncing off a café awning and into the arms of a passing doctor. The café was closed for the day and the awning was out only because a mechanism had jammed.

On the Run

Former British Army soldier Mike Buss from Swindon, England, completed 517 1/4 mi (832.4 km) on a treadmill over seven grueling days. He ran the equivalent of nearly three marathons a day, sleeping for just two hours a day, and lost two toenails in the process.

Weird Inhalation

After Artyom Sidorkin started coughing blood and complaining of chest pains, surgeons in Russia found a 2-in-long (5-cm) spruce tree inside his lung. He must have inhaled the piece of tree, which then got lodged in his lung, causing it to become seriously inflamed.

Self-service

After badly cutting his leg in an accident at home, a 32-year-old man became so frustrated at having to wait an hour at Sundsvall Hospital in northern Sweden that he picked up a needle and thread and sewed up the cut himself.

Tugged Off

In June 2009, a man from Shenzhen, China, was competing in a game of tug-of-war when he had his hand pulled off.

Born Twice

Doctors in Texas performed prenatal surgery at 25 weeks to remove a grapefruit-sized tumor from Macie McCartney, while she was still inside her mother's womb. The procedure involved pulling out the uterus of mother Keri and then half of Macie's body. Once free from the tumor, Macie was returned to the womb, where she recovered and grew for another ten weeks before being "born" again.

Snowshoe Beard

David Traver of Anchorage, Alaska, was the winner of the 2009 World Beard and Moustache Championships with his 20½-in-long (52-cm) beard woven to resemble a snowshoe.

Baby Frozen

Sixteen-week-old Finley Burton of County Daurham, England, was put in a hospital "deep freeze" for four days to keep him alive when complications arose after heart surgery. His heart had started to beat alarmingly quickly, so his body was placed in a "cool bag," through which cold air was pumped to keep his temperature down. This slowed his metabolism, which in turn slowed his heart rate.

Large Family

After giving birth to two sets of quadruplets (in 2004 and 2005), Dale Chalk of Sydney, New South Wales, Australia, had twins in 2009, giving her a total of 11 children under the age of seven.

Dangerous Operation

In March 2010, U.S. Army medical staff at Bagram airfield in Afghanistan wore armor in the operating room while removing a live high-explosive round from the scalp of a soldier from the Afghan Army.

Single Handed

Despite being born with just one hand, Kevin Shields from Fort William, Scotland, is an accomplished rock climber and has even mastered treacherous ice climbs.

Baby's Tail

Surgeons in China performed an operation to remove a 5-in-long (13-cm) tail from the body of a four-month-old baby girl. Hong Hong, from China's Anhui Province, was born with the tail, but it quickly doubled in size. X-rays had shown that it was connected to a fatty tumor within her spinal column.

Reverse Walker

Rotating his feet nearly 180 degrees, Bittu Gandhi of Rajkot, Gujarat, India, can walk backward while facing forward!

Parasitic Twin

Eighteen-month-old Kang Mengru of Henan Province, China, had her dead twin removed from her stomach. Her parents were puzzled by her increasingly swollen stomach, which made her look pregnant, until medical scans revealed that she was carrying the parasitic fetus of her unborn twin in her belly. In such rare cases—affecting one in 500,000 births—one twin in the womb grows larger than the other and envelops its smaller sibling. The second fetus never fully develops, but continues to grow within the first baby, feeding off it like a parasite.

Too Many Toes

In 2010, doctors at a hospital in Shenyang, China, operated on a six-year-old boy who had eight toes on each foot and 15 fingers owing to a rare genetic mutation known as central polydactyly. After a 6½-hour operation, medics had successfully removed 11 extra digits.

A Bicycle Made for Two

Although Charles B. Tripp had no arms and Eli Bowen had no legs, they were able to ride a bicycle—together. Known to circus audiences as "The Armless Wonder" and "The Legless Wonder," they simply combined their physical attributes on a tandem bicycle—Tripp pedaling with his legs and Bowen steering with his arms.

Charles B. Tripp was born without arms in 1855 in Woodstock, Ontario, Canada, but soon learned to dress himself and write using his feet. Remarkably, he made his living as a skilled carpenter until joining Barnum's Circus, which was the start of a 50-year career as a performer. He specialized in penmanship, portrait painting and paper cutting—holding the implements between his toes. Around the turn of the century, he developed an interest in photography and became known as "The Armless Photographer." He died in 1939 in Salisbury, North Carolina, at the grand age of 84.

Eli Bowen was born in Ohio in 1844. He was one of ten children, all of whom were able-bodied except for Eli who had seal limbs, or phocomelia, a condition that left him with no legs and with two feet of different sizes growing from his hips. As a child he walked on his arms, perfecting a technique whereby he held wooden blocks in his hands that enabled him to swing his hips between his arms. The strength he gained from this helped him become a talented acrobat and, at the age of 13, he joined his first circus troupe.

Despite his condition, Eli was considered by many to be the most handsome man in showbusiness and, at age 26, he married Mattie Haight who was ten years his junior. The couple had four healthy sons. Eli continued performing into his eighties, and his death, from pleurisy in 1924, was just days before he was due to appear at The Dreamland Circus at Coney Island, New York.

Eli Bowen with his wife and son.

Charles Tripp having a cup of tea.

Lick Off

Actor Nick Afanasiev from California has an incredible role all to himself—as the owner of America's longest tongue! Stretching to an unbelievable 3.5 in (9 cm), it means that Nick can lick his own nose and even his elbow, a bizarre feat that most people find impossible.

Snake Twins

In June 2009, in Xiaogan, eastern China, Hui Chung gave birth to conjoined twins, who were known as the "snake babies" because they were attached at the waist. The siblings shared one long body with a head at each end, and as they did not have external sexual organs, it was impossible to say what sex they were.

Long Hair

When 79-year-old Tran Van Hay died in Kien Giang, Vietnam, in February 2010, his hair was more than 22 ft (6.7 m) long and weighed 23 lb (10.5 kg). He began to let his hair grow more than 50 years ago, because he often became sick after a haircut. As his hair grew, he balanced it on his head like a basket.

Miracle Escape

A Japanese toddler who wandered onto rail tracks in Suzaka City escaped with only scratches after a train came to a halt on top of her. After spotting the girl, the driver applied the emergency brakes and the train stopped with the girl beneath. She survived because she was trapped in the 20-in (50-cm) gap between the train and the tracks.

Scorched Footprints

For two weeks in 2009, Sikeli Nadiri left a trail of scorched footprints on grassland around his home village in Fiji. There was no explanation as to why the grass had burned away beneath his feet, as he had not stepped on any chemicals or anything else that would cause scorching.

Nickel Allergy

Kim Taylor from Northamptonshire, England, is unable to touch hundreds of everyday items like keys, coins, zippers, scissors, door handles and saucepans because she is severely allergic to nickel. She takes her own wooden-handled cutlery to restaurants and has to cover everything nickel—even her eyeglasses, bra clasp, and buttons—in nail varnish so that her skin doesn't ever come into contact with the metal.

Turtle Boy

Maimaiti Hali from Heping, China, was born with a hard, mutated growth covering most of his back, its shell-like appearance leading bullies to call him "Turtle Boy." The growth was removed from the eight-year-old's back in a two-hour operation in 2010 and replaced with skin grafts from his scalp and legs.

Rope Bed

Gao Yang of Liaoning Province, China, can sleep on a single length of rope tied between two trees for up to seven hours at a time. He was taught special balancing skills at age 12 but it took him nearly a quarter of a century to master this feat by practicing on a 10-ft-high (3-m) rope in his local park every morning.

Cat Boy

A boy in Dahua, China, has bright blue eyes that glow in the dark and enable him to see in the pitch black. Nong Youhui can read perfectly in complete darkness and also has good vision during the day. Medical experts think he was born with a rare condition called leukodermia, which has left his eyes with less protective pigment and made them more sensitive to light.

Sum Girl

A 15-year-old schoolgirl with a love of math was awakened from a coma when her father began asking her simple sums. Vicki Alex of Northamptonshire, England, had been unconscious for three days and had failed to respond to other attempts to stimulate her brain, but after her father's intervention she soon regained full consciousness.

Body-building Granny

At age 73, grandmother Ernestine Shepherd of Baltimore, Maryland, gets up at 3 a.m. and spends her days running, lifting weights and working out. She runs 80 mi (130 km) a week—the equivalent of three marathons—bench-presses 150 lb (68 kg) and lifts 20-lb (9-kg) dumbbells.

Heart Stopped

Joseph Tiralosi of Brooklyn, New York City, miraculously survived after his heart stopped beating for 45 minutes. The 56-year-old father had gone into sudden cardiac arrest inside the emergency room at New York-Presbyterian/Weill Cornell Medical Center, and it was nearly an hour before doctors succeeded in getting his heart going again. Usually if a person cannot be revived within six minutes, they die. Equally incredibly, he came through the whole episode without suffering any form of brain damage.

Sandwich Bag

To keep up the body temperature of a tiny premature baby, medics at Worcestershire Royal Hospital in England used the smallest insulating jacket they could find—a 6-in (15-cm) plastic sandwich bag from the hospital kitchens. The improvised insulator did the trick and saved the life of little Lexi Lacey who had been born 14 weeks early weighing just 14 oz (396 g) and had been given only a ten percent chance of survival.

Mini Man

At age 22, Wu Kang from Wuhan, China, wears the clothes of a nine-month-old baby and stands just under 2 ft 3 in (68 cm) tall. Wu suffers from panhypopituitarism, which decreases the secretion of hormones, including growth hormones, produced by the pituitary gland in the brain.

Breathe In!

Steve McFarlane of South Jordan, Utah, can displace some of his internal organs to suck in his stomach with spectacular effect.

Free Flights

Thirty-one-year-old Liew Siaw Hsia gave birth on an AirAsia flight over Malaysia in October 2009, and as a result the company granted her and her child free flights for life.

Second Face

A baby born in China's Hunan Province has two faces. Kangkang was born in 2009 with a transverse facial cleft that extends nearly all the way up to his ears, making it look as if he is wearing a mask.

Gold Tattoo

A business in Dubai offers temporary body tattoos made of real gold. The 24-carat gold-leaf tattoos are in demand for glitzy parties and weddings and can be bought for as little as $50. The company is also offering tattoos in platinum.

Poke-a-Nut

During a 2009 martial-arts demonstration in Malacca, Malaysia, Ho Eng Hui pierced four coconuts with his index finger in 31.8 seconds.

Making Antivenom

Snake antivenom is commonly produced by injecting horses with snake venom, then collecting the appropriate antibodies from their blood.

Mass Extraction

Between the ages of seven and 12, Chelsea Keysaw of Kinnear, Wyoming, underwent three oral surgeries to remove a total of 13 extra permanent teeth and 15 baby teeth.

Foot Skills

Born without arms, Ren Jiemei from Shandong Province, China, has learned to use her feet to eat, wash, comb her hair, draw pictures and cut paper. She is so skilled with her feet that when she uses them to thread a needle she is always successful on the first attempt—in fact, she is said to be the best embroiderer in her village. In her school days, she often topped the class despite having to write with her feet and use her mouth to turn book pages.

Route 66

Ron Jones of Bartlesville, Oklahoma, gets his kicks out of having Route 66 tattoos all over his body. He has more than 80 tattoos dedicated to destinations along the 2,448-mi (3,940-km) highway, including the Ariston Café in Litchfield, Illinois, and the arch on the Santa Monica Pier in California, which marks the end of the road.

Einstein Scan

An X-ray of Albert Einstein's skull fetched more than $35,000 at a 2010 auction in Beverly Hills, California. The genius scientist had the scan in 1945, ten years before his death at age 76.

Tattooed Mom

Bishop's daughter and mother-of-three Jinxi Boo, from southern California, has almost her entire body covered in tattoos. She has a tattoo of a black-and-white dairy cow (because she's vegan), portraits of her family, and her favorite musicians (Gwen Stefani, Björk, Cyndi Lauper and Meg White), plus a spectacular octopus tattoo across her throat and chest that took 26 hours to complete. A trip to Disneyland as a teenager inspired her love of tattoos, but she did not have her first design—a small cherry on her ankle—until she was 30.

Caught Toddler

Two-year-old Zhang Fangyu survived a 100-ft (30-m) fall in Hangzhou, Zhejiang Province, China, in June 2011 after she climbed out of a 10th-floor window and was caught by a woman walking in the street below. Her rescuer, Wu Juping, suffered multiple fractures to her arm.

Skydiving Champ

Despite losing both his legs in a bomb explosion in Northern Ireland in 1992, former paratrooper Alistair Hodgson of Cumbria, England, is a freestyle skydiving champion and has made more than 5,000 jumps.

Arm Wrestler

Joby Mathew from Kerala, India, may be only 3 ft 5 in (1.05 m) tall but he is a champion arm wrestler. Despite having severely underdeveloped legs, he is able to defeat able-bodied opponents who are twice his height. He can also jump up steps using only his hands and perform push-ups on just one hand.

Miracle Boy

Seventeen-month-old Jessiah Jackson of Leland, North Carolina, fell from a chair in July 2010 and a metal hook pierced his skull. It penetrated 2 in (5 cm) into his brain, but he survived.

Rusty Nail

A man had a rusty 4.7-in-long (12-cm) nail removed from his left kidney in Zhengzhou, Henan Province, China. The nail had been in Mr. Gao's body for 20 years following an accident at home. Although it had cut into his stomach and entered his body, he had sterilized the wound and it healed. In time, a membrane formed around the nail, preventing it penetrating deeper into his body.

Glass Eater

Wang Xianjun of Sichuan Province, China, has eaten more than 1,500 lightbulbs. He started snacking on broken glass when he was 12 because it was "crispy and delicious," and now regularly eats a bulb for breakfast. He smashes the bulb and swallows it piece by piece while sipping from a glass of water. Although his bizarre diet has apparently not affected his health, it did cost him his marriage. He had kept his glass munching a secret from his wife, but when she caught him, she thought it was too weird and they separated.

Blood Camp

The Indian political party Shiv Sena collected 24,200 bottles of human blood in a single day at a blood donation camp in Goregaon.

Saved by Implants

When a gunman opened fire with a semiautomatic assault rifle in a dentist's office in Beverly Hills, California, Lydia Carranza's life was saved by her size-D breast implants, which took the force of the blow and stopped bullet fragments from reaching her vital organs.

Impaled by Tree

A 13-in-long (33-cm) tree limb crashed through the windshield as Michelle Childers of Kamiah, Idaho, and her husband were driving down the road, impaling her through the neck. Amazingly, she survived.

Sticky Situation

Irmgard Holm, 70, of Phoenix, Arizona, sealed her eye shut after mistakenly using quick-drying glue instead of eye drops. She had confused the two products' similar-looking bottles. Doctors cut off the glue covering her eye and washed out the remainder to prevent serious damage.

Titanic Tumor

Doctors in Buenos Aires, Argentina, removed a tumor weighing 50 lb 11 oz (23 kg) from the womb of a 54-year-old woman in 2010. It had been growing inside her body for 18 months. She entered a hospital for the operation weighing 308 lb (140 kg), but after the removal of the tumor she was discharged weighing just 231 lb (105 kg).

Head Returned

Lewis Powell, a conspirator in the assassination of U.S. President Abraham Lincoln, was hanged in 1865 and was buried headless. His skull had been missing for 127 years when it was found in storage in the Smithsonian Museum and returned to the body.

Tongue Typist

Legally blind and unable to use his hands, Josh LaRue of New Concord, Ohio, wrote a book by tapping out the words in Morse Code using his tongue.

Bee Therapy

Bed-ridden multiple sclerosis sufferer Sami Chugg from Bristol, England, was able to get back on her feet after being stung 1,500 times by bees. The Bee Venom Therapy, carried out over a period of 18 months, involved holding a bee in a pair of tweezers and deliberately stinging an area of skin around her spine.

Chinese Accent

After suffering a severe migraine headache in March 2010, Sarah Colwill of Plymouth, Devon, England, suddenly started speaking with a Chinese accent—despite never having been to that country. Doctors say she has Foreign Accent Syndrome, a rare condition that damages the part of the brain that controls our speech and word formation.

Monster Stone

A kidney stone the size of a coconut was removed by surgeons in Hungary from the stomach of Sandor Sarkadi. Whereas even the largest kidney stones are seldom bigger than a golf ball, this one measured a whopping 6¾ in (17 cm) in diameter and weighed 2½ lb (1.1 kg).

Accidents Happen

SHARP REMINDER

Having penetrated a man's skin, a nail is lodged in the bones of his index and middle fingers.

X-rays were first observed in 1895 by German physicist Wilhelm Roentgen, who found them accidentally while experimenting with vacuum tubes. A form of electromagnetic radiation, they have gone on to become one of the most useful tools in medical practice, employed for identifying everything from broken bones to accidentally swallowed toothbrushes.

SAFETY PIN

A safety pin lodged in the esophagus of a woman.

KEY LOCATION

This X-ray shows that this seven-year-old boy swallowed a key.

Bumpy Landing

In June 2009, window cleaner Alex Clay from Eau Claire, Wisconsin, fell six floors, bounced off a concrete first-floor roof, and landed on the ground—surviving with nothing worse than a broken foot bone and a cut on his leg.

Botox Cure

A stroke victim who had been paralyzed for more than 20 years was able to walk again after being injected with Botox, a substance usually associated with smoothing wrinkles. Having been told by doctors that he would never regain his mobility, Russell McPhee of Victoria, Australia, was able to stand up and walk a few yards just a month after his first Botox injection.

Chopstick Removal

A Chinese man had a chopstick removed from his stomach 28 years after swallowing it. Mr. Zhang had swallowed the chopstick in 1982, but thought it had been digested until he started suffering stomach pains. X-rays revealed that the remains of the chopstick were still lodged inside him. Surgeons in Shanghai extricated it by making a small incision in his stomach.

Chance Discovery

An X-ray of a 35-year-old woman from Para, Brazil, who complained of earache revealed that she had over 20 steel needles in her body. She had inserted the needles into herself as a child.

Fatal Pick

In September 2008, a man from Manchester, England, died from a nosebleed caused by his aggressive nose picking.

Horned Man

Jesse Thornhill of Tulsa, Oklahoma, has two devil horns on his head, created by surgically implanting Teflon lumps under the skin to stretch the scalp. The heavy-metal fan also boasts tattooed eyebrows, lengthened earlobes, and implant earrings on his head.

Echo Location

A blind English boy has learned to "see" again after adopting a technique used by dolphins and bats to detect where objects are. Jamie Aspland from Ashford, Kent, navigates his way around obstacles by means of echolocation, whereby he utters high-pitch clicks and then interprets the sound that rebounds off the surfaces around him.

Tortoise Woman

For nearly 30 years, Sun Fengqin from Inner Mongolia carried a 55-lb (25-kg) tumor on her back, which resulted in her being nicknamed "Tortoise Woman." The tumor started as a yellow birthmark but grew so large that in the end she struggled to walk upright.

Rubber Man

Vijay Sharma of Rajasthan, India, is so flexible that he can pass his body through a tennis racket, wind his arms around his back so that his hands grip each other at the front of his waist, wrap his legs over his head, and drink from bottles that he has gripped between his toes.

Souvenir Finger

After losing part of his small finger, Matthew Tipler of Bend, Oregon, took the tip, encased it in clear plastic, and made a keychain out of it.

Amnesia Victim

In 2009, a man later identified as Edward Lighthart walked out of a park in Seattle, Washington, with $600 in his sock but with no idea of who he was and how he got there— the victim of a rare form of dissociative amnesia.

Tall Teen

At age 14, Brazilian teenager Elisany Silva towers over her sisters because she is already 6 ft 9 in (2.06 m) tall. She is so tall that she had to stop going to school because she could not fit on the bus. Medical experts believe she could be suffering from gigantism, a condition in which the body produces excessive amounts of growth hormones. If left untreated she could continue to grow up to 6 in (15 cm) more a year.

Hidden Needle

Doctors in China's Henan Province removed a needle from a man's brain that may have been there for 50 years. Following a seizure, Lin Yaohui, 51, was rushed to hospital where X-rays revealed the 2-in-long (5-cm) metal needle embedded in his skull. As an adult's skull is hard, surgeons believe the needle must have penetrated his head before he was 18 months old.

Bearded Lady

When she suddenly started to grow facial hair in the 1920s, Mrs. Baker B. Twyman of Peoria, Illinois, supported her family by joining the circus as a bearded lady. She later had the surplus hair surgically removed.

Sneezed Bullet

A man who was shot in the head during New Year's Eve celebrations in Naples, Italy, survived after sneezing the bullet out of his nose. The .22 calibre bullet went through the right side of Darco Sangermano's head, behind his eye socket, and lodged in his nasal passage. Bleeding heavily, he was rushed to a hospital but while waiting to be seen by doctors, he sneezed and the bullet flew out of his right nostril.

Name Jinx

The parents of a boy who has failed to grow since being born on Dwarf Street claim the name has jinxed their child. Four-year-old Liu Chengrui from Wuhan, China, still weighs just 11 lb (5 kg) and stands only 2 ft (60 cm) tall.

Eye Twitch

Barbara Watkins of Halifax, England, suffers from a rare and bizarre condition that causes her to wink thousands of times a day. She has blepharospasm, an incurable condition that causes frequent muscle contractions around the eyes and affects just a handful of people in every million.

High Life

Husband and wife Wayne and Laurie Hallquist of Stockton, California, measure a combined height of 13 ft 4 in (4.07 m). He stands 6 ft 10 in (2.1 m) and she is 6 ft 6 in (1.97 m).

Extra Bones

Dan Aziere of Danbury, Connecticut, suffers from multiple hereditary exostoses, a rare genetic disorder that causes extra bones to keep growing in his body. He estimates that he has about 50 excess bones—some as large as 4 in (10 cm) long—and since the age of five he has had more than a dozen operations to remove them.

Tiny Tot

At 21 years old, Hatice Kocaman from Kadirli, Turkey, has the body mass of an eight-month-old baby. She suffers from a rare bone disease and stands just 28 in (70 cm) tall and weighs only 15 lb (6.8 kg).

Belly Button Bears

Artist Rachel Betty Case from Bethlehem, Pennsylvania, turns belly button fluff into tiny bears. She collects the lint from the belly buttons of male friends and sells her cute fluffy creations in small glass jars.

Eight Limbs

Before having an operation to remove them when he was seven years old, Deepak Paswaan of Bihar, India, had four extra limbs—the result of being born with the arms, legs, and buttocks of a parasitic twin protruding from his chest. Although the parasitic twin's arms were small and withered, its legs grew at the same rate as Deepak, meaning the youngster had to carry a heavy weight around.

Talented Toes

Since having both arms amputated at age ten after an accident, Liu Wei of Beijing, China, has learned to do everything with his feet. He uses his toes to eat, dress himself, brush his teeth and surf the Internet. He even plays the piano with his toes and earned a standing ovation when he performed on the TV show *China's Got Talent*, which he then went on to win.

Bullet Surprise

A 35-year-old Polish man who went to a hospital in Bochum, Germany, worried about a small lump on the back of his head, was unaware that he had been shot five years earlier. It was only when doctors removed a .22 caliber bullet from his skull that he remembered receiving a blow to the head around midnight at a New Year's Party.

Metal Muncher

Doctors in Cajamarca, Peru, removed 2 lb 3 oz (1 kg) of metal from a man's stomach, including nails, coins, copper wire and scrap metal. Requelme Abanto Alvarado said he had been eating metal for months and had once swallowed 17 5-in (13-cm) nails in one day.

Not Twins

In 2010, Angie Cromar from Murray, Utah, found herself pregnant with two babies at the same time—but they weren't twins. She was born with a rare condition called didelphys, meaning two uteruses, and she had conceived in both—at odds of one in five million.

New Language

A 13-year-old Croatian girl woke from a 24-hour coma speaking fluent German. The girl was no longer able to speak Croatian but was able to communicate perfectly in German, a language that she had only just started studying at school.

Self-amputation

Ramlan, an 18-year-old construction worker who was trapped by a fallen concrete girder in the rubble of a building that collapsed during a 2009 earthquake in Padang, Indonesia, survived by sawing off his own leg.

Toddler Plunge

Two-year-old Zhu Xinping had a miraculous escape after falling from the 21st floor of an apartment block in Jianyang City, Sichuan Province, China. She escaped with nothing worse than a broken leg after landing on a freshly dug pile of soil that cushioned her fall.

Long Lobes

Jian Tianjin, a farmer from Taiwan, has stretchy earlobes that make his ears 6½ in (16 cm) in length. His lobes are so long and flexible that they reach his shoulders and can be wound around his chin.

Hairy Hands

Since becoming the first American to undergo a double hand transplant, Jeff Kepner from Augusta, Georgia, has noticed that his new hands are considerably hairier than the rest of his body because the donor had more hair than him.

Gall Stones

Doctors in Shenyang, Liaoning Province, China, removed more than 880 stones from the gall bladder of a 67-year-old woman. Mrs. Miao's gall bladder was so full of stones it had swollen to the size of a fist, forcing doctors to remove the whole bladder. They estimated that the stones had been forming inside her for about 20 years.

Sucked Hair

After her car swerved off the road in Colorado, Cynthia Hoover survived for five days in the freezing wilderness of the Rocky Mountains by sucking water from her wet hair into her mouth. She was eventually found because she managed to crawl 450 yd (410 m)—despite having 11 broken ribs, a punctured lung and several broken vertebrae—to where she heard voices coming from a disused mine.

Still Singing

After suffering a stroke, singer Ann Arscott of Birmingham, England, was left unable to speak—but she could still sing. She has aphasia, a condition caused by damage to the areas of the brain responsible for language. It impairs speech, but some people with it can still sing, as music activates a different part of the brain.

Celebrity Tattoos

Steve Porter from Nottingham, England, has 12 autographed pictures of celebrities—including Alice Cooper, Anastacia and Ozzy Osbourne—inked onto his skin as tattoos. In total, he has more than 20 tattoos of actors and rock stars covering his body.

Body Bacteria

There are as many as ten times the number of living bacteria and bugs in and on our bodies as there are human cells. Of the estimated 100 trillion microbes, the most densely populated areas of flesh are the belly button, the bottoms of the feet and between the fingers.

Sneezed Nail

Prax Sanchez, 72, of Colorado Springs, Colorado, had an MRI scan for an ear problem, which dislodged a nail in his head that he then coughed up after the procedure. He had no idea that the nail was there and it could have been decades old.

First-aid App

During the 65 hours that U.S. filmmaker Dan Woolley was trapped following the Haitian earthquake in January 2010, he used an iPhone first-aid application to treat his fractured leg and head wound.

Deep Sleep

A Polish man woke up from a 19-year coma to find the Communist Party no longer in power and food no longer rationed. After being hit by a train in 1988, railway worker Jan Grzebski also slept through the weddings of four of his children and the births of 11 grandchildren.

Facial Transplant

Thirty Spanish doctors at the Vall D'Hebron Hospital in Barcelona worked for 22 hours in March 2010 to perform a full facial transplant on a patient, which included skin, nerves, muscles, nose, lips, cheekbones, teeth and a jawbone. The recipient, a 31-year-old man, is eventually expected to regain up to 90 percent of his facial functions.

Star Wars Tattoos

Star Wars fan Luke Kaye from Wiltshire, England, has undergone more than 100 hours of pain to have his body tattooed. His back, arms and legs are covered with tattoos of over a dozen characters from all six *Star Wars* movies, including Luke Skywalker, C-3PO and Darth Vader.

Churchill's Chompers

A pair of gold-plated false teeth owned by former British Prime Minister Winston Churchill sold at auction for £15,000 ($24,000) in 2010. Without his dentures, Churchill would never have been able to make his rousing wartime speeches—in fact, they were so valuable to him that he carried a spare set at all times.

Long Locks

Asha Mandela from Clermont, Florida, has hair that measures over 19 ft (6 m), longer than a pickup truck. Asha has not had her hair cut for an astonishing 25 years.

Furry Features

Supatra Sasuphan from Bangkok, Thailand, was born with Ambras Syndrome—or congenital hypertrichosis—a rare genetic disease that causes excessive hair growth on the face and other parts of the body.

It affects one person in a billion, and there are fewer than 40 known cases in the world. There is no permanent cure for the condition, but nine-year-old Supatra doesn't let it affect her life and enjoys the same activities as her schoolfriends. She hopes eventually to become a teacher.

Parachute Plunge

When her parachute became entangled seconds after she exited an airplane above South Africa, skydiver Lareece Butler plunged 3,000 ft (915 m) before hitting the ground—she survived with a broken leg, broken pelvis, bruises and concussion.

Seven-foot Worm

Sailing on board the ship *Elizabeth* from Cork, Ireland, to Quebec, Canada, in June 1825, 12-year-old Ellen McCarthy fell ill and coughed up three intestinal worms, the longest of which measured 7 ft 3 in (2.2 m).

Lightning Strike

Dog-walker Brad Gifford of Kettering, England, had a miraculous escape after he was knocked unconscious, burst both eardrums, and exploded into flames when a 300,000-volt bolt of lightning struck him on the ear. The lightning was traveling at 14,000 mph (22,500 km/h) and had heated the air around it to 54,032°F (30,000°C)—five times hotter than the surface of the Sun.

Illustrated Lady

Julia Gnuse of Foothill Ranch, California, got her first tattoo to cover unsightly blisters on her legs, but she became hooked and now has tattoos over 95 percent of her body, including her face. Known as "The Illustrated Lady," her body drawings include jungle scenes, cartoons, and the cast of *Bewitched*.

Magnetic Fingers

By having tiny magnetic implants inserted in their fingers, people are able to pick up metal items, such as paper clips or bottle tops, seemingly by magic. Some people have even had magnets inserted in the backs of their hands or on their ears!

Big Baby

At ten months old, Lei Lei, a baby from Hunan Province, China, weighed 44 lb (20 kg)—equivalent to the weight of an average six-year-old.

Back to Life

A 73-year-old woman was brought back to life 30 minutes after her heart stopped beating during a hospital test in Changsha, China. Usually a person dies if they cannot be revived within six minutes.

Ate Finger

In a protest over unpaid wages, a Serbian union official chopped off his finger and ate it. Zoran Bulatovic, a union leader at a textile factory in Novi Pazar, was so angry because some of his fellow workers had not been paid for several years that he used a hacksaw to chop off most of the little finger on his left hand and then ate it to underline the fact that the workers could no longer afford to eat conventional food.

Beatle Tattoo

Beatles fan Rose Ann Belluso of Downington, Pennsylvania, took a sign to Paul McCartney's Philadelphia show in August 2010 asking him to sign her back with a marker pen that she had brought along. After the singer called her up on stage and obliged, she decided to make the inscription permanent the next day by getting a tattoo artist to ink over the signature.

Puff, Puff… Boom!

Unlucky Andi Susanto of Indonesia lost six of his teeth when a cigarette he was smoking mysteriously exploded in February 2010.

Lucky Break

When Raymond Curry overturned his car near his home in Northumberland, England, he was rushed to the hospital with a fence post speared through his chest. At the hospital, doctors were relieved to see that the post had amazingly missed all of his vital organs. They found a four-leafed clover stuck to his back!

Saving Lives

Ben Kopp, a U.S. Army Ranger Corporal, was killed while saving six soldiers in a firefight and then helped save the lives of 75 others by donating his organs and tissues.

Little Miss Dynamite

Dr. Thienna Ho, 5 ft (1.5 m) tall and weighing barely 95 lb (43 kg), deadlifted 104,846 lb (47,557 kg) in one hour in San Francisco. The barbell she lifted weighed 46 lb (21 kg)—nearly half her body weight. She has previously completed more than 5,000 sumo squats in one hour.

Sprouting Pea

Doctors in Cape Cod, Massachusetts, investigating the cause of a patient's sickness, were stunned to find that he had a pea plant growing in his lung. They believe Ron Sveden, from nearby Brewster, had eaten a pea at some time in the previous couple of months but that it had gone down the wrong way, and the seed had split inside him and started to sprout, growing to about ½ in (1 cm) in size.

Self-styled

Etienne Dumont, a journalist from Geneva, Switzerland, has some of the most stunning body modifications in the world. He is tattooed from head to toe with vibrant images including skulls, flowers and animals, but most striking are the designs covering his face and a hole stretched in his chin, held open by a transparent disk through which you can see his teeth. He also has a synthetic horn implant protruding from his scalp and has also used progressively larger disks to stretch his earlobes.

Body of Work

A closer look at these images reveals that they are all created using the human body. By painting directly onto skin, artist Craig Tracy of New Orleans, Louisiana, manipulates the natural shape of his models against a meticulously designed background, creating mind-blowing illusions without the use of computer trickery.

Craig uses photographs to plan the image and then models often sit for hours at a time as he applies the paint, with each painting taking on average one day to complete.

IMMACULATE

Immaculate features a hand-painted and airbrushed background. Once the models are in position, Craig adds the final paint to their body.

BUTTERFLY

Named after the butterfly
shape visible on the nose
of the panther, Craig
completed Butterfly in one
mammoth 24-hour session,
with only one hour of sleep
for both him and his model.

Crochet Lions

English "crochetdermist" Shauna Richardson spent two years hand-crocheting three huge lions, each measuring 25 ft (7.5 m) long and 10 ft (3 m) high. She crocheted the skins in wool, accurately tracing the animals' muscular contours, over a polystyrene and steel framework. Shauna also crochets life-size pieces, which have included wild boars, bears and baboons.

New York Bears

Joshua Allen Harris placed inflatable polar bears made from discarded plastic bags above ventilation grates in the New York City subway so that the animals inflated and deflated with the passing of underground trains.

Traveling Bible

A unique 1,500-page traveling Bible, written in 66 languages—one language for each book of the Old and New Testament—has toured more than 150 countries. The huge 15-lb (7-kg) book, which measures 18 × 12 in (45 × 30 cm), set off on its tour from the Philippines in October 2008.

Baseball Mementos

Mitch Poole, clubhouse manager with the Los Angeles Dodgers baseball team, turns milestones into mementos by painting significant game balls with details of the achievement. It is traditional for a clubhouse manager to retrieve the ball when an important hit, run, steal or win takes place, and for more than 20 years Mitch has decorated hundreds of balls. Using acrylic paint, he writes the player's name, opponent, accomplishment, date, box score and other information on the ball.

A New Leaf

Victor Liu collects dried old leaves from the streets around his home in Hebei Province, China, and very painstakingly carves into them beautiful images of subjects such as Barack Obama, Marilyn Monroe, the *Mona Lisa* and the Statue of Liberty.

Original Nintendo

In February 2010, a video-game collector paid $13,105 for an original Nintendo entertainment system and five game cartridges.

Painting with Wheels

Ian Cook of Birmingham, England, created an artwork of a racing car 33 x 16½ ft (10 x 5 m)—painted with the wheels of remote-control cars, go-karts, a racing car, a sports car, a motorbike and a six-ton truck. He took a huge canvas, applied paint and then drove across it, creating the image with the different sizes and patterns of the tires. He said painting with the truck was a challenge because the back wheels were twice as wide as the front ones so it was difficult to see what he was doing.

Sand Sculpture

A group of 30 artists took 75 days to create a 73-ft-tall (22-m) sand sculpture at the Zhoushan Sand Sculpture Festival in China. The sculpture depicted a Nigerian story of how a hummingbird managed to become king of all animals.

Daily Grind

Instead of paint or ink, Bend, Oregon, artist Karen Eland creates replicas of famous artworks with coffee. Since her first espresso painting in 1998, she has completed more than 90 illustrations—many of which incorporate coffee drinking—including Leonardo da Vinci's *Mona Latte*, *Whistler's Mocha*, and *Rodin's The Drinker*.

Stage Epic

German producer Franz Abraham has created a stage version of the Roman epic *Ben-Hur* featuring 400 actors, 900 costumes, 50 scene designs, 46 horses, 120 doves, five chariots, two eagles and two vultures. The action takes place in a 26,000-sq-ft (2,415-sq-m) arena covered with 10 in (25 cm) of sand, and uses 30 mi (48 km) of cable, 250 moving lights and 25 tons of sound equipment.

Big Business

In Minneapolis, Minnesota, in 2009, entrepreneur Lief Larson presented a work contact with a giant business card that measured a noticeable 60 x 34 in (150 x 85 cm).

BB-ball Gaga

Sculptor and artist John O'Hearn of Gainesville, Florida, makes colorful mosaics from thousands of Airsoft BBs—the ¼-in (6-mm) plastic balls used in a BB gun. Among his designs are a portrait of Florida Gators quarterback Tim Tebow from 46,308 BBs, which measures 4 x 6 ft (1.2 x 1.8 m), and this mosaic of singer Lady Gaga that is 4 x 8 ft (1.2 x 2.4 m) and contains 61,509 BBs.

Splendid Sari

A team of weavers in Chennai, India, spent 4,680 hours making a $100,000 sari that was woven with precious metals and gems.

Big Monet

At the 2010 Normandy Impressionist Festival, 1,250 fans of 19th-century French artist Claude Monet gathered in Rouen and held painted panels above their heads to create a giant, 6,460-sq-ft (600-sq-m) replica of his 1894 work *Rouen Cathedral at the End of the Day*. The result was captured by cameras perched 90 ft (27 m) above the city hall.

Bone Images

Swiss-born artist and photographer François Robert, who is now based in the U.S.A., produces works of art from real human bones. He spent hours arranging bones into striking shapes for his photographic collection *Stop the Violence*, which featured bone images of a gun, a tank, a bomb, a grenade, a Kalashnikov rifle and a knife. He hit upon the idea after trading a wired-together human skeleton, found inside some school lockers he had bought, for a box of 206 human bones.

High Horse

Tony Dew from York, England, hand-carved a wooden rocking horse that stands 11 ft 10 in (3.6 m) high and 16 ft (4.9 m) long—more than twice the size of most real horses.

Cart Art

Ptolemy Elrington trawls rivers and lakes near his studio in Brighton, England, for abandoned metal shopping carts and turns them into enchanting sculptures of animals, insects and birds. By breaking up the carts and welding them into the desired shapes, he has created such designs as a heron, a frog (with bulging eyes from the cart's wheels), a dragonfly with a 6-ft (1.8-m) wingspan, and this kingfisher eating a fish.

Pothole Scenes

Urban artists Claudia Ficca and Davide Luciano from Montreal, Canada, travel North America transforming unsightly street potholes into works of art. They have been photographed in the guise of a woman washing her clothes in a pothole, a priest baptizing a baby in another, and a scuba diver taking a dip.

Same Glass

For more than 35 years on an almost daily basis, Peter Dreher of Wittnau, Germany, has painted a portrait of the same drinking glass in the same position in his studio. He has so far completed more than 4,000 paintings of the glass.

Lego Repairs

German artist Jan Vormann travels the world fixing crumbling walls and monuments with LEGO®. Among areas he has brightened up with the toy bricks are the old quarter of Tel Aviv in Israel and New York's Bryant Park.

Midnight Knitter

Under the cover of darkness in early 2010, an unknown person dubbed the "Midnight Knitter" draped tree branches and lampposts in West Cape May, New Jersey, with small, brightly colored woolen sweaters.

Movie Veteran

Aachi Manorama, a veteran of India's Tamil film industry, has appeared in more than 1,500 movies and 1,000 stage performances.

Gum Dog

Gareth Williams of the U.K. created this sculpture of a dog, which was exhibited at London's Royal College of Art in 2009, with hair clippings from his own head stuck together with pieces of used chewing gum.

Sitting in Silence

Over a period of nearly three months in 2010, Serbian performance artist Marina Abramović spent 700 hours simply sitting and staring across a table at members of the public at New York's Museum of Modern Art. She sat on a chair for seven hours a day, six days a week, for her installation *The Artist Is Present*. Around 1,400 people—including singer Björk and model Isabella Rossellini—sat opposite her and returned her silent gaze. Some managed an entire day; others lasted just a few minutes.

Cool Music

Norwegian composer Terje Isungset has recorded several albums with instruments made entirely of ice, including percussion, horns and trumpets.

Early Watch

In 2009, art experts discovered a 450-year-old painting that featured an image of a watch. The portrait, painted by Italian Renaissance artist Maso da San Friano around 1560, shows Cosimo I de' Medici, Duke of Florence, holding a golden timepiece. Watches first appeared shortly after 1500, making this one of the oldest paintings to depict a true watch.

Tower Cozy

Robyn Love of New York City crocheted a yarn cozy for a wooden water tower on Broadway. Over a period of three weeks, she and six assistants used 60 balls of yellow and black yarn to transform the tower into a huge yellow pencil, complete with point.

Expensive Doll

A French doll designed by Paris artist Albert Marque in 1915 was sold at auction in Atlanta, Georgia, for $263,000 in 2009. Only 100 examples of the doll were ever made and each was individually costumed, in styles ranging from 18th-century French court to traditional Russian folklore.

Holiday Snaps

A series of 19th-century watercolor paintings of European beauty spots by an unknown female British holidaymaker was sold in London for more than $5,000 in 2010. The paintings of such picturesque locations as Bavaria, the Swiss Alps, and the Belgian city of Bruges were made in journals as holiday snaps by the woman following vacations she took with her husband in 1850 and 1853.

Living Dolls

When British artist Boo Ritson tells her subjects she wants to paint them, she means it literally. Boo covers her human volunteers in layers of water-based paint to create giant action figures, which she then photographs. She specializes in American symbols, which means that as well as painting subjects such as cheerleader and cowboy living dolls, she has also applied the technique to donuts.

Tattooed Pigs

Belgian artist Wim Delvoye tattooed pigs with Louis Vuitton designer logos for an exhibit called *Art Farm*. He tattooed the LV logos on the animals when they were piglets and watched the designs increase in size as the pigs' bodies grew.

Some Yarn!

Over the period of a week, Austin, Texas, artist Magda Sayeg covered a Mexico City bus from front to back with brightly colored knitted yarn. She has also knitted woolen coverings for trees, car antennas, and signs in the U.S.A., as well as for the Louvre Museum in Paris.

Typed Portraits

Keira Rathbone of Dorset, England, uses manual typewriters—some up to 70 years old—as her paintbrushes to create portraits of famous people, including Barack Obama, Marilyn Monroe and supermodel Kate Moss. After deciding which of her collection of 30 typewriters she wants to use, she turns the roller and selects different characters— numbers, letters and punctuation—to make the required shapes.

Sound your Horn!

A giant, working vuvuzela horn 115 ft (35 m) long and 18 ft (5.5 m) in diameter was placed above a highway in Cape Town, South Africa, in 2010.

$11 Million Book

A copy of the book *Birds of America*, written and illustrated by Haitian-born John James Audubon in the early 19th century, was sold for more than $11 million in December 2010. Only 119 complete copies of the large-format book, which has foldout pages measuring 39½ x 29½ in (100 x 75 cm), are in existence, and all but 11 of those are in museums and libraries. To obtain such accurate likenesses of birds, Audubon stalked his subjects across the U.S.A. and shot them before hanging them from wires and painting them.

Behind the Smile

Dr. Vito Franco of the University of Palermo, Sicily, Italy, believes the enigmatic smile on the face of Leonardo da Vinci's *Mona Lisa* was the result of very high levels of cholesterol. After studying the painting closely, the doctor says he can detect a build up of fatty acids around her left eye.

Tan Art

James Titterton of London, England, endured a full body wax and eight sunbed sessions to have a fish, a cockerel and a ship's anchor bronzed onto his flesh. He masked off parts of his chest, arms and legs with vinyl stickers of the various images before having the outlines tanned on to his skin. Dressed in only underpants, he then exhibited his tanned artwork at a gallery in Sussex.

Hay Castle

In January 2010, visitors flocked to Rob Marshall's sheep farm in West Victoria, Australia, to see a castle measuring 100 x 20 ft (30 x 6 m) that he had built out of hundreds of bales of hay. The castle remained in situ for six weeks until Rob dismantled it and used the bales to feed his sheep.

Tree Sculpture

Inspired by a silver birch tree, Swedish furniture chain IKEA created a huge tree sculpture made only from white kitchen appliances—including a washing machine, a dishwasher and a microwave oven—that was erected outside London's Barbican Centre in 2010.

Guitar Windmills

Mimicking The Who guitarist Pete Townshend's windmill actions, Spencer Borbon of San Francisco whirled his arm around 79 times in 30 seconds at the 2009 San Francisco Treasure Island Music Festival.

Tracker Bob

Bob "Tracker Bob" Hiemenz of Flora, Illinois, has a collection of more than 60,000 eight-track audio tapes. Since acquiring his first tapes in 1985, he has spent about $7,000 on his passion, which covers everyone from Abba to ZZ Top.

Bard Boost

Performing William Shakespeare plays to cows can help boost milk production. After the Changeling Theatre Company entertained Friesian cows at a farm in Kent, England, with *The Merry Wives of Windsor*, milk yields increased by four percent.

Finger Portraits

U.K.-based artist Kyle Lambert creates amazingly lifelike portraits of celebrities, including Jennifer Aniston and Beyoncé, using an iPad.

Curiouser Creation

Los Angeles art group L.A. Pop Art wrote out every word from the first 11 chapters of Lewis Carroll's novel, *Alice In Wonderland*, to create an illustration from the story. From a distance it appears to be solid color, but almost every inch of the artwork is formed from Lewis Carroll's own words, written clearly in felt-tip pens. The text was written upside down so that the artists didn't smudge the ink.

244

Inflated Animals

Chinese artist Yang Maoyuan creates animal sculptures with a difference—he takes the skins of dead animals and inflates them to monstrous sizes, often dyeing them in lurid colors.

Beijing-based Yang travels to Hebei in northern China to buy horse, goat and sheep skins. He then stitches and processes the skins before blowing them up so that their bodies become bloated and round. He chooses animals from his Mongolian ancestry, making them larger than life to reflect his oldest dream symbols, and gives them a round shape that represents harmony in China. To make his sculptures even more grotesque, he gives some of the sheep two or three heads.

Yang's bright blue, three-headed, many-legged goat.

Yang's art has been a hit in galleries worldwide.

247

Plastic Fantastic

Sayaka Ganz creates amazing wildlife sculptures from items of discarded plastic found in garbage cans and thrift shops, or donated by friends—and her finished works sell for more than $12,000.

Sayaka, who was born in Japan but now lives in Fort Wayne, Indiana, has made models of penguins, an eagle, a horse, a cheetah and a fish, varying in length from 18 in (45 cm) to 8 ft (2.4 m) and incorporating plastic sunglasses, cutlery, baskets and cooking utensils. The biggest sculptures contain up to 500 pieces of junk and take nine months to make. She sorts all her plastic into 20 color groups in her basement and then ties the chosen items onto a wire frame to create each sculpture. Sayaka studies photographs showing her animal subjects from different angles so that she can perfect the lines of motion. She says, "I get great satisfaction from fitting these objects together to create a beautiful form that seems alive."

Chocolate Train

In October 2010, London, England, food artist Carl Warner unveiled the *Chocolate Express*, a 6-ft (1.8-m) train sculpture made from chocolate, and running on chocolate tracks. It took ten days to build and also incorporated chocolate rolls, Wagon Wheels, Crunchie bars and Dime bars.

Toast Portrait

Laura Hadland from Leicester, England, created a portrait of her mother-in-law, Sandra Whitfield, from 9,852 slices of toast. Laura and 40 friends used nine toasters to brown the slices from 600 loaves of bread to varying degrees before arranging them to make a lifelike mosaic measuring 32 ft 8 in x 42 ft 3 in (10 x 13 m).

Girl Gucci

At just 13 years old, Cecilia Cassini of Encino, California, is already an accomplished fashion designer. After receiving a sewing machine for her sixth birthday, she went on to design clothes for children and adults, and a number of celebrities have worn her designs.

Lord of the Sticks

Patrick Acton of Gladbrook, Iowa, spent three years building a replica of the *Lord of the Rings* city Minas Tirith from 420,000 matchsticks.

Photographic Memories

Munish Bansal of Kent, England, has taken pictures of his children every day for 13 years. He has filled more than 600 albums with over 8,500 digital images of his daughter Suman, 12, and her 10-year-old brother, Jay, since the day they were born.

Part Art

Artist Franco Recchia from Florence, Italy, constructs models of cityscapes from the discarded parts of old computers. He uses circuit boards, casings, processing chips and various other computer components as his building blocks.

Golden Monopoly

San Francisco jewelry designer Sidney Mobell has created a Monopoly set made with solid gold and jewels. The dice are encrusted with diamonds and these alone cost $10,000.

Porcelain Seeds

In 2010, London's Tate Modern gallery staged a work called *Sunflower Seeds* by Chinese artist Ai Weiwei. The piece consisted of more than 100 million individually handmade porcelain replicas of seeds.

The Candy Man

Mexican artist Cristiam Ramos makes amazing candy portraits of celebrities. Instead of paint, he uses Gummi Bears, licorice, M&M's®, and after-dinner mints as his artistic materials. His works include likenesses of Elvis and Michael Jackson from hundreds of M&M's®, and a portrait of Lady Gaga from gumdrops, M&M's®, and yellow licorice.

Monster Mona

A giant version of Leonardo da Vinci's *Mona Lisa* went on display in a shopping mall in Wales in 2009—50 times bigger than the 16th-century original. It covered a massive 2,600 sq ft (240 sq m) and was big enough to fit 22 buses inside. A total of 245 people worked on the project under artist Katy Webster, and it took them 987 hours to create, using 23 gal (86 l) of paint.

Couscous City

French-Algerian artist Kader Attia built a scale model of the ancient city of Ghardaia, Algeria, entirely out of cooked couscous.

Wicker Men

In Romania, a team of 16 craftsmen created a huge wicker basket that was large enough to hold one million loaves of homemade bread. It took nine days to make, measured 59 x 33 ft (18 x 10 m) and was 31 ft (9.5 m) tall.

Celebrity Pumpkins

Gardener David Finkle carves impressive portraits of famous people—including Barack Obama, Michael Jackson and Simon Cowell—out of pumpkins that grow on his small farm at Chelmsford in Essex, England.

Concert For Dogs

Australia's Sydney Opera House staged a concert for dogs in 2010. More than a thousand dogs turned up for the 20-minute Music For Dogs event, which was organized by U.S. musician Laurie Anderson and her rock-star husband Lou Reed. It featured a concerto of high-pitch whistles, whale calls, synthesizers and strings—some inaudible to human ears.

Dental Display

To entertain and relax his patients, dentist Ian Davis from London, England, has created a series of sculptures featuring miniature men scrubbing, cleaning, and repairing teeth. The men can be seen digging out fillings with tiny pickaxes and polishing and scaling teeth with the help of scaffolding—and all the teeth he uses are taken from the casts of real patients' mouths.

Marilyn with Wings

Mexican artist Enrique Ramos created his portrait of Hollywood icon Marilyn Monroe from hundreds of rainforest butterflies. Enrique has also created an image of U.S. President John F. Kennedy in the same way. Both insect portraits are on display at the Ripley's Believe It or Not! Odditorium in London, England.

Mini Me

Indonesian photographer Ari Mahardika has "cloned" himself dozens of times for a series of intricate montages. Using a self-timer to take photos of himself in different poses against a white background, he then shrinks the portraits into mini-me characters, positioning them so that it looks as though he is interacting with himself.

Lost Movie

A lost Charlie Chaplin film valued at $60,000 was bought on eBay for $5.68 by a British collector in 2009. Morace Park of Essex, England, purchased the battered olive green film canister listed as "an old film" and was amazed to discover that the movie in question was *Zepped*, a 1916 Chaplin propaganda film poking fun at the zeppelin, the German instrument of terror during World War I. As recently as 2006, a movie expert stated that the seven-minute movie had almost certainly been lost forever.

First Exhibition

When Leo Haines was born with cerebral palsy and a terminal condition affecting his lungs and heart, he was given only six months to live. However, in 2010 the five-year-old from Somerset, England, stunned doctors by opening his first art exhibition. He began painting alongside his grandmother and has since completed more than 40 works, which are said to be reminiscent of famous U.S. abstract artist Jackson Pollock.

Bean Mosaic

A candy shop in Brighton, England, displayed a colorful mosaic of Queen Elizabeth II made from 10,000 jelly beans.

Dollar Mosaics

A Latvian artist creates mosaics made entirely out of U.S. dollar bills. Irina Truhanova sketches an outline of her subject before filling it in with snippets of the bills. Her creations include the Statue of Liberty, a Bentley car, and Russian President Vladimir Putin.

Urban Dancers

As part of its 2009 "Bodies in Urban Spaces" project, Dance Umbrella, choreographed by Willi Dorner, placed its performers in unlikely locations around the center of London, England. Passersby stumbled across dancers squeezed between pillars, wrapped around lampposts, folded into a bicycle rack, and clinging to a wall like Spider-Man.

Junior Drummer

At just three years of age, Howard Wong's rock drumming has attracted nearly ten million hits on YouTube even though he can barely see over the top of his drum kit. Howard from Penang, Malaysia, first started playing at the age of 18 months and now performs regularly with his father's band.

Typewriter Art

Cerebral-palsy sufferer Paul Smith of Roseburg, Oregon, who died in 2007, became a world-famous artist by creating masterpieces using manual typewriters. He achieved his amazing images by pressing the symbols at the tops of the number keys, and as his mastery of the typewriter grew, he developed techniques to create shadings, colors, and textures that made his work resemble pencil or charcoal drawings. Over the years, he created hundreds of artworks—each one taking him up to three months— including landscapes, animals and portraits.

Underwater Gallery

Diving enthusiasts in Lithuania have opened the country's first underwater picture gallery. Twenty large-format photographs by local artists were put on display beneath the surface of Lake Plateliai, and the organizers hope to expand the project to include sculptures, stained glass and watercolor paintings. The idea originated after a couple from a diving club put their wedding picture underwater so that they could enjoy it every time they dived.

Mosaic Mural

More than 130 artists and 500 children worked for three years to create a ceramic mosaic mural in Hanoi, Vietnam, that measures nearly 2½ mi (4 km) long. The brainchild of artist Nguyen Thu Thuy, the mosaic depicts images of Vietnam's history, life and culture.

Poo Shoes

British artist INSA created a pair of 10-in-high (25-cm) stiletto shoes with platforms made from elephant dung. He sourced the waste from the same family of elephants that provided the material for a famous series of elephant-dung collage paintings by Turner Prize-winning British artist Chris Ofili in the 1990s.

Glass Holograms

Using special pencils, multiple layers of painted glass, and between 14 and 30 glass panes, artist Xia Xiao Wan from Beijing, China, is able to transform ordinary 2-D glass into stunning 3-D holographic images.

Bargain Buy

A decade after buying 65 photographic plates at a garage sale in California for just $45, Rick Norsigian found that they could be the work of celebrated U.S. nature photographer Ansel Adams and therefore be worth around $200 million.

Roadkill Hats

Fashion designer James Faulkner of Edinburgh, Scotland, has created a range of hats from roadkill. Inspired by the idea of using a dead magpie he found by the roadside to complement a friend's black-and-white dress, he has developed a range of 36 animal hats, using the wings, feathers and fur of squashed pigeons, rabbits, foxes, pheasants and crows.

Playing with Food

Brazilian artist and photographer Vanessa Dualib creates cartoon animals from misshapen food and then takes pictures of them against appropriate backdrops before they go rotten. Among her 70 characters are radish mice, blowfruit fish, a potato dinosaur and Pepe the pepper.

27-hour Concert

Gonzales, a Canadian musician, played a 27-hour concert in Paris, France, in 2009. His 300-song set ranged from Britney Spears to Beethoven.

Whistle-stop Tour

German guitarist Vicente Patiz drove more than 600 mi (960 km) to give concerts in eight countries—Germany, Belgium, the Netherlands, France, Luxembourg, Switzerland, Lichtenstein and Austria—in just 24 hours.

Bamboo Dance

More than 10,700 people assembled on March 12, 2010, to perform the Cheraw dance together in Aizawl, Mizoram, India. They spread out over an area of about 1¾ mi (3 km) to dance an eight-minute routine with bamboo sticks.

Miscellaneous Mosaic

Kris Kuksi, a sculptor and painter from Kansas, creates macabre yet beautiful sculptures assembled from hundreds, sometimes thousands, of discarded toys, figurines and general trash. His work has been bought by celebrities and exhibited around the world.

Kris explains how *Lies and Persuasion* came together: "My pieces are a collection of many different things. I started out by gathering miscellaneous figurines, small rocks, jewelry—anything I could incorporate. After I found some essential "supplies" that I felt were important for the individuality of the piece, I built a foundation, and everything after that is just assemblage. When it's all finished, the piece gets various coats of paint.

"*Lies and Persuasion* has so many little things in it and, interestingly enough, the skull forms in the piece are actually the same skull split in half. I'll buy anything, anywhere, if I feel it's needed for a piece. I'd say that the whole assemblage, that is, the creation itself—withholding the mental preparation and shopping—lasted about a month."

Sticky Sculpture

When a popular adhesive tape company challenged people to come up with the best sculpture made entirely from sticky tape, it received some incredible entries. Artist Annie K. stuck together this giant jellyfish that appears to be floating in the air and ensnaring a bicycle in its tentacles. Some of the entries included an office desk made from 36 rolls of tape and a drum kit made from 48 rolls—that's over 7,770 ft (2,368 m), or enough tape to wrap around an aircraft carrier seven times.

Microbial Art

Dr. T. Ryan Gregory of the University of Guelph, Canada, is a pioneer of microbial art, where scientists design patterns by brushing fungi, deadly bacteria, and dye around a petri dish. He creates images by using a small paintbrush and E. coli in liquid medium. These are then allowed to grow in a laboratory incubator, but the "living paint" soon dies, so the pictures are only temporary.

Noncontact Instrument

The theremin is an electronic musical instrument that is played without any contact from the player! Named after Russian professor Léon Theremin, who invented it in 1919, it consists of two metal antennae that sense the position of the player's hands and send corresponding electric signals to a loudspeaker.

Cardboard Scream

Artist Mark Langan from Cleveland, Ohio, re-created Edvard Munch's haunting painting *The Scream* using discarded cardboard boxes. He spent 90 hours cutting up five old boxes with a craft knife and layering them to create a 3-D picture that measured 2.2 in (5.5 cm) deep. His creation sold for $2,500.

Ant Invasion

Dutch artist Henk Hofstra painted some 500 giant red ants over the town of Drachten for his work *Invasion of the Ants*. The ants each measured 10 x 6½ ft (3 x 2 m) and were created over three nights in May 2010. They were placed so that they appeared to be invading the De Lawei Theater, which was celebrating its 50th anniversary.

Quick on the Draw

Singaporean artist Peter Zhou, aka Peter Draw, drew nearly 1,000 people nonstop, without food, for 24 hours.

Rubber Beasts

Artist Ji Yong-Ho from Seoul, South Korea, makes animal sculptures from old tires. Using the flexibility of the rubber to imitate skin and muscles, he has created powerful lions, dogs, rhinos and this 10-ft-long (3-m) shark, each work taking three months to make and selling for up to $75,000. To vary the skin texture, he uses different kinds of tread. For example, the neck and forehead of his rhinoceros are made from broad-treaded tractor tires layered beneath a rough outer skin of motorcycle tires.

Giant Chair

Furniture craftsman Radoslav Russev carved a wooden chair that was almost 15 ft (4.5 m) high and weighed more than 770 lb (350 kg). He made the oversized chair, which was placed in the main square of Razgrad, Bulgaria, from 70 cubic ft (2 cubic m) of pinewood.

Leather Portraits

Welsh artist Mark Evans creates huge portraits of famous people—in leather. Using knives as his "brushes," he has scraped impressions of Muhammad Ali, Sir Winston Churchill and model Naomi Campbell into leather hides. He discovered his talent by accident after spilling blood on a new leather jacket. He tried to repair it with a palette knife but scratched too hard and ended up etching a portrait of Jimi Hendrix onto the back of the jacket.

Dead Flies

Magnus Muhr collects dead flies from windows and lamps around his house in Sweden, places them on white paper, draws in legs and a crazy background, and then photographs them. The photos show the insects appearing to dance, sunbathe, dive, ride horses and perform acrobatic circus routines.

Many Parts

Bollywood actress Priyanka Chopra played all 12 characters in the 2009 movie *What's Your Rashee?* Each character was one of the 12 zodiac signs.

Board Game

In 2009, board-game fanatic Luanga Nuwame created a 900-sq-ft (84-sq-m) wooden board game based on the city of Mississauga, Ontario, Canada… with real people as the pieces. He also built a huge dice with which to play it.

Washington's Fine

New York Society Library says George Washington owes it $300,000 in library fines. Its ledgers show that the first U.S. President borrowed two books that he should have returned on November 2, 1789, but are now over 220 years overdue.

French Anthem

Claude-Joseph Rouget de Lisle composed "The Marseillaise" in 1792 in return for a bottle of wine. The tune became the anthem of French Revolutionaries and was later adopted as the French national anthem. Ironically, Rouget de Lisle was a royalist who was thrown into prison during the Revolution and narrowly escaped being guillotined.

Serenading Sharks

Andy Brandy Casagrande IV, an American wildlife cinematographer, strummed a waterproof guitar and played a song underwater to sharks off the coast of Mexico—without a cage. He penned "The Great White Shark Song" to raise awareness of shark conservation and decided the best way to make his point was to don scuba gear and play his tune in shark-infested waters.

Cereal-ism

With the help of 150 students, high-school teacher Doyle Geddes of Smithfield, Utah, used 2 tons of breakfast cereal to create a massive reproduction of Vincent van Gogh's painting *Starry Night* measuring 72 x 90 ft (22 x 27 m).

Costly Comic

A copy of the 1938 edition of *Action Comics No. 1* sold in March 2010 for $1.5 million on an auction website. The issue, which features Superman's debut, originally sold for 10 cents.

Decorative Recycling

Florida-based artists Alain Guerra and Neraldo de la Paz create stunning sculptures from discarded clothing. They drape old garments over a wire frame to form colorful designs including a rainbow, a snake and a series of clothing trees that represent all four seasons of the year.

Last Suppers

For his *Last Suppers* series, British artist James Reynolds re-created the final meals requested by American Death Row prisoners. He filled a succession of orange prison-issue trays with their genuine last meals, which included a single black olive; an onion, a packet of chewing gum and two bottles of Coke; and six raw eggs.

Dirt Shirts

Remembering how they always used to end up with manure on their clothes when they helped on the family farm as kids, Patti Froman Maine of Corry, Pennsylvania, and her brother Sonny Froman designed a range of T-shirts that are deliberately coated in the stuff. Their CowChipShirts don't smell and come in colors such as Udder Rose and Silage Brown.

Gold Painting

Russian artist Elena Zolotaya created a 10-ft-wide (3-m) picture painted entirely with 14-carat gold.

Tall Order

For a wager, Norway's Ola Helland collected over one million giraffe pictures in 440 days. He was backpacking through South America when, as a keepsake to remember all the new friends he had met, he asked each to draw him a giraffe. When a friend bet him he couldn't collect a million, Ola set up a website and was soon deluged with giraffe pictures from 106 countries, including a giraffe made from a banana, and another made out of bread.

New Books

Each year, in the U.S.A. alone, about 30 million trees are used to make paper to print new books.

Many Hands

At the 2010 Baltimore Book Festival in Maryland, 512 people contributed to a single piece of art. Local author K. Michael Crawford erected an easel with a blank canvas and invited passersby to add to the picture.

Turning Heads

After going bald in his twenties, Philip Levine of London, England, began using his scalp as a canvas for art. Every week, body painter Kat Sinclair transformed Philip's designs into a different piece of head art. He turned his head into a disco ball covered with 1,000 crystals, had it painted with flowers, cartoon characters and smiley faces, and even had acupuncture needles inserted into his scalp in the shape of a butterfly.

Morten Viskum, The Hand with the Golden Ring II, 2010.

Helping Hand

For his painting *The Hand with the Golden Ring*, Norwegian artist Morten Viskum said he used the hand of a human corpse as a paintbrush. He claims that he's been working with a severed hand as a brush for over a decade, and uses it to apply animal blood, acrylic paints and sometimes glitter to his canvases.

Deep Drawings

Chilean artist Fredo creates
mind-boggling 3-D pencil
drawings that appear
to rise out of the page.
Despite its 3-D appearance,
all his work is pencil on flat
paper. At only 17 years old,
Fredo is already exhibiting
his work in Chile.

Strand of Beads

In October 2009, the city of Providence, Rhode Island, created a strand of red-and-white beads that measured 1,349 ft (411 m) long!

Late Returns

In 2009, a former student at Camelback High School, Phoenix, Arizona, returned two library books that had been checked out half a century earlier, and enclosed a $1,000 money order for the fines. The books had been taken out in 1959, but the borrower's family moved to another state and the books were mistakenly packed away.

Toothpick City

Scott Weaver of Rohnert Park, California, spent thousands of hours during a 34-year period building a toothpick model of every major landmark in San Francisco, using more than 100,000 toothpicks. The construction, titled *Rolling Through the Bay*, stands 9 ft (2.7 m) tall, 7 ft (2.1 m) wide and 2 ft (60 cm) deep. It has survived four house relocations, an earthquake, and Trooper—one of Weaver's four Great Danes—who once obliterated Fisherman's Wharf and about 100 hours' work with a careless wag of his tail.

Human Hoover

Artist Paul Hazelton of Kent, England, has made a model of a complete bedroom—including a TV, armchairs, and a wardrobe—out of dust! Known as the "Human Hoover," he collects dust from furniture, pictures and window sills, and then transforms the bunches of tiny particles into 3-D sculptures by wetting, shaping and drying them. Some of his dust models—which also include a briefcase, a moth and a humanoid—are 20 in (50 cm) high.

Hot Lips

Makeup artist Rick DiCecca applied lipstick to more than 300 women in one hour at Macy's Department Store, Chicago, Illinois.

Lego Ship

For nearly a week, 3,500 children used 513,000 LEGO® bricks to build a 25-ft-long (7.6-m) model of a container ship in Wilhelmshaven, Germany.

Pistol Puzzle

GarE Maxton, a machinist-artist from Michigan, created a 125-piece metal puzzle sculpture that can be assembled into a working, muzzle-loading pistol.

Observation Test

To help improve their powers of deductive observation, a group of New York City police officers visited the Metropolitan Museum of Art to discuss with an expert what conclusions they could draw from the contents of pictures by the likes of Caravaggio and Guercino.

Party Pooper

With the help of local schoolchildren from Sichuan Province, China, sculptor Zhu Cheng made a replica of the famous *Venus de Milo* statue—from panda dung. The poop statue later sold for $45,000.

Intrepid Builder

Using 250,000 pieces of LEGO®, Ed Diment took nine months to build a 22-ft-long (6.7-m) replica of the World-War-II aircraft carrier U.S.S. *Intrepid* in the conservatory of his home in Portsmouth, England. The finished model weighed more than 500 lb (227 kg).

Underground Music

Norwegian singer Unni Lovlid staged two sell-out 2010 concerts in a Victorian drain 20 ft (6 m) underground in Brighton, England. The sewer could accommodate 25 audience members wearing hard hats.

Tabletop Landscapes

New Jersey photographer and artist Matthew Albanese devises spectacular images of windswept tropical islands, tornadoes and volcanoes by building models from everyday items.

The azure sea in his tabletop *D.I.Y. Paradise* is actually melted sugar and tin foil, and the island is made from salt. He carefully arranged cotton balls over the scene to create clouds, and even the palm trees are not as they seem—the leaves are formed from feathers.

Matthew has also made convincing icebergs from sugar and waterfalls from salt, and re-created the surface of Mars with paprika, cinnamon, nutmeg, and chili powder. His tornadoes are made from steel wool and he has created an impressive Aurora Borealis using a shower curtain, a corkboard and strobe lighting. His photographs of these homemade natural phenomena sell for over $900 each.

Ticket Tower

British artist Robert Bradford created scale models of three U.K. landmarks—St. Paul's Cathedral, Edinburgh Castle and Blackpool Tower—from a total of 115,000 used train tickets.

Moon Scent

Printers in Edinburgh, Scotland, have created a scratch 'n' sniff artwork that smells like the Moon. They developed it by talking to former NASA astronaut Charlie Duke, who was a member of the Apollo 16 mission in 1972, and who described the Moon's surface as smelling like spent gunpowder.

Victory at Last

Using an original wooden beam from the H.M.S. *Victory*, sculptor Ian Brennan from Hampshire, England, spent 17 years carving a 47-in-long (1.2-m) model of Admiral Horatio Nelson's 18th-century flagship. The model contains 200 ft (60 m) of rope, 104 miniature guns and 37 sails.

Cow Maze

In a field near Berlin, Germany, workers cut corn and hemp into the shape of a giant cow. The maze depicted the bovine digestive system and was designed by the country's Federal Institute of Risk Assessment to promote healthy eating habits.

Apple Killer

Together with photographer Paul Fairchild, San Francisco artist Michael Tompert staged an exhibition of butchered and mangled Apple products. Tompert has shot, burned, hammered and sawed his way through a range of merchandise and even ran over seven iPods with a diesel locomotive. His greatest challenge was an iPad, which survived a series of blows from a sledgehammer, before finally exploding after its insides were heated with a soldering torch. He says he's trying to make people think about their relationship with these highly popular items.

Human Ashes

Dutch artist Wieki Somers makes 3-D printed sculptures of common household appliances—including bathroom scales, a vacuum cleaner and a toaster—out of human ashes.

Gallery Blunder

Polish experimental artist Leon Tarasewicz sued a gallery for $30,000 after it ripped up one of his paintings and threw it in a trash can in the mistaken belief that it was a large bunch of scrap paper used for getting excess paint off brushes. The 25-ft-high (7.6-m) exhibit had been on display in the gallery in Katowice, but staff thought that it had been left behind by decorators.

Microscopic Models

Origami artist Mui-Ling Teh of Thornhill, Ontario, Canada, makes paper models so tiny—as small as 0.08 in (2 mm) long—that they look like a speck to the naked eye. She makes her microscopic models of objects such as birds, flowers and airplanes with scissors and tweezers. She first began to experiment with origami at age ten when she made small models out of candy wrappers.

Auto Robot

A 33-ft-tall (10-m) version of Transformer Optimus Prime made from the bodies and tires of old cars and motorcycles was unveiled at Beijing's Green Dream Park in 2010. The *Autobot* sculpture weighed six tons and was assembled from five truckloads of recycled parts.

Huge Hammock

Hansy Better Barraza, a professor at Rhode Island School of Design, created a 33-ft-long (10-m) hammock, covering an area of 264 sq ft (24.5 sq m) in Boston, Massachusetts, in 2010. The sculpture consisted of 4,278 ft (1,304 m)—that's nearly a mile—of "rope" made from recycled bottles woven over curved steel pipes.

Smelly Issue

Issue No. 23 of the German magazine *mono.kultur* was infused with 12 smells suggested by Norwegian scientist, artist and odor expert Sissel Tolaas. Using a technique called microencapsulation, the smells were printed into the pages of the magazine, with the reader rubbing the paper to release them.

Beef Bikini

For the September 2010 cover shot of Japanese magazine *Vogue Hommes Japan*, U.S. singer Lady Gaga wore a bikini made of raw meat.

Screw Mosaic

Saimir Strati spent two weeks creating a mosaic of a U.S. banknote 8 ft (2.4 m) high and 16 ft 1 in (4.9 m) long from 300,000 industrial screws. The giant bill features a portrait of the ancient Greek poet Homer in the center.

Natural Sculptures

Peter Riedel, an artist and photographer from Toronto, Canada, spent five hours creating 42 temporary outdoor sculptures in the city's Humber River by balancing rocks and boulders on top of each other. He never uses glue in his works but arranges the rocks so that they don't fall.

Tasty Shoes

Israel's Kobi Levi has designed shoes in the shapes of bananas, cats, shopping baskets, dogs, rocking chairs—and one pair with a pink stiletto heel that makes it look as though the wearer has stepped in a piece of chewing gum.

Illusion Confusion

There is a lot more to this portrait of legendary artist Salvador Dalí than meets the eye. It is in fact a large 3-D illusion, consisting of a shark, a bull's head and a seal, among many other objects. These bizarre items appear to be randomly piled up but are actually meticulously placed to complete the image from just one perspective. Bernard Pras, the artist from Belgium, has been re-creating famous pictures out of junk for more than 30 years.

Man-made Monsters

Using only man-made materials, Californian artist Doug Higley makes monsters for showmen to display at flea markets and fairs across the world. He has created fake mummified and petrified creatures, bogus mermaids, shrunken heads, chupacabras, freaky jungle pygmies and atomic death worms. His work has been exhibited in 34 countries and one of his mermaids appeared at Buckingham Palace, London. He also once created 42 mermaids for a car-dealer promotion in the U.S.A. and Canada, whereby potential customers were invited to see the "strange creature" found in the trunk of a trade-in vehicle and take a test drive. The gimmick sold thousands of cars!

Still Famous

In the year following his death on June 25, 2009, Michael Jackson's estate earned one billion dollars.

Small Portions

Using acrylic paints and a magnifying glass, French artist Stephanie Kilgast creates miniature clay models of food in 1:12 scale. She painstakingly molds the clay with scalpels, blades, art knives and toothpicks, and has made more than 600 cakes, pastries, fruit and full meals, including a full English breakfast with baked beans, bacon, sausages and fried eggs.

Ancient Shoe

Archeologists in Armenia have found a leather shoe more than 5,500 years old. The shoe, which was stuffed with grass, was discovered in a mountain cave where it had been kept in excellent condition thanks to a thick layer of sheep excrement that acted as a protective seal.

Corn Maze

Bob Connors cut images of Stewie and Brian, two of the characters from the animated TV comedy *Family Guy*, into a seven-acre cornfield maze at his farm in Danvers, Massachusetts.

Fashion Ferrari

A full-size replica of a Ferrari Formula-1 car was made out of $60,000 worth of designer clothing. Eight people worked for five hours at a store in London's Carnaby Street to turn 1,999 items of clothing—including 1,682 red T-shirts, 88 pairs of jeans, 64 pairs of shoes and 31 belts—into a 14-ft-long (4.3-m) model car. The wheels were made from water bottles, the wing mirrors from sunglasses and the tires from black jeans.

Avid Reader

Nonagenarian Louise Brown from Dumfries and Galloway, Scotland, has borrowed 25,000 library books in her lifetime. She has read up to a dozen books a week since 1946 without incurring a single fine for late returns.

Poem Boxing

Japan hosts the National Poem Boxing Championships where contestants fight it out with words in three-minute rounds. The poets step into a boxing ring and read out verses on a wide range of subjects, hoping to secure a win. In the final round, the last two combatants still standing must improvise a poem incorporating a random word that the judges tell them to use.

Same Shot

Except for the years of World War II, Ria van Dijk had a photograph taken of herself at the same shooting gallery in Tilburg, the Netherlands, every year for 74 years. The first picture was taken in 1936 when she was 16.

Phone Dress

A London fashion company has introduced the M-Dress, a little black dress that also serves as a cell phone. The dress, which has a tiny antenna in its hem, allows wearers to make and receive calls by putting their SIM card under the label. To take a call, they raise their hand to their ear; to end it they let it fall to their side.

Tentacle Terror

In 2008, artists Filthy Luker and Pedro Estrellas positioned huge inflatable green octopus tentacles through the windows of an unnamed building in France.

Wooden Chain

Markley Noel of Hickory Corners, Michigan, carved a 480-ft-long (146-m) wooden chain from a single 25-ft-long (7.6-m) maple plank. The chain, which has 1,993 links, each 4 in (10 cm) long, took him seven years to make.

Pencil Tips

Dalton Ghetti of Bridgeport, Connecticut, has been creating miniature graphite masterpieces from the tips of pencils for more than 25 years, including a sculpture of Elvis wearing shades, carved from a single pencil tip. He uses three tools—a razor blade, a sewing needle and a sculpting knife— but no magnifying glass. He digs into the graphite with the needle, then scratches and creates lines, turning the pencil slowly in his hand. One piece—a pencil with interlinking chains—took him two-and-a-half years. He has made more than 100 pencil-tip shapes in total, such as a saw, a screw, a key on a chain, a boot, a chair and all 26 letters of the alphabet.

Roll the Dice

Ari Krupnik, a software engineer from Silicon Valley, California, builds mosaics of famous people from hundreds of dice, achieving different shades of gray according to which face is up. He created a portrait of revolutionary leader Che Guevara from 400 dice and one of George Orwell, author of *Animal Farm*, from 1,925 dice. He has also made a 3-D image of actress Uma Thurman from hundreds of M&M's®.

Pretty Paddies

Each year, the farmers of Inakadate Village, Aomori Prefecture, Japan, use different-colored varieties of rice to create works of art spanning entire rice paddies.

Blind Draft

U.S. novelist Kent Haruf writes the first draft of each of his books blind! He takes off his glasses, pulls a stocking cap down over his eyes, and types his words in darkness.

Rubik's Replica

Five artists in Toronto, Canada, spent two months making a replica of Leonardo da Vinci's *The Last Supper* measuring 8½ x 17 ft (2.6 x 5.2 m), using 4,050 Rubik's Cubes.

Vast Violin

In 2010, a dozen workers in Markneukirchen, Germany, created a playable violin that measured 13 ft 11 in (4.3 m) tall, 4½ ft (1.4 m) wide, and weighed more than 220 lb (100 kg).

Gum-wrapper Dress

Elizabeth Rasmuson of Garner, Iowa, made her 2010 high-school prom dress out of hundreds of gum wrappers that she and her boyfriend, Jordan Weaver, had been collecting for six months. She also made him a matching vest out of blue-and-white gum wrappers.

In the Dark

London's Tate Modern gallery unveiled a giant installation in 2009—40 ft (12 m) of pitch darkness. It was created by Polish artist Miroslaw Balka who said that the darkness was a metaphor for life.

Party Poopers

U.S. rock band Kings of Leon had to abandon a concert at the Verizon Amphitheater, St. Louis, Missouri, in July 2010 after they were bombarded with pigeon droppings. An infestation of birds in the rafters above the stage led to bassist Jared Followill being hit several times during the band's first two songs, including in the face.

Tiny Tiger

A Taiwanese artist has created a painted tiger sculpture that is smaller than a grain of rice. Chen Forng-Shean spent three months carving the 0.04-in-high (1-mm) tiger from resin. He has also made delicate miniature sculptures from sand, dental floss, rice, ant heads and fly wings.

Garbage Pictures

Richard Broom of Lincolnshire, England, spent hours photographing litter along Britain's roadsides and posting them on an Internet blog in an attempt to get the government to tidy up the country—but his photos, including discarded paper cups, old cans, a broken toilet, and bottles of urine, proved so popular that they have turned into highly collectable art.

Mini Mansion

Peter Riches of Hove, England, spent nearly 15 years creating an elaborately decorated doll house and sold it for $80,000—that's enough to buy a real home in some places. His miniature 23-room mansion boasted a music room with grand piano, a hand-crafted games room with snooker table, and a library with more than 1,000 individually bound books. He made the shell of the house from plaster and hand-etched 32,000 bricks on its walls. He cut the 5,000 roof tiles from cardboard. The finished house measured 4 ft (1.2 m) wide, 3 ft 3 in (1 m) high and 2 ft 7 in (80 cm) deep.

Cloud Graffiti

U.S. pop artist Ron English created cloud graffiti in the skies above New York City in September 2009. He hired a skywriting plane and got it to spell the word "cloud" in puffy white dots several times over the city.

Chalk Drawing

Head of a Muse, a simple black chalk drawing on paper by Renaissance painter Raphael, sold at an auction in London, England, for $47.9 million in December 2009.

Pinhead Nativity

In 2009, Italian craftsman Aldo Caliro sculpted a nativity scene—featuring hand-carved figures of the Virgin Mary, Joseph, and an angel, plus a tiny baby Jesus in his crib—on the head of a pin! He painted the figures with a single paintbrush hair. He had previously carved tiny nativity scenes on a lentil and a coffee bean.

Long Story

It will be nearly 1,000 years before the cover of the May 2009 issue of *Opium* magazine can be read in its entirety. It will take that long for the successive layers of ink to degrade—at the rate of one word per century—thereby revealing a nine-word tale created by U.S. conceptual artist Jonathan Keats.

Lego® Plane

LEGO® enthusiast Ryan McNaught built a $5,500 replica of the world's biggest passenger plane—the Airbus A380—with more than 35,000 bricks. It took him more than eight months to build the model, which is 7 ft (2.1 m) long and 6 ft (1.8 m) wide, in the garage of his home in Melbourne, Victoria, Australia.

Blood Painter

Rev Mayers never runs out of the unique ink he uses for his paintings, because it's one hundred percent his own blood on the canvas. The extreme artist from Sydney, Australia, has the blood extracted from his arm using a syringe, the way a doctor would extract blood. He then applies the precious fluid with an airbrush or a paintbrush. More detail and depth becomes visible as the art ages. Rev estimates that he has so far used in excess of 12 pints of his own blood in his paintings, more than most adults have in their entire body.

Precise Worker

U.S. bestselling horror writer Stephen King, originally from Portland, Maine, writes exactly ten pages (around 2,000 words) a day, whether he's in a creative mood or not.

Head Stand

Kris Sleeman of the Dallas extreme performance group Traumatic Stress Discipline appears to feel no pain.

At the grand opening of the Ripley's Believe It or Not! Odditorium in San Antonio, Texas, he lay face down in a pile of freshly broken glass bottles, and then invited Ripley employee Viviana Ray to stand on his head. Kris's pain-defying feats also included having a concrete block on his chest shattered by a sledgehammer while lying on a bed of nails.

Florida Monster

Two boys playing on the beach near St. Augustine, Florida, in 1896 spotted the carcass of a huge creature half buried in the sand. It seemed to have a number of tentacles, some up to 30 ft (9 m) long, prompting the belief that it was some kind of giant octopus. However, a similar blob washed up in Chile in 2003 turned out to be a decomposing sperm whale. When some marine creatures decay, their form changes so much that they can look like unidentified sea monsters.

Wonder Well

Chand Baori, a stepped well 100 ft deep (30 m) in the village of Abhaneri, Rajasthan, India, was built more than a thousand years ago with 13 stories and 3,500 steps.

Missing Belt

For reasons unknown, Jupiter loses or regains one of its two belts every ten to 15 years. The planet usually has two dark bands in its atmosphere—one in its northern hemisphere and one in its southern hemisphere—but pictures taken by astronomers in April 2010 showed that the Southern Equatorial Belt had disappeared. The dark belts are clouds created from chemicals such as sulfur and phosphorus, which are blown into bands by 350-mph (560-km/h) winds.

Human Punchbag

Xiao Lin, a fitness coach from Shenyang, China, rents himself out as a punchbag for stressed women who want to let off steam. The women pay $15 for a 30-minute session during which they can hit him as hard and as often as they like.

Traffic Calming

City transportation officials in Cambridge, Massachusetts, tried to calm drivers annoyed at receiving parking tickets by putting instructions on the reverse side about how to relax by bending the body into simple yoga positions.

Metal Spheres

Over recent decades, miners in Klerksdorp, South Africa, have dug up hundreds of ancient metal spheres that look entirely man-made. However, they were found in Precambrian rock dating back 2.8 billion years—that's over 2.79 billion years before Neanderthal man! The mysterious spheres measure about 1 in (2.5 cm) in diameter and some are etched with three parallel grooves running around the middle.

Unique Stone

The Mystery Stone of Lake Winnipesaukee, New Hampshire, has distinctive markings that make it unique. The egg-shaped stone—found encased in a lump of clay in 1872—has intricate man-made carvings and a hole bored through both ends, but its origins and purpose remain unknown and no matching stones have ever been discovered.

Baghdad Battery

An ancient clay vessel was an early example of a battery— even though batteries were not rediscovered for another 1,800 years. The 2,000-year-old Baghdad Battery contained a copper cylinder and an oxidized iron rod, both held in place by asphalt. When filled with an acid or alkaline liquid, it was capable of producing an electric charge.

Ape Man

On an expedition to Venezuela in 1920, Swiss geologist François de Loys claimed to have stumbled across a 5-ft-tall (1.5-m), red-haired, tailless ape that walked upright like a human. He shot the animal and photographed it, using a long stick to prop up its head, but the corpse went missing before it could be examined. If genuine, it would have been the first ape ever discovered in the Americas, thereby rewriting the theory of primate evolution, but scientists decided that the photo was merely a common spider monkey whose tail was conveniently hidden or chopped off.

Super Sub

Cyril Howarth from Lancashire, England, spent $75,000 on converting a 70-ft-long (21-m) canal narrow boat into a replica of a World-War-II German U-boat. Unlike other submarines, this vessel stays strictly on the surface.

Own Juror

William Woods was about to stand trial in Ottawa, Ontario, Canada, in 1999 on charges of dangerous driving, but the trial had to be postponed because Woods was summoned for jury duty—for his own case.

Political Clown

A professional clown was elected to represent São Paulo in Congress after picking up 1.3 million votes in the 2010 Brazilian general elections. Tiririca (real name Francisco Oliveira) received the highest number of votes for any federal deputy across the country with his catchy TV slogans including: "What does a federal deputy do? I have no idea, but vote for me and I'll let you know."

Too Close for Comfort

Two people found themselves in an unbelievable predicament after being thrown from their motorcycle in Hubei Province, China, in 2010. They flew headfirst into the mouth of a drainpipe just 1 ft 8 in (50 cm) wide and were stuck fast. Fortunately, passersby saw their feet protruding from the polluted water pipe and notified firefighters, who dug the couple free in just ten minutes.

Head for Heights

A six-year-old boy slipped through window bars of an eighth-floor apartment in Hubei Province, China, but ended up dangling by his ears 60 ft (18 m) above the ground after they got trapped in the bars because the rest of his head was too wide to pass through.

Bottleneck Mystery

A 60-mi (96-km) traffic jam trapped thousands of vehicles on the Beijing–Tibet expressway for 11 days in August 2010—but then it completely disappeared overnight without any apparent explanation.

Dancing Cop

Dressed in police blues, white gloves, and an officer's cap, Tony Lepore dances while directing the traffic at an intersection in Providence, Rhode Island. He began his dance routine in the 1980s through boredom and although he retired from the police department in 1988, he returns each year for two weeks to entertain passersby.

Mother Cat

Peter Keonig, a Buddhist bank robber serving five years for armed robberies in Germany, had his request for his cat to be granted visiting rights to him in jail rejected by a court—despite his plea that the animal is the reincarnation of his mother.

Cesspit Hell

A Chinese man was rescued in 2010 after spending two days stuck up to his neck in a toilet cesspit. The man had slipped while using an outhouse toilet in Wuyuan, Inner Mongolia, and had fallen into the pit below. Unsurprisingly, as soon as he was freed, he ran to a nearby pond to have a wash!

Lost Letters

While on a 2010 field trip to the Alps, Freya Cowan, a geography student from the University of Dundee, Scotland, stumbled across a U.S.-bound mailbag from the Malabar Princess, an Air India plane that crashed near the summit of Mont Blanc while en route to London in 1950, killing all 40 passengers and eight crew on board. Some of the correspondence inside the mailbag was still in such good condition that she set about sending 75 letters and birthday cards on to their intended recipients 60 years late.

Alien Autopsy

A display at the U.F.O. Museum at Roswell, New Mexico, re-creates the alleged autopsy of a dead alien killed when his spacecraft crashed in the area in 1947. The dummy extraterrestrial was originally made for the 1994 movie *Roswell*.

Band of Holes

Nearly 7,000 man-made holes are located on a plain near Peru's Pisco Valley—but their origins and purpose remain unknown. The Band of Holes stretches for 1 mi (1.6 km) and some of the holes are up to 7 ft (2.1 m) deep.

Aliens Welcome

Bob Tohak has believed in U.F.O.s since he was a kid. He is so eager to make contact with aliens that he has put a 42-ft-high (13-m) U.F.O. landing port on his property in Poland, Wisconsin. "I'm just hoping that something will show up," he says.

Ambulance Stolen

An Illinois man was arrested for stealing an ambulance in Mount Horeb, Wisconsin—with a patient and paramedics still inside it.

Ashes Live On

For $3,000, U.K.-based firm And Vinyly will press a person's ashes or those of their pet into a playable record featuring their favorite music, a personal message or their last will and testament. The ashes are sprinkled onto a raw piece of vinyl and then pressed by plates. When the plates exert pressure on the vinyl to create the grooves, the ashes are pressed into the record. Customers can also have their own album-cover portrait, created by mixing their ashes into the paint.

They're Here!

A 2010 April Fool's report in a Jordanian newspaper wreaked havoc in one town. Its front-page article described a U.F.O. landing near Jafr, 185 mi (300 km) from Amman. Residents panicked, keeping their children home from school; and Jafr's mayor even sent security forces in search of the aliens. He was about to empty the town of its 13,000 residents when newspaper journalists came clean.

Straight Line

Four ancient historical sites—Easter Island in the Pacific Ocean, the Nazca lines in southern Peru, the Inca city of Ollantaytambo, also in southern Peru, and the Great Pyramid of Giza, Egypt—are all exactly aligned along a straight line. Other world wonders that are within just one-tenth of a degree of this alignment include Persepolis, the capital of ancient Persia; Mohenjo Daro, the ancient capital of the Indus Valley; and the lost city of Petra in modern-day Jordan.

Near Miss

Pilot David Hastings from Norwich, U.K., revealed a close encounter with a U.F.O. when flying over the Mojave Desert in the U.S.A. in 1987. He said a mysterious black shape came at his plane head-on, then flashed overhead. Seconds later the object was moving at high speed at the plane's side. Hastings took photos and showed them to U.S. Navy officers, but they refused to comment.

Ghost Ship

Carrying a shipment of coal, the Carroll A. Deering was found run aground off the coast of North Carolina on January 31, 1921—but its 11-man crew had vanished. There was no sign of the crew's belongings or the ship's navigating instruments, log or clock, yet evidence in the galley indicated that food was being prepared for the following day's meals.

Fire Starter

A ghostly young girl was pictured in a building on fire in the town of Wem, England, in 1995. Many were convinced that the photograph captured the ghost of a girl that died after accidentally setting the same building alight in the 17th century. In 2010, after the photographer had died, it was suggested that the 1995 photograph was a fake. The ghostly girl in the fire had been copied from a 1922 Wem postcard, which was spotted in the local newspaper by an eagle-eyed reader.

Cow Suit

Milkman Tony Fowler from Leicestershire, England, wore a black-and-white cow suit to receive his M.B.E. from Queen Elizabeth II at Buckingham Palace in June 2010. The Friesian outfit should have had a tail at the back, but Fowler's dog chewed it off.

Unwanted Coins

A stockpile of dollar coins worth more than $1.1 billion is languishing in storage because Americans prefer dollar bills. If stacked, the pile of coins would reach seven times higher than the altitude of the International Space Station.

Royal Residence

Janet and Philip Williams have turned their four-bedroom home in Woonona, New South Wales, Australia, into a royal museum, attracting thousands of visitors each year. They have more than 12,000 items of House of Windsor memorabilia, ranging from a life-size model of Queen Elizabeth II to a pair of Prince Charles and Princess Diana slippers. Even the toilet is decorated like a royal throne, complete with purple velvet trim.

$9,000 Toothpick

In December 2009, a toothpick that once belonged to British author Charles Dickens sold for $9,150 at an auction in New York City.

Lint Leonardo

Laura Bell of Roscommon, Michigan, has made a replica of Leonardo da Vinci's painting *The Last Supper* out of laundry lint that measures 13 ft 8 in x 4 ft 4 in (4 x 1.3 m). She bought towels in the colors she wanted, laundering them separately to achieve the right shades. To obtain the amount of lint she needed to make the picture, she had to do about 800 hours of laundry and it then took her another 200 hours to re-create the famous Renaissance masterpiece.

Same Sneakers

As part of a bet he made with his Spanish teacher, high-school freshman Ben Hedblom of Tampa, Florida, wore the same pair of sneakers every day for four years until he graduated—even though they wore away so that his toes eventually stuck out the front and he had to encase the shoes in plastic bags on rainy days.

Reptilian Row

A row over loud music between two South Carolina motel guests ended with one being accused of slapping the other in the face with the head of a 4-ft (1.2-m) python. The suspect was charged with assault and the weapon— the python—was handed over to his family for safe keeping.

Manure Message

To celebrate his wife Carole's 67th birthday, farmer Dick Kleis used a manure spreader to spell out HAP B DAY LUV U in a field visible from the living room of the couple's home in Zwingle, Iowa. It took him three hours and four loads of liquid manure to create the message—he was going to add a heart, too, but he ran out of manure.

Jesus Lives

When a 50-year-old man was taken to a hospital with minor facial injuries after being hit by a car in Northampton, Massachusetts, in May 2010, he gave his name as Lord Jesus Christ. Police officers checked his I.D. and confirmed that it was indeed his legal name.

Bogus Tycoon

Echoing the real-life escapades of Frank Abagnale Jr. in the movie *Catch Me If You Can*, a 17-year-old boy from Yorkshire, England, posed as an aviation tycoon for six months. He tricked British companies into believing he was about to launch his own airline and that he had a fleet of jets. When the ruse was uncovered, the boy was found to be suffering from a form of autism, which enabled him to recall the exact detail of every airline's flight schedule.

Just the Job

Jason Sadler of Ponte Vedra Beach, Florida, earned more than $85,000 in 2009, promoting different businesses by wearing their T-shirts.

Magic Gel

"Aerogel" was created in 1931 by U.S. scientist Samuel Stephens Kistler following a bet with a colleague over who could replace the liquid in gel with a gas without causing shrinkage. Even though it is 99.8 percent air, the unique substance aerogel can withstand temperatures of up to 2,550°F (1,400°C) and is strong enough to support 2,000 times its own weight.

Lost Army

Twin brothers Angelo and Alfredo Castiglioni believe they have found the remains of a 50,000-strong Persian army, said to have been drowned in the sands of the Sahara Desert 2,500 years ago. The Italian archeologists have discovered bronze weapons, a silver bracelet, an earring and hundreds of human bones that are thought to have belonged to the lost army of Persian King Cambyses II, whose men were reportedly buried in a terrible sandstorm in 525 BC.

Toy Parts

Dr. William H. Sewell invented an artificial heart pump prototype with parts from an Erector set toy while at Yale Medical School.

Invisible Man

Scientists at Tokyo University have developed camouflage technology that makes people disappear. A coat made of a high-tech reflective material has a video camera placed in it, which sends film to a projector. This, in turn, bounces the moving image off the front of the coat, making the wearer appear transparent, even when the fabric is creased.

Stench Busters

The city of Beijing, China, has installed 100 high-pressure deodorant guns, which can spray dozens of liters of fragrance per minute, to combat the stench from one of the city's many overflowing landfill sites. Beijing's 17 million people generate nearly 20,000 tons of waste every day—7,700 tons more than the capacity of municipal disposal plants.

Solar Slug

Elysia chlorotica, a green sea slug that lives along the Atlantic seaboard of the U.S.A., runs on solar power. Scientists at the University of Maine have discovered that it photosynthesizes using genes "stolen" from the algae it eats.

Magnetic Lift

Scientists have successfully levitated fruit, insects, frogs and mice by applying a repelling effect on the water molecules in their bodies with powerful magnets.

Quake-proof Bed

Wang Wenxi from Shijiazhuang, China, has invented an earthquake-proof bed. When an earthquake strikes, a strong board automatically slides into place, protecting the person from falling debris. His secure bed has cupboards at both ends with water, canned food, a hammer, and a megaphone to help the occupant survive for several days beneath rubble.

Strad Beaten

A violin made of wood that had been treated with fungus for nine months was judged better than a $2-million 1711 Stradivarius in a sound test conducted in Germany before an audience of 180 people. Scientists say a fungal attack changes the cell structure of the wood, giving it a warmer, more rounded sound.

Perfect Fit

In Peru, the ancient site of Sacsayhuaman features three huge stone walls built so expertly that it is impossible to insert a piece of paper between the different-shaped stones, some of which are 9 ft 10 in (3 m) high and weigh 200 tons.

Ectoplasm

Communicating with the dead was a popular pursuit in the early 20th century, and mediums who went into a trancelike state were often seen to produce a peculiar white substance called ectoplasm from their mouth, ears, nose or navel.

Participants at seances would then watch in amazement as the ectoplasm was apparently transformed into spiritual faces, fully functional arms and even entire bodies. It also appeared to give mediums the power to perform astonishing feats of telekinesis, such as raising tables and chairs without any physical contact. But was it all genuine or just an elaborate hoax?

BEYOND DOUBT?

German physician Baron Albert von Schrenck-Notzing always imposed strict conditions to ensure that mediums could not fake ectoplasm. For this experiment, noted Polish medium, Stanislawa P., was sewn into a special fraud-proof coat, but still appeared to create ectoplasm from her mouth.

HOLMES MYSTERY

While in a trance in Winnipeg, Canada, in 1929, Scottish medium Mary Marshall produced nasal ectoplasm. At the center of it was a face that her spirit guide—Walter—claimed was that of Sherlock Holmes creator Sir Arthur Conan Doyle, himself a confirmed believer in spiritualism. The necklace worn by Mary in the photograph is an "apport"— an object that materialized during the seance, but was not there before or after the event.

GHOSTLY FACE

At a 1912 seance, ectoplasm from French medium Eva C. (Eva Carrière) formed into the shape of a man's head, which, according to an observer, then made bowing movements. Eva C. was renowned for being able to produce ectoplasm, but skeptics said it was nothing more than chewed paper or fabric that had been regurgitated. Once, after the flow of ectoplasm had been reabsorbed into her mouth, she was given a powerful emetic and when she failed to vomit, the doubters were satisfied that she had not swallowed anything to fake the ectoplasm.

Solar Detector

The Super-Kamiokande Detector is a gigantic cylindrical stainless steel tank, measuring 136 ft (41 m) high and 129 ft (39 m) in diameter, located more than half a mile (0.8 km) underground in Japan. Holding 50,000 tons of water, it is lined with 11,146 ultra-sensitive light detectors and serves as a scientific observatory to monitor solar neutrinos—particles that are produced in the Sun by nuclear fusion. This will help us understand what goes on inside the Sun and how matter was created in the early Universe. The Detector is located underground to shield the experiments from cosmic rays and background radiation.

Renewed Vows

Margaret and John Beauvoisin of Hampshire, England, celebrated their diamond wedding anniversary by taking their vows again. The couple got married in 1948 and have renewed their vows every year since 1950, only missing out in 1949 because John was stationed in Bermuda with the Royal Navy.

Doll House

Bettina Dorfmann from Dusseldorf, Germany, owns more than 6,000 Barbie dolls—and some are worth up to $10,000. An entire room of her house is devoted to displaying 1,500 of them while another 3,000 Barbies from her collection are on show at exhibitions and museums around the world.

Pink Lady

Los Angeles actress Kitten Kay Sera has worn nothing but pink for over 25 years. "The Pink Lady," as she is known, even wears pink to funerals and once dumped a boyfriend because he was colorblind and therefore unable to appreciate the joy of pink. She dyes her Maltese dog, Kisses, in her favorite color using beetroot-juice baths.

Snake Smuggler

After customs officers in Kristiansand, Norway, discovered a tarantula in the bag of a ferry passenger who had traveled from Denmark, they decided to conduct a full body search. On investigation, they also found 14 royal pythons and ten albino leopard geckos taped to the man's torso and legs.

Cash Flow

A 47-year-old Ukrainian man got his arm stuck in a public toilet in Chernigov for three hours after trying to retrieve $24 that he had dropped. With the man trapped up to his elbow, rescuers had to use hydraulic shears to cut him free. He emerged unharmed but $24 poorer, while the toilet itself was completely destroyed.

Subway Hideaway

A 13-year-old boy who thought he was in trouble at school spent 11 days hiding on the New York City subway in 2009. Francisco Hernandez Jr. hid on the D train he normally rides during his short commute from his Brooklyn home to school. He slept on trains and survived on junk food he bought from newsstands along the route.

Pillow Talk

In a special ceremony in March 2010, Korean Lee Jin-gyu married a large pillow adorned with a picture of female Japanese animated character, Fate Testarossa. He put the pillow in a wedding dress for the service, which was conducted before a priest. He takes the pillow everywhere—and when he and his pillow bride go to a restaurant, the pillow gets its own seat and its own meal.

Upside-down House

A totally upside-down house opened as a tourist attraction in the grounds of a zoo in Gettorf, Germany, in 2010. Standing on a pointed roof and supported by steel beams in the attic, the 23-ft (7-m) house boasts an upside-down kitchen, as well as a completely inverted bathroom, living room and bedroom. Workers screwed 50 separate pieces into the "floor" (actually the ceiling), including beds, tables and a microwave oven. Needle and thread were used to keep bed linen in place.

Bearly Believable!

A 2010 survey showed that more than one-third of British adults still take a childhood teddy bear to bed with them at night.

Leisurely Stroll

Paul Railton was fined $100 in 2010 for taking his dog for a walk while driving alongside in his car. He was spotted driving at low speed along a country lane in County Durham, England, holding his Lurcher's leash through the car window as the dog trotted next to him.

Upside Down

Wang Xiaoyu, a barber from Changsha, Hunan Province, China, gives haircuts while standing on his head. A trained martial artist, he performs his headstands on a table to achieve the right height for cutting customers' hair.

Blamed Vampire

A Fruita, Colorado, woman who drove her car into a canal in June 2010 blamed the accident on a vampire. She said she was driving on a dirt road late at night, when she spotted a vampire in the middle of the road and hastily put the car in reverse. When troopers arrived, they found the woman's car in the canal, but there was no sign of the vampire.

Concrete Breaker

Kung fu champion Chris Roper from Suffolk, England, can break a 26-in-thick (66-cm) block of concrete with his foot, a 20-in (51-cm) block with his elbow, and a 12-in (30-cm) block with his bare hand.

Car Coffins

Automobile fan Danny Mendez of Winchester, California, has designed a range of $1,500 fiberglass coffins in the shapes of classic cars. Each Cruisin' Casket features motorcycle headlights, alloy wheels from golf carts, and extending side exhausts that serve as handles for pallbearers. In the absence of a death in the family, the coffins can also double as ice coolers.

Guardian Angel

Police in Fribourg, Switzerland, hired a roadside angel to stop motorists driving too fast. Dressed all in white, the angel, played by a bearded actor, stood at different locations and flapped his wings at speeding drivers.

Sailing in Circles

A nautical novice who thought he was sailing around the coast of Britain in a counterclockwise direction ended up circling a small island off Kent instead. He was rescued by a lifeboat after running out of fuel off the 8-mi-wide (13-km) Isle of Sheppey, whose shore he had been hugging day and night on the principle of keeping the land to his right. He had not realized that Sheppey was an island.

Road Hogs

A section of road near Eureka, Missouri, is covered with asphalt made from recycled pig manure, courtesy of a nearby hog farm.

Mayo Misery

A consignment of mayonnaise fell off the back of a truck in Hyogo, Japan, causing an eight-vehicle pileup as cars and motorcycles skidded wildly on the crushed sauce. The highway had to be closed for five hours.

Strong Hair

In November 2009, Manjit Singh from Leicester, England, pulled a double-decker London bus 70 ft (21 m)—using only his hair. By attaching a clamp to his thick ponytail, he managed to pull the seven-ton bus through Battersea Park. The feat made up for his disappointment in 2007, when he had been unable to pull a similar bus with his ears.

Wake Up!

An Australian mining company has invented a hat that wakes up sleepy truck drivers. The hi-tech SmartCap is fitted with brain monitoring sensors, and if the driver seems to be drifting off, the cap sends a message to a computer screen in the truck cab, which then flashes a warning.

Facebook Phenomenon

People across the world spend more than 700 billion minutes a month surfing through the website of Facebook, the Palo Alto, California-based social networking site. Since Facebook was launched in 2004, more than 500 million people have joined the site— that's around eight percent of the world's population.

Burning Mystery

When 92-year-old Dr. John Irving Bentley was found in the bathroom of his home in Coudersport, Pennsylvania, in December 1966, all that remained of him was a pile of ashes and the lower half of his right leg. He is thought to have been a victim of spontaneous human combustion, a phenomenon where people suddenly burst into flames for no apparent reason. Although almost his entire body had been consumed by an intense heat, the fire was confined to a small area and, apart from a hole in the floor where he had been standing, the rest of the room was largely undamaged. The rubber tips on his walking frame were still intact and a nearby bathtub was hardly scorched.

Auto Inferno

Jeanna Winchester was riding in a car with a friend in Jacksonville, Florida, in 1980 when she was mysteriously engulfed in bright yellow flames. There was no spilled gas, she had not been smoking, and the car window was up. Jeanna survived, although she suffered severe burns. The car interior, however, was virtually undamaged, with just a slight browning on Jeanna's white leather seat.

Charred Remains

In March 1997, the charred remains of 76-year-old John O'Connor were found in a chair some distance from the hearth of his living room in County Kerry, Ireland. Only his head, upper torso, and feet remained unburned, yet there was little smoke damage to the room or the furniture.

Fatal Fire

Mrs. Olga Worth Stephens, 75, of Dallas, Texas, suddenly burst into flames while waiting in her parked car in 1964 and died before anyone could rescue her. The car was undamaged and firemen concluded that nothing in the vehicle could have started the fatal blaze.

Paper Puzzle

Anna Martin of West Philadelphia, Pennsylvania, was found incinerated at home in 1957, her body totally consumed by fire except for a piece of her torso and her shoes. The medical examiner estimated that temperatures must have reached at least 1,700°F (925°C)—far too hot for anything in the room to remain uncharred, yet newspapers lying just 2 ft (60 cm) away were found intact.

Subway Pushers

Human "pushers" are hired to work on Tokyo's subway system to help cram more people into the overcrowded train cars.

Burning Dress

A dress being worn by Mrs. Charles Williamson of Bladenboro, North Carolina, unaccountably burst into flames in 1932. Her husband and daughter ripped off the blazing dress with their bare hands yet none of the three suffered any burns. Over the next four days, various items in the house suddenly caught fire, but each time the flames, which had neither smoke nor smell, vanished after the article had burned itself out.

Vaporized Flesh

At Blackwood, Wales, in 1980, a man's body was found burned beyond recognition in his living room. The armchair that he was sitting in was hardly damaged—neither were some plastic objects nearby—but the fire was so intense that it left a coating of vaporized flesh on the ceiling.

Versatile Performer

Yang Guanghe, from China's Guizhou Province, can perform more than 30 different stunts—including standing on lit lightbulbs, lifting buckets of water with his eyelids, using an electric drill on his nose, standing on upturned knives, pulling a car with his eyelids, and inserting a live snake into one of his nostrils then pulling it out from his mouth.

Crystal Tears

Between March and November 1996, a 12-year-old Lebanese girl, Hasnah Mohamed Meselmani, produced glass crystal tears from her eyes. She wept tiny crystals at an average rate of seven a day, and although they were razor-sharp, she felt no pain. Physicians were mystified by her condition, which stopped as suddenly as it had started.

Mystic Cat

Oscar the cat has correctly predicted the deaths of over 50 patients at the Steere House Nursing and Rehabilitation Center in Providence, Rhode Island, by curling up next to them some two hours before they die. For more than two years, he was present at every death in the home—except one when relatives asked him to leave the room. Nurses once placed Oscar on the bed of a patient they thought was close to death, but he immediately went to sit beside someone in another room. The cat's judgment proved better than that of the medics, because while the second patient died that evening, the first lived for two more days.

House of Cards

Bryan Berg of Santa Fe, New Mexico, built a model of the Venetian Macao Resort-Hotel in Las Vegas from 218,792 playing cards, without using glue or tape. It took 44 days and 4,051 decks of cards to complete the model that measured 33 x 10 ft (10 x 3 m) and weighed 600 lb (272 kg).

Great Shakes

Dorena Young of Wallsburg, Utah, has a collection of more than 3,600 salt-and-pepper shakers. She has been collecting them for more than 60 years and has ones shaped like boats, cats, dogs, deer, vegetables, hats, lighthouses and sea horses. She even has a pair of J.F.K. and Jackie Onassis salt-and-pepper shakers.

Sneaker Line

Collecting more than 10,500 sneakers sent in by readers, *National Geographic Kids* magazine unveiled a 1.65-mi (2.65-km) line of shoes, tied together by their laces, at Washington, D.C.

Ringing Rocks

Ringing Rocks Park in Upper Black Eddy, Pennsylvania, is home to a field of boulders, which, when hit with a solid object such as a hammer, produce melodious bell-like tones.

Daring Plunge

Amateur kayaker Christie Glissmeyer from Hood River, Oregon, paddled down the 82-ft-high (25.2-m) Metlako Falls at Eagle Creek, Oregon, in May 2010—a plunge that was nearly twice the height of any waterfall she had previously run.

Dust Bunnies

These cuddly looking bunnies are actually composed of household detritus, including Christmas tree needles, discarded toddler toy parts, dryer lint, toenail clippings, and human hair. Suzanne Proulx, from Erie, Pennsylvania, took 2½ years to collect enough dirt and dust to make 16 of her *Dust Bunnies*. Suzanne's first bunnies were a humorous comment on the dust and dirt that seemed to invade her house and multiply like wild rabbits. They are also about rebirth and renewal, taking what has been thrown away and creating something new.

Skeleton Staff

When the Post-Mortem Club held its annual breakfast in Chicago in 1934, the guest of honor was the skeleton of its late founder, Mr. J. M. McAdou of Florida, who had died the previous year. The club was an organization of naprapaths (practitioners of a manual medical technique similar to osteopathy) and had a rule that stated each member should leave them his skeleton so that it could attend future meetings... although probably not vote.

Bacterial Rain

Over a three-week period in August 1994, gelatinous blobs rained down over Oakville, Washington State, leaving animals dead and people with flu-like symptoms. The blobs contained human white blood cells and two types of bacteria, one of which is found in our digestive system, but no one knows exactly where the blobs came from.

Slimy Cure

According to the African religion of Ifa Orisha, drinking the juices and mucus of Giant African snails can cure the sick.

Fish Deaths

In December 2010, more than 80,000 drum fish were found dead along a 20-mile (32-km) stretch of the Arkansas River and 10,000 red drum fish were mysteriously washed up dead in Chesapeake Bay, Maryland.

Hairy Journey

In 2007–8, German adventurer Christoph Rehage walked nearly 2,887 mi (4,646 km) across China from Beijing to Urumqi and took a picture of himself every day—so that he could document the growth of his beard.

Plain of Jars

Hundreds of ancient stone jars, some weighing up to 6 tons, can be found scattered across several square miles in northern Laos. Their purpose remains a mystery, but they may have been used to house the bodies of dead people until decomposition, after which the remains would have been removed for burial or cremation.

Polar Riddle

When video footage showed a large, white beast lying on the shore, British TV presenter Naomi Lloyd excitedly told viewers that a polar bear from the Arctic had been washed up in Bude, Cornwall. It subsequently emerged that the animal was actually a cow that had been bleached white by seawater.

Game Proposal

A New York City video-game fan proposed to his girlfriend with gold coins in a specially designed level of Super Mario World. Having persuaded her to play the game, he used a level-editing program called Lunar Magic to spell out "Lisa will you marry me?" on screen. He then recorded her delighted reaction in a video posted on YouTube.

Grave Visits

When ten-year-old Florence Irene Ford was buried after dying of yellow fever in 1871, her distraught mother Ellen had steps built down to the head of the casket and a glass window installed so that she could comfort her child during the thunderstorms that had always terrified her during her short life. On many nights, Ellen would ride up to the cemetery in Natchez, Mississippi, and go underground to sit with her dead daughter and read or sing to her.

In the early 1990s, a woman took her 13-year-old daughter to visit the Ford grave at night. After descending the steps, the woman suddenly emerged screaming with a strange green glow all over her. As she rolled on the grass the glow diminished until a cemetery worker was able to scoop it into his hands. He later said it felt like compressed air or a tennis ball. He then released it into the air where it went up, sparkled, and finally disappeared.

Raining Birds

More than 5,000 dead red-winged blackbirds rained from the sky over Beebe, Arkansas, on January 1, 2011, littering the streets with corpses. Three days later, another 500 birds—dead or dying—fell onto the Louisiana Highway in Pointe Coupee Parish. Scientists say the birds, disturbed by New Year's Eve fireworks or a passing train, may have died after flying at night and crashing into trees, houses and power lines.

Marfa Lights

For over a century, witnesses have been spooked by the Marfa Lights, a strange light phenomenon occurring around the Mitchell Flats, outside Marfa, Texas. Descriptions range from small dancing lights in the sky to a single, stationary bright light that changes color. In a failed attempt to solve the mystery, a former World-War-II pilot even chased the lights in an airplane.

Ghost Yacht

A 40-ft-long (12-m) yacht, the Kaz II, was found drifting off the coast of Queensland, Australia, in 2007, with its engine running and a table laid for dinner but no sign of its three-man crew. The radio was working, the computers were running, and the lifejackets were still on board, but there was no evidence of foul play and no bodies were ever found.

Garden Fairies

Phyllis Bacon believes a fairy fluttered into her life and out again one evening in her garden in London, England. She wasn't even looking through the camera when she held it at arm's length and clicked the button to take a picture of her backyard. She spent months scouring the Internet for butterflies, beetles and moths that might match the image, but came up with nothing.

Real Fairies?

As reported in *Ripley's Believe It or Not! Enter If You Dare*, two cousins, Frances Griffiths and Elsie Wright, rocked the world in 1917 when they said they had photographed fairies in a leafy glen near Elsie's home in Cottingley, England. The five photographs were highly convincing and were published by Arthur Conan Doyle,

author of the Sherlock Holmes novels, with an accompanying article. Many experts in photography and psychic research, who examined the pictures and questioned the girls, came to the conclusion that the images were genuine. It was only in the 1980s the girls admitted to faking the pictures with cardboard cutouts and

hatpins. However, when Frances Griffiths' daughter appeared on the BBC TV show *The Antiques Roadshow* on January 4, 2009, with a camera given to her by Conan Doyle, she revealed that her mother claimed right up to her death that the fifth and final photograph, taken on a separate occasion and shown here, was genuine.

Rat Supper

By using a special scanning technique, scientists Henrik Lauridsen and Kasper Hansen from Aarhus, Denmark, were able to take X-rays of a python digesting a rat. The rat can be seen gradually disappearing during the course of 132 hours (5½ days) after the snake had swallowed it.

Bullet Blocker

Colombian tailor Miguel Caballero runs a boutique in Mexico City where jackets and shirts are not stacked by size but by how well they will stop a bullet. He uses secret materials, the most expensive of which, called Black, is so light that it can be scrunched up like paper but will protect the wearer from a bullet fired at point-blank range.

Black Hole

Scientists at the Southeast University in Nanjing, China, have created a pocket-size black hole—an 8½-in-wide (21.5-cm) disk that absorbs all the electromagnetic radiation thrown at it. The metal disk has 60 concentric rings that affect the magnetic properties of passing light, bending the beams into the center of the disk and trapping them in a maze of etched grooves.

Shrinking Coins

A powerful electromagnetic field can shrink a coin to half its diameter. The technique is known as high-velocity metal forming, a process that creates an invisible, pulsed magnetic field that batters the coin with a strong shock wave, forcing it to change its physical shape in the blink of an eye.

Speed of Sound

Sound travels 4.3 times faster in water than it does in air. When something vibrates, it causes molecules to bump into each other. As water molecules are closer together, the vibrations transfer faster between themselves.

Robot Olympics

At the 2010 International Robot Olympics held in Harbin, China, humanoid robots from 19 countries competed in 17 disciplines, including running, walking, boxing, kung fu and dancing. All robots had to be less than 2 ft (60 cm) tall and be built with a head, two arms and two legs. The opening event, the 5-m (5-yd) sprint, was won in a time of 20 seconds.

Yellow Deposit

An unexplained greenish-yellow goo fell from the skies and splattered houses and streets in Snyder, New York State, on January 18, 2011. As temperatures dropped, homes were coated in yellow or green icicles.

Resuscitating Roadkill

A 55-year-old man was arrested on a remote highway northeast of Pittsburgh, Pennsylvania, after he was seen performing mouth-to-mouth resuscitation on roadkill. Witnesses said the possum in question was not just playing dead, it had been deceased for some time.

Frozen with Heat

Water can be frozen solid—by applying heat! Supercooled water, which can stay liquid down to −40°F (−40°C), will freeze as it is being heated, as long as the temperature also changes the electrical charge of the surface with which the water is in contact.

Wee Folk

Two tree pods shaped like fairies are kept in a glass box at the Wat Phrapangmuni Temple near Sing Buri, Thailand. According to popular belief, these Naree Pons (or pod people) appeared to the Buddha as beautiful women while he meditated in a secluded area. They then vanished and left behind a miniature humanoid pod form on a nearby tree.

Ghostly Pleas

Sightings of the ghosts of tormented slaves from the 1830s have been reported at Lalaurie House, New Orleans. Servants who begged the assistance of outsiders when the house was burning are seen running back inside, slamming doors, shouting repeatedly. Several people have seen ghostly faces of the dead peering from upper windows.

Flaming Fireball

A massive fireball lit up the sky over five U.S. states—Missouri, Iowa, Wisconsin, Illinois and Indiana—on the night of April 14, 2010. Puzzled scientists say it could have been a meteor, a chunk from an asteroid, or rocket debris.

Eerie Face

The image of a child's face dating back over 100 years was found burned onto an old oven door at a restaurant in Saint John, New Brunswick, Canada, in the 1980s. A lady visitor to the property at 31 Leinster Street had gone into the cellar to inspect the original brick oven, but when the dirt was cleaned away the smiling face of a young girl became visible in the iron door. It is believed the family living there in the late 19th century had used the oven as a crematorium to dispose of their dead daughter. The image on the door was caused by carbons given off by the body during burning, the bright light of the fire having acted as a lens.

Advanced Mechanism

When the Antikythera Mechanism was recovered from a shipwreck near Crete in 1900, the writing on its case indicated that it was made around 80 BC—but an X-ray revealed a system of differential gears not known to have existed until AD 1575. It is believed to be an ancient mechanical computer designed to calculate astronomical positions, but its sophistication is in fact comparable to a 19th-century Swiss clock.

Ghostly Vision

When Kevin Horkin downloaded this photo and saw a pale young woman peering from a window on the first floor of Gwrych Castle in Abergele, he knew something spooky was afoot. The huge Welsh castle has been derelict since 1985 and the floor crumbled away years ago, so no one could possibly have been standing there. Countless sightings, orbs, cold spots and cases of objects moving have been recorded at Gwrych, said to be the most haunted building in Wales.

Mary, the Hanged Elephant

Mary was a 5-ton Asian elephant who was hanged for her so-called crimes on September 12, 1916. Her story is a cautionary tale of circus abuse during the early 20th century. She had been prodded behind the ear by her trainer as she bent down to nibble on watermelon rind, so she grabbed him with her trunk and stamped on his head, killing him. Labeled a highly dangerous beast, the public demanded her death. She survived being shot with two dozen rounds, so it was decided to hang her. Mary was hanged from an industrial crane, the rope tied around her neck the following day in Erwin, Tennessee.

Stone Balls

In the Costa Rican jungle in the 1930s, workmen found more than 300 man-made stone balls, many perfectly spherical and varying in size from as small as a tennis ball to huge boulders 8 ft (2.4 m) in diameter and weighing 15 tons. The stones date back at least 500 years, but nobody knows who made them and how they achieved such perfect spheres.

Phone Home

A man has spent two years living in a cramped phone booth in Dalian City, Liaoning Province, China. He sleeps by curling up into a ball on top of cushions and hangs his spare clothes from the roof.

Elephant Collision

Driving home from church in Enid, Oklahoma, a couple collided with an elephant that ran across the highway after escaping from a nearby circus. The elephant was unharmed apart from a broken tusk.

Paid Piper

Tourism bosses in Vienna, Austria, found a way to frighten off rats from the city's sewers—by playing the bagpipes. *The Third Man* tours, which walk the sewers made famous by Orson Welles' cult 1949 movie, were closed down when health chiefs ruled that the risk of rat bites was too great, but now they're back in business after hiring a bagpiper whose shrill sounds remarkably send the rodents running for cover.

Quiet Companion

Alan Derrick of Somerset, England, lived in a house with the dead body of his friend hidden behind a sofa from 1998 to 2008.

Dam Coincidence

J.G. Tierney drowned in 1922 while surveying the future site of the Hoover Dam. In 1935, his son Patrick became the last person to die in the dam's construction when he fell from an intake tower.

Milk Miracle

For several hours on September 21, 1995, Hindu religious statues all over the world drank milk. When a worshiper at a temple in New Delhi, India, offered milk to the trunk of a statue of the elephant-headed deity Ganesha, the liquid was seen to disappear. Soon Hindu temples in the U.K., Canada, Dubai and Nepal were reporting similar occurrences. Scientists were baffled by the phenomenon, which stopped before the end of the day when statues suddenly refused the milk.

Elephant Electrocution

In an attempt to prove the dangers of Nikola Tesla's alternating current (AC) and the safety of his competing direct current (DC) for use in the home, Thomas Edison electrocuted an elephant in 1903. Topsy was an elephant with Forepaugh Circus at Coney Island's Luna Park, New York City, who had killed three men in three years, and her owners wanted her destroyed. Edison suggested electrocution, a method that had been used for human executions since 1890. Topsy was fed carrots containing potassium cyanide before a current of 6,600 volts was sent through her body, killing her in seconds. A crowd of 1,500 witnessed the event, which Edison also filmed.

Robotic Jellyfish

Scientists in Germany have developed a range of biologically inspired robotic jellyfish that can swim. The battery-powered jellyfish are propelled through the water by eight electrically driven tentacles, the construction of which is based on the anatomy of fish fins. With the help of sensors and control software, the jellyfish steer themselves and can communicate by means of 11 infrared light-emitting diodes, enabling them to work together as a team and to avoid bumping into each other.

Robot Wedding

A wedding that took place in a Tokyo, Japan, restaurant in May 2010 was conducted by a robot. Bride Satoko Inoue and groom Tomohiro Shibata were directed through the ceremony by I-Fairy, a 4-ft (1.2-m) robot, who wore a wreath of flowers and a set of wires that led to a human controller who was sitting at a nearby computer.

Who Goes Hare!

In 1971, a rabbit was shot by Jasper Barrett near his home in Jefferson, South Carolina. On being prepared for the pot by his wife and a friend, the outline in black of a woman's face was found on the skinned flesh of one foreleg. It was about an inch (2.5 cm) across and had a rosebud mouth, curly hair and long lashes. Within a week, 4,000 people had trekked to see the face and police were called to control the crowds.

Healing Hand

Surgeons in China saved a young girl's hand by grafting it on to her leg for three months. Nine-year-old Ming Li lost her left hand when she was run over by a tractor on her way to school in Zhengzhou, Henan Province. Her arm was too badly crushed to reattach the hand to her wrist so doctors grafted it on to her right calf instead, before transplanting it back on to her arm once it had healed.

Iceman's Relatives

Nearly 20 years after discovering the mummified body of a 5,300-year-old man—known as Oetzi the iceman—in a melting Alpine glacier, scientists have extracted DNA from a bone in his pelvis with a view to tracking down his living descendants.

Strong Stomach

Julika Faciu from Piatra Neamt, Romania, allowed 50 motorbikes and a 3-ton jeep to ride over his stomach, one by one.

Underground City

A series of streets, houses and tombs belonging to an Egyptian city dating back more than 3,500 years has been located by radar. Austrian archeologists used radar imaging to show the outlines of Avaris, the ancient capital of the Hyksos people, beneath fields and modern buildings in the Nile Delta.

Clean Teen

As a teenager, James Brown from Nottinghamshire, England, had a collection of 50 vacuum cleaners—and his love for them has led to him opening Britain's first vacuum cleaner museum. He can identify different brands of vacuum cleaners in his collection simply by the sound they make.

Dried Shark

A seafront store in Taiwan offers whole dried sharks for sale at a price of 6,500 Hong Kong dollars (U.S. $844) per 1 lb 5 oz (600 g). Shark fins are a popular delicacy in Chinese soup, while other parts of the shark are considered to have beneficial medicinal properties.

Homemade Reactor

Mark Suppes, a 32-year-old web designer for fashion house Gucci, has built his own homemade nuclear fusion reactor on the third floor of a Brooklyn, New York City, warehouse. He took two years to build it, using $35,000 worth of parts he bought on eBay.

Unfinished City

Having spent years constructing 30-ft-high (9-m) walls from perfectly hewn basalt, the inhabitants of the ancient city of Nan Madol, in the Micronesia region of the Pacific, mysteriously abandoned it, leaving some of the walls unfinished.

Homemade Plane

In July 2010, 82-year-old Arnold Ebneter of Woodinville, Washington State, flew his homemade lightweight airplane, the E-1, nonstop from Everett, Washington State, to Fredericksburg, Virginia—a journey of 2,327 mi (3,746 km) —in 18 hours 27 minutes.

King Charles

Charles Wesley Mumbere worked as a nurses' aide for years in the U.S.A., but on October 19, 2009, he reclaimed his crown as head of the mountainous kingdom of Rwenzururu in Uganda, ruling over about 300,000 people.

Rolling, Rolling, Rolling...

Lotan Baba, the "Rolling Saint" of India, spreads his message of peace by rolling on the ground from town to town across the country. He rolls 6–8 mi (10–12 km) a day and estimates that over the years he has rolled about 18,650 mi (30,000 km). His enthusiasm for rolling may be partly explained by the fact that as penance he once spent seven years standing upright, in the same place.

Fire Trim

Italian-American hairdresser Pietro Santoro cuts hair using a naked flame at his barber shop in Washington, D.C. He says that cutting hair with fire gives it more body.

Debt Unpaid

Former British Prime Minister Winston Churchill (1874–1965) died owing 13 rupees to the Bangalore Club of Bangalore, India. The club has maintained the ledger showing that debt and displays it—but refuses to allow anyone to pay his tab.

Ripley's Hero

Daring Thai snake charmer Khum Chaibuddee, also known as the "King of Cobras," was honored as a Ripley's Ambassador by the Ripley's Believe It or Not museum in Pattaya, Thailand, in 2010. He celebrated by performing with his deadly cobras and even kissing them, his signature trick. In *Ripley's Believe It or Not! The Remarkable Revealed*, we reported that a fearless Khum had kissed 19 highly poisonous cobras one by one on the head without being bitten.

INCREDIBLE AMBASSADOR

Lively Landings

Giant 300-ton Boeing 747s coming in to land at Princess Juliana Airport on the Caribbean island of Saint Martin fly just 60 ft (18.4 m) above the heads of vacationers on Maho Beach.

They fly so low that they blow sand into the faces of plane spotters gathered below. The beach is right next to the runway, which, at 7,054 ft (2,170 m), is the shortest in the world to regularly accommodate 747s.

Over the autobahn Leipzig Hall Airport, Germany.

Low tide Barra Airport, Scotland.

Smoothed ice and snow ice runway in Antarctica.

Crossing the highway Gibraltar Airport.

Beige World

After examining the amounts of light emitted by galaxies, scientists at NASA have concluded that the Universe is not really black at all—more a dull beige. They say that the shade is constantly changing and has become much less blue over the past ten billion years because redder stars are now more dominant.

First Computer

Unveiled in 1946 at the University of Pennsylvania, ENIAC (short for Electronic Numerical Integrator and Computer) was the world's first general-purpose computer. It weighed 30 tons and occupied an entire room. Amazingly, its computing ability can be re-created today on a silicon chip smaller than your thumbnail.

Anti-flu Suit

A Japanese menswear company has developed a suit that it claims protects the wearer from the deadly H1N1 strain of influenza. The $550 suit, produced by the Haruyama Trading Company, is coated with the chemical titanium dioxide—an ingredient of toothpaste and cosmetics—that reacts with light to break down and kill the virus on contact.

Oh, Crumbs!

The Swiss-based Large Hadron Collider, the world's most powerful particle accelerator and probably the most complex machine ever built, was shut down in 2009 after a bird passing overhead dropped a piece of bread on a section of machinery, which caused parts of the accelerator to overheat.

Skiing Robot

A skiing robot that can navigate slalom courses has been developed by researchers at the Jozef Stefan Institute in Slovenia. The robot, which is about the size of an eight-year-old child and uses regular skis, has a pair of computer systems. One of them is attached to cameras to help plot the robot's course down the slope, the other is attached to gyroscopes and force sensors to keep it stable.

Plasma Knife

To help stem the loss of blood from serious wounds, the U.S. military has been testing a plasma knife, with a blade consisting of heated, ionized gas, which can cut through flesh just as easily as a steel scalpel. The plasma knife seals off the damaged flesh, stopping the bleeding and protecting against infection.

Phone Control

The iDriver app enables motorists to drive a car using their cell phone. Devised by researchers from Berlin, Germany, the app has a steering wheel, separate buttons for accelerating and braking, and is capable of directing a 2-ton minivan.

Large Dish

The Large Zenith Telescope at the University of British Columbia in Canada uses a mirror made from a spinning dish of liquid mercury nearly 20 ft (6.1 m) in diameter.

Bell Tribute

On August 4, 1922—the day of the funeral of Alexander Graham Bell—all telephone services in the U.S.A. and Canada were shut down for one minute as a tribute to the inventor, who, in the 1870s, had invented the world's first workable telephone.

Rotten Eggs

As part of a safety campaign in 2010, Puget Sound Energy, a utility company in Washington State, added the stench of rotten eggs to its gas bills. Natural gas is odorless, but providers add a chemical with a sulfurlike aroma to the gas so that leaks can be detected.

Smells good

Body Art

Hong Kong radiologist Kai-Hung Fung has created stunning images of the human body that look like works of art. Dr. Fung scans the patient using a conventional computer topography (CT) scan, generally used for diagnosing brain and cardiac problems, before feeding the information into a computer and adding vivid color.

Bite size

Say what?

317

Wrong Funeral

After reading a death notice in her local paper in Merthyr Tydfil, Wales, stating that upholsterer Ron Jones had passed away, Margaret Griffiths sat through the funeral service for her old friend—only to discover later that she had got the wrong Ron Jones. The confusion arose because there were two men named Ron Jones of similar age in the town and both had worked as upholsterers.

Strange Venue

Jason and Rachael Storm decided to start their life together in 2008 by getting married at a place where it usually comes to an end—a funeral home in St. Joseph Township, Michigan, where the groom was a director.

Mobile Chapel

A 1942 firetruck owned by Rev. Darrell Best, of Shelbyville, Illinois, has been converted into a mobile wedding chapel called "Best Man." It has stained glass windows, an altar, two wooden pews and a fully working pipe organ.

Huge Hole

A 66-ft-wide (20-m) sinkhole opened up overnight in the yard of the Zhang family home in Leshan, China. Several fruit trees disappeared down the hole, which was more than 130 ft (40 m) deep and stopped less than 3 ft (1 m) from the house.

Crab Dispenser

A food vending machine in Nanjing, China, sells live crabs. Designed by Shi Tuanjie, the machine offers live hairy crabs and accompanying bottles of vinegar. The crustaceans vary in price from $2 to $7, according to size. The crabs, a tasty delicacy in the region, are packed into plastic boxes and chilled to 40°F (5°C), leaving them sedated but still alive. An average of 200 crabs a day are sold, and customers are promised compensation of three live crabs should their purchase happen to be dead.

Snow Palace

To create a fairy-tale setting for his ultimately successful marriage proposal to Christi Lombardo in February 2010, Ryan Knotek built a snow castle near his home in Parma, Ohio. Using blocks of snow, he constructed a one-room, one-story palace topped with roof spires and furnished inside with a portable heater to keep the winter chill away.

Flamboyant Funeral

Flamboyant Hong-Kong lawyer Kai-bong Chau, 75, was buried in March 2010 with paper replicas of his gold and pink Rolls-Royce cars and a selection of his most colorful outfits. Paper models of cars, homes and money are traditionally burned at Chinese funerals to provide the dead with comfort and luxuries in the afterlife.

Young Undertaker

In September 2010, George Simnett set up his own funeral business in Leicestershire, England—at age 17.

Blessed Computers

To attract bankers and financiers from the City of London to his church, the Rev. Canon David Parrott performed a service in which he blessed their cell phones and laptop computers.

Fast Food

Patrick "Deep Dish" Bertoletti from Chicago is one of the world's most successful competitive eaters. In 2008, he became an official pizza-eating world champion, devouring 47 slices of 16-in (41-cm) deep dish in 10 minutes. Most people might not finish even half of one large pizza in that time.

Highlights of Patrick's career include finishing off more than 10 lb (4.5 kg) of Key lime pie in 8 minutes and 275 pickled peppers in 10 minutes. These and many more appetite-busting achievements mean that Patrick is ranked in the top five eaters in the world by the sport's Major League Eating organization. In 2010, in Black Hawk, Colorado, Patrick swallowed 3 lb 11¾ oz (1.7 kg) of deep-fried bull's testicles in 10 minutes.

You don't need to be extremely heavy to be an eating champion; in fact many eating champions are in good shape. Culinary-school graduate Patrick weighs in at 190 lb (86 kg), relatively lightweight given his 6-ft-2-in (1.88-m) frame and the vast amounts of food he consumes at eating competitions—

regularly gulping down more than 10,000 calories in a few minutes. Fittingly, Patrick works as a chef and hopes to open his own restaurant—serving regular-sized portions.

Patrick's Menu		
Food	Amount	Time
Blueberry pie	9 lb (4 kg)	8 minutes
Slushie	22 fl oz (650 ml)	9 seconds
Hotdogs	55	10 minutes
Pizza (16 in/41 cm)	47 slices	10 minutes
Hamburgers	94	8 minutes
Chicken wings	227	30 minutes
Chili spaghetti	11½ lb (5.2 kg)	10 minutes
Ribs	8½ lb (3.8 kg)	12 minutes
Subs (8 in/20 cm)	14	10 minutes

All at Sea

American sailor Reid Stowe returned to shore in June 2010 after spending more than three years at sea without touching dry land. He set off from New Jersey in his 70-ft (21-m) schooner Anne in April 2007 and docked in Manhattan at the end of a 1,152-day voyage, to be greeted by his girlfriend, who had joined him on part of the voyage, and their 23-month-old son, whom he had never seen before.

Bullion Bugatti

Made from solid 24-carat gold and platinum and featuring a large, flawless diamond on the front grille, the Bugatti Veyron Diamond must be the most expensive toy car ever made. It may be only toy-sized, weighing 15 lb (7 kg) and measuring 10 in (25 cm) in length, but it costs a cool $2 million to buy—that's almost twice as expensive as a real, regular-sized Bugatti Veyron! Jewelry designer Stuart Hughes from Liverpool, England, and Swiss model expert Robert Gulpen spent two months creating this intricate replica, which also features functional steering and a detailed engine.

Hang Time

An Oklahoma driver escaped disaster after reversing his Mercedes sedan through the exterior wall of a parking garage—seven floors up! The driver's foot had become stuck on the gas pedal, but luckily the vehicle lodged itself halfway through the exterior wall. Falling debris damaged several cars, but no one was injured and the driver exited his vehicle safely.

High Security

The $400-million yacht, 557 ft (170 m) long, owned by Russian billionaire Roman Abramovich, is equipped with a swimming pool, two helipads, a mini-submarine and a missile defense system.

Highway Party

Some 20,000 tables were set up along a 37-mile (60-km) section of a German autobahn between Dortmund and Duisberg for a street party with a difference. The high-speed road was closed to motorists and turned over to cyclists, skaters, and picnickers in an event attended by more than three million people.

Bacon Kevin Bacon

J & D's Foods in Seattle commissioned Pennsylvania artist Mike Lahue to create a sculpture of actor Kevin Bacon, from crispy bacon bits! The tasty Hollywood head took three months to complete, but unfortunately it is inedible owing to a protective lacquer coating. A bacon-obsessed food company from Seattle, J & D's Foods produce bacon soda, "baconnaise" mayonnaise, bacon popcorn, envelopes that taste of bacon when you lick the seal and even bacon lip balm. Their company slogan is "Everything should taste like bacon."

Curry Boom

In 1950, there were only six Indian restaurants in the whole of Great Britain, but by 2004 their number had grown to around 9,000.

Persistent Offender

A Saudi-Arabian student racked up $97,000 in driving fines—the result of 400 traffic violations in Dubai over a period of less than two years.

Slow Getaway

A burglary suspect in Hillsborough County, Florida, was quickly captured after trying to evade arrest by escaping on a lawn mower.

Spoon Fed

Surgeons in Rotterdam, the Netherlands, removed 78 different items of cutlery from the stomach of 52-year-old Margaret Daalmans after she had gone to the hospital complaining of stomach pains. X-rays showed she had swallowed dozens of forks and spoons as a result of her insatiable appetite for cutlery.

Field Day

James Field from Sheffield, England, made 42 bungee jumps in one hour—that's nearly one jump a minute—from a crane that was raised 160 ft (49 m) in the air near Tower Bridge, London.

Lucky Leap

During a traffic accident in August 2009, Carl Brewer of Canton, Ohio, saved himself by leaping from his motorcycle onto the back of a moving pickup truck.

Ship Found

In 2010, archeologists excavating the World Trade Center site in New York City discovered the remains of a wooden ship believed to have been buried there more than 200 years ago.

327

The Lost Squadron

A World-War-II fighter plane was rescued and restored to flying condition after spending 50 years buried beneath 268 ft (82 m) of solid snow and ice in Greenland.

The Lockheed P-38F Lightning, since nicknamed "Glacier Girl," was part of an eight-strong squadron making its way across the Atlantic to fight in Europe in June 1942. Bad weather forced the squadron to crash-land on a remote ice cap in Greenland. The crews were rescued after ten days on the ice, but the planes had to be sacrificed.

Later attempts to recover the aircraft proved unsuccessful because decades of snowstorms and shifting ice had carried them 2 mi (3.2 km) from their original location, and buried them so deep no one could find them. Then, in 1988, Glacier Girl was tracked down by a combination of magnetometers (to detect underground magnetic fields) and radar. A daring rescue and restoration project then swung into action.

Glacier Girl flying above Nevada in 2006. More than 80 percent of the new aircraft was built from original parts retrieved from deep beneath Greenland's ice and snow. In October 2002, before a crowd of 20,000 spectators, Glacier Girl took to the skies once again—60 years after her fateful crash in the Arctic. Now the plane can be seen at air shows across the U.S.A.

Sparkling Blades

War correspondent Michael Yon captured an unusual phenomenon while working in Afghanistan. When U.S. Air Force helicopters come in to land, the dust in the air reacts with the spinning blades to create static electricity that throws out bright sparks around the chopper. Michael named this the Kopp-Etchells effect, after U.S. soldier Benjamin Kopp and British soldier Joseph Etchells, both of whom Yon knew and whom died in the conflict.

Back to Life

A 1929 Austin 12/4 car that had been languishing idly in a garage in Lincolnshire, England, instantly roared into life in 2010 when its starter handle was turned for the first time in nearly 50 years. The car had been owned by Roger Bulled's late father, Leslie, who had last driven it in 1961.

Hypersonic Flight

Flying off the coast of southern California in May 2010, an unmanned X-51A Waverider aircraft flew for more than three minutes at Mach 5—that's five times the speed of sound and more than 3,800 mph (6,115 km/h).

Wrong Nuts

In May 2009, a car traveling down a Swiss highway lost all four of its wheels at the same time. The owner had used the wrong nuts to secure them.

Police Tractor

To combat crime in rural areas of Lincolnshire, England, a farm tractor has been converted into a police vehicle, complete with a flashing blue light.

Off the Rails

One of the most bizarre rail accidents in history occurred in 1895, when a steam locomotive thundered into the Montparnasse station in Paris, France, at full speed. The engine plowed through the platform and then the station wall, crashing into the street 30 ft (9 m) below and killing a pedestrian. The train had been 2 mi (3.2 km) from the station and traveling at 55 mph (90 km/h) when the driver realized that the brakes had failed. Despite the driver's best efforts, the locomotive hit the station at 35 mph (55 km/h). All those aboard escaped serious injury.

Helicopter Rescue

A Swiss van driver and his vehicle had to be rescued by helicopter after his GPS sent him up a remote mountain footpath near Bergun. Robert Ziegler found himself stranded on the narrow track, unable to go forward or turn around.

Lost Torpedo

The Taiwanese navy offered a reward of nearly $1,000 in 2010 after sailors aboard the submarine Sea Dragon lost a torpedo during a routine training exercise.

INCREDIBLY STRANGE

Flame Thrower

Fed up with car drivers cutting him off on the road, James Bond fan Colin Furze from Lincolnshire, England, designed the ultimate revenge—a gadget that fires 15-ft-long (4.5-m) flames out the back of his moped.

Toilet Car

Dave Hersch of Lakewood, Colorado, spent four years designing a twin-bowl motorized toilet capable of reaching speeds of 30 mph (48 km/h). His "toilet car" has a 6.5 horsepower motor, can seat two people, and features six toilet rolls and a magazine rack.

Busy Airport

London's Heathrow Airport is six times the size of the country of Monaco and has three chaplains—Anglican, Catholic, Free Church—and representatives for the Jewish, Muslim, Hindu, Buddhist and Sikh faiths. Nearly 70 million passengers pass through the airport each year, and 10 percent of Britain's perfume sales take place there.

Ejector Scare

A civilian passenger in a South African Air Force display plane accidentally activated the ejector seat while reaching for something to steady himself during a spectacular midair maneuver. The startled passenger instantly shot through the jet's Perspex canopy and was blasted 300 ft (90 m) into the sky by the rocket-powered emergency chair. He subsequently floated down to the ground on a parachute that opened automatically.

Barbie Ban

Forty-year-old Paul Hutton of Essex, England, was banned from the road after being caught drunk driving in a toy Barbie car that had a top speed of 4 mph (6 km/h). The electric car was designed for three-to-five-year-olds.

Much Traveled

German police who stopped a double-decker Latvian tour bus in Berlin in 2010 found that it had 1.1 million mi (1.8 million km) on the clock—enough to take passengers to the Moon and back twice.

Jet Bus

It wouldn't take long to get to school in Paul Stender's jet-powered school bus. School Time is equipped with a massive Phantom jet-fighter engine with the power of more than 250 family automobiles, propelling the 35-ft (10.5-m) bus to speeds of more than 350 mph (560 km/h). Paul has also built a 10,000-horsepower Dodge pickup that can reach up to 400 mph (645 km/h), and a jet-powered outhouse featured in *Ripley's Believe It or Not! Seeing is Believing*.

Sausage Drama

A cleaner was taken to hospital in May 2010 after his head and shoulders were sucked into a sausage machine at a factory in Danvers, Massachusetts. The victim, who was not seriously hurt, was cleaning the inside of a cylinder that draws marinade into the meat, when the machine was accidentally switched on.

Gigantic Grill

Jack Henriques, an engineer from Gloucestershire, England, has built a giant barbecue that can cook 1,000 sausages or grill 500 burgers at once. He spent three months welding together the steel grill, which weighs 2 tons and measures 16 ft (5 m) long, 6 ft 3 in (1.9 m) wide, and 11½ ft (3.5 m) tall. The $15,000 barbecue, which requires 14 bags of coal to fill fully, is so big it can cook seven whole lambs, three whole pigs, or two whole cows at the same time.

Super Salami

A monster salami measuring 7 ft 3 in (2.2 m) long and weighing 143 lb (65 kg) went on show at the Agricultural Trading Exhibition in Anhui, China, in February 2010.

Volcano Barbecue

When Iceland's Fimmvörðuháls volcano erupted in April 2010, Reykjavik chef Fridgeir Eiriksson cooked soup, flaming lobster, monkfish, and shallots using the volcano's 390°F (200°C) lava as an oven. Two customers paid $1,000 to enjoy the special Champagne dinner on the bubbling volcano.

Flying Car

A company from Massachusetts has devised a road car that can convert into an airplane in just 30 seconds. The Terrafugia Transition, which has four wheels, two folding wings, and a propeller at the rear, can reach speeds of 80 mph (130 km/h) on the ground and 115 mph (185 km/h) in the air. It can be stored in a conventional garage, yet has a flight range of more than 490 mi (790 km).

335

Wall of Death

The crowd peers over the Wall of Death as the powerful motorbikes roll into the ring. The sound inside the track grows deafening as the motorbikes accelerate, tires rumbling. As they pick up speed, the bikes climb the steep, wooden walls until the riders flash inches past the faces in the audience.

Tubular tracks with steep walls, Walls of Death, or Motordromes, evolved in the early 20th century. Riders would start at the bottom of the circular track, increasing their speed and the angle, until they were racing at just over 55 mph (88 km/h) at right angles to the wooden wall. One slip could spell disaster—early Wall of Death riders had little or no safety equipment, often neglecting to wear helmets because the force of gravity would make it hard to keep their head straight. Soon riders started to increase the risk, racing two or three abreast, crossing each other. Eventually, the races introduced motorcars, too. Optimum speed was essential. If the bikes went slower than 55 mph (88 km/h), they would drop off the wall; too much faster and the riders were in danger of blacking out as the centrifugal force could drain blood from the brain. Motordromes are now rare—few exist in North America and Europe, but they are still popular in Asia.

Cookie Crum, still riding motorbikes and now living in Oregon, was one of the few female Motordrome riders. She first started to ride the Wall of Death in 1949, at only 17 years old, and she toured the U.S.A. for eight years. Cookie also rode in what became known as "liondromes." To thrill the crowd even further, fully grown lions were let loose on the boards, the idea being that they would chase the rider around the ring. Incredibly, they were also trained to sit in vehicles as they tore around the Motordrome (see far left).

Stuntmen perform death-defying feats on motorbikes and in cars whizzing around the walls of "Wells of Death" at fairs across India. A modern twist on the original Walls of Death, these dromes attract large crowds wherever they spring up.

Yellow Lines

Sally Baker left her Peugeot 206 on a street in Manchester, England, because the road had unrestricted parking—but when she returned she found the vehicle was facing the other way, had double yellow lines painted underneath, and had a parking ticket on the windshield. In her absence, council workmen had hoisted her car into the air so that they could paint double yellow "no parking" lines beneath it.

Bike Burial

When Harry "The Horse" Flamburis, a Hells' Angels motorcycle club leader from Daly City, California, died, he was buried with his motorbike.

Lamborghini Replica

Truck driver Chen Jinmiao of Hunan Province, China, built a replica Lamborghini supercar—complete with the famous wing doors—for just $3,000. He downloaded the drawings from the Internet and bought materials from markets and bargain stores to construct a working car with a top speed of 50 mph (80 km/h)—compared to a real Lamborghini's 200 mph (320 km/h).

Personal Potholes

In an attempt to finance the repair of its crumbling roads, the village of Niederzimmern, Germany, put its many potholes up for sale in 2010. For $68, people could buy a hole in the road, and in return the authorities repaired it and put a personal message on top. TV channels and newspapers soon bought some of the potholes for advertising.

Melon-coly Motorists

A busy motorway near Basel, Switzerland, was closed for two hours after a Spanish truck carrying melons lost its load and splattered fruit all over the road. Drivers in the 3-mi-long (5-km) traffic jam eased the pain of their delay by getting out of their cars and helping themselves to the melons.

Homemade Sub

In October 2009, Tao Xiangli, a farmer from Beijing, China, made a successful maiden voyage in his homemade submarine. Without any expert advice, he spent 18 months building the 4-ft-10-in-high (1.5-m), 21-ft-long (6.5-m), one-man, battery-powered sub from used scrap. The body is made out of five oil drums, the sonar is improvised from a stethoscope, and the periscope is an old camera. He tested the vessel by taking it down to the bottom of a local river and staying on the riverbed for nearly five minutes.

Gatorbike

Jim Jablon from Florida has made a wild custom motorbike from a real-life alligator. Each year a number of wild alligators in the state are culled to control the population, and Jim decided to put one to good use. The reptilian chopper, named the GatorBike, took over a year to build, and features the full skull and skin of an alligator. Worth $80,000, the bike was created to raise funds for Jablon's wildlife rehabilitation park, which has its own rescued alligators alongside other animals, such as Arctic, the large albino Burmese python pictured around Jim's neck.

Built to Last

School caretaker Owen Hook of Cambridgeshire, England, has ridden the same bicycle for nearly 60 years. He bought the top-of-the-line three-speed Raleigh cycle in 1953 and still rides it half a mile (0.8 km) to and from work every day.

Sound Asleep

A French teenager who fell asleep between rail tracks escaped injury when a high-speed train passed right over him. The driver of the TGV train between Paris and Quimper noticed the 19-year-old lying stretched out on his stomach between the rails, but the train was traveling so fast that it continued for another 900 yd (820 m) before it was brought to a halt, passing right over the man who remained sound asleep throughout.

Maiden Flight

After six years of design and construction, a Chinese cobbler, who left school with only a basic education, completed a maiden flight in his homemade airplane. Huang Jianjun of Hunan Province spent more than $15,000 on the project—and in June 2010 his plane soared to a height of over 1,640 ft (500 m) before safely landing.

Emergency Landing

Pilot Matt Conway was forced to make an emergency landing on a busy Atlanta, Georgia, highway after his plane experienced engine problems. He touched down on Interstate 85, a few miles from Peachtree DeKalb Airport, and skidded to a halt without hitting any cars. However, the plane did block four lanes, causing a long traffic jam until it was hauled away a few hours later.

Modern Sailing

To cut fuel costs by 20 percent and reduce greenhouse emissions, the 10,000-ton German cargo ship MV *Beluga Skysails* is partially powered by a huge kite. In a throwback to old sailing ships, the 433-ft-long (132-m) vessel is pulled by a computer-guided 1,720-sq-ft (160-sq-m) kite, which is tethered to a 49-ft-high (15-m) mast.

Viking Land Boat

Matt Norris of Austin, Texas, spent two years building a 45-ft-long (14-m) human-powered road vehicle in the style of a Viking longboat. Made of steel and corrugated plastic, it glides on trailer tires, has the axle of a golf cart, and is propelled by its crew of 13 people who "row" a system of pulleys and cables.

Banana Ketchup

Made from mashed banana, sugar, vinegar and spices, banana ketchup is a popular Filipino condiment that is often colored red to resemble tomato ketchup. It was first produced during World War II when there was a shortage of tomato ketchup but an abundance of bananas.

Long-life Burger

Wellness consultant Karen Hanrahan of Chicago, Illinois, has kept a burger for more than 14 years—without doing anything to preserve it—and it still looks as fresh as the day she bought it!

Bottle Track

Li Guiwen, a military driver from Beijing, China, gently steered a car along a track made up of two rows of upright bottles for more than 195 ft (60 m). His journey along the 1,798 bottles of beer took 8 minutes 28 seconds.

Taos Hum

For years, people in and around the town of Taos, New Mexico, have been able to hear a curious low-frequency noise known as the Taos Hum. Not audible to everyone, it has been described as sounding like a distant diesel engine, but its source has never been traced.

Inflatable Weapons

Russian balloon manufacturer Rusbal has created a range of full-size inflatable weapons—including fighter planes and tanks (see above)—that look realistic to the enemy from as near as 330 ft (100 m). The country's defense department commissioned the models as decoys in order to protect real combat units from strikes.

Such inflatables are not a new invention. During World War II, the British army used blow-up rubber tanks as decoys. Designed to look just like a U.S. Sherman tank—and easily carried by four men—they were deployed before the Normandy Landings in 1944 in an attempt to deceive the German Army.

Fake Porsche

Austrian artist Hannes Langeder spent six months building a life-size Porsche sports car from plastic pipes, tape, and cardboard. The aluminum-foil-covered Ferdinand GT3-RS has no engine, but is powered by a hidden bicycle, which is why it has handlebars instead of a steering wheel.

Waterfall Diver

A former chauffeur, Di Huanran now makes his living by diving from waterfalls at Jingpo Lake, Heilongjiang Province, China. It was there, in 1983, that he first plunged nearly 75 ft (23 m) down the Diaoshuilou Waterfall into the fast-flowing waters below, and he has since made thousands of dives.

Bridge of Bottles

Jack Waterfall who comes from Cambridgeshire, England, designed a 118-ft-long (36-m) bridge made from 14,100 plastic milk bottles. The bridge represented the amount of plastic that people in Cambridgeshire use each day by lunchtime.

Holy Boy

An 11-year-old boy decided not to go back to school in Boston, Massachusetts, in 2009 after he was declared the reincarnation of a Buddhist holy man who first died in 1250. Instead, Jigme Wangchuk has moved to Darjeeling, India, where as the head of a Buddhist sect he will spend ten years in virtual seclusion. His parents say they realized he was not like other children when he went into trances and talked about his "past life," giving vivid descriptions of a temple he had never visited.

Base Jump

Two days after the official opening of the 2,720-ft-high (828-m) Burj Kalifa tower in Dubai, BASE jumpers Al Neyadi and Omar Alhegelan, who have made more than 17,000 skydives between them, plunged 2,204 ft (672 m) from the structure. After free falling for 10 seconds, they unfurled parachutes to sail another 30 seconds to the ground.

Cone Fall

Shortly after takeoff, a 20-lb (9-kg) engine tailcone, measuring 4 ft (1.2 m) long and 3 ft (90 cm) in diameter, plummeted thousands of feet from a Delta Air Lines jet and landed on the lawn of a home in Roosevelt, New York. None of the crew noticed that the part had fallen off, and the plane—a Boeing 777—was able to complete its journey from Kennedy Airport to Tokyo, Japan.

Lion Burger

To mark the 2010 soccer World Cup in South Africa, a restaurant in Mesa, Arizona, added lion burgers to its menu. Cameron Selogie's Il Vinaio restaurant offered the burger (from farm-raised lion) at $21, served with spicy homemade fries and roast corn on the cob.

Ring Recovery

A man who promised his wife of three months that he would find his wedding ring after it fell into Wellington Harbour, New Zealand, in 2008 finally recovered it 16 months later. Ecologist Aleki Taumoepeau was checking the harbor for invasive plant species when the ring fell into 10 ft (3 m) of water. He threw an anchor overboard to mark the spot and although initial searches failed, his persistence eventually paid off.

Pier Pressure

Over a period of two years, Hazel Costin and Jay Preller of Somerset, England, kissed at the end of all 55 British piers before getting married on Brighton Pier. They had originally met on the Grand Pier at Weston-super-Mare.

Steel Suit

During World War I, the U.S.A. developed the Brewster Body Shield, a suit of armor designed to protect soldiers from bullets. It consisted of a breastplate and headpiece and was made from steel plates to repel machine gun fire at 2,700 ft per second (820 m per second). It weighed a heavy 40 lb (18 kg).

School Flight

When a ferry service was stopped in late 2009, the school children of Papa Westray in Scotland's Orkney Islands were forced to take a 96-second air flight to school each day.

Mini Motorbike

Santosh Kumar of Mysore, India, built an electric motorcycle less than 18 in (45 cm) long and less than 1 ft (30 cm) tall, but capable of carrying a person.

Long Leak

The World-War-II ruin of the battleship U.S.S. *Arizona* is still leaking oil into the ocean nearly 70 years after it was sunk in Pearl Harbor, Hawaii.

Monster Limo

The Midnight Rider, a giant tractor-trailer limo, is 70 ft (21 m) long, 13 ft 8 in (4.2 m) high, has 22 wheels, weighs about 50,560 lb (22,930 kg) and has room for 40 passengers. Owned by Pamela Bartholomew Machado from California, the monster vehicle, which costs $1,000 an hour to hire, boasts three lounges, a bar and a bathroom. A full tank of gas costs about $700 and a full oil change costs around $1,000.

Treasure Hoax

When Patty Henken bought an old rocking chair at an auction in 2008, she found in the stuffing a typewritten note describing a lead chestcontaining $250 in U.S. gold coins that was supposedly buried 15 ft (4.5 m) underground in a vacant lot in Springfield, Illinois. She dug unsuccessfully for the treasure, only to discover later that the note's signatory, "Chauncey Wolcott," was the pen name of a prolific prankster, John "Jay" Slaven, who died in 1976.

Horse-drawn Hummer

Jeremy Dean of New York City spent $15,000 on his Hummer H2 sport utility vehicle, and then turned it into a horse-drawn carriage.

Warthog Alert

In November 2009, an Air Zimbabwe plane made an emergency stop after hitting a warthog on the runway in Harare, Zimbabwe.

Wheelie Wizard

Tyler Shepard, the "Wheelie Wizard" of Middletown, Ohio, rides near-vertical wheelies on a Honda XR 50 motorbike without a front wheel. His wheelie shows include such incredible feats as riding his one-wheeled bike in a wheelie while blindfolded, and maintaining a wheelie for 1 hour 30 minutes nonstop during a parade.

Bottle Boat

Four months after leaving San Francisco, California, the Plastiki, a 60-ft (18-m) catamaran built from 12,500 recycled plastic bottles, reached Sydney, Australia, in July 2010 at the end of a 9,550-mi (15,370-km) voyage across the Pacific Ocean. The boat's bottles were lashed to pontoons and held together with glue made from cashew nut husks and sugar cane. Even the sails were made from recycled plastic.

Lucky Escape

A driving lesson on Good Luck Road, Lanham, Maryland, ended with a large family car crashing through the wall of a ground-floor apartment and finishing up on a bed where the homeowner had been lying just minutes earlier.

Last Orders

Matthias Krankl of Maulburg, Germany, was banned from driving by police after converting a beer crate into a motorized mini quad bike.

Versatile Vehicle

Dave March of the Californian company WaterCar has created the Python, a $220,000 amphibious supercar that can reach speeds of 125 mph (200 km/h) on land and 60 mph (96 km/h)—faster than many speedboats—on water. All the driver has to do before entering the water is put the gears into neutral, engage the jet drive, then push a button to raise the wheels.

Zipper Boat

Japanese artist Yasuhiro Suzuki has designed a boat that looks like a zipper—and the wake it leaves behind it in the water makes it look like it's unzipping the ocean as it goes along.

Kicking the Bucket

Gaetano Di Furia's coffin was carried to his funeral in Lincolnshire, England, in the bucket of a JCB digger. His family chose it instead of a traditional hearse because he had always enjoyed driving JCBs at work.

Floating Palace

At 1,187 ft (362 m) long, the Finnish-built liner *Oasis of the Seas* is four times the length of a football field and, at 236 ft (72 m) high, it is taller than Nelson's Column in London. Over 3,300 mi (5,310 km) of electrical cabling and 150 mi (240 km) of pipework run through the ship, which took 8,000 man years to build (three years in actual time). Around 160,000 gal (600,000 l) of paint were used to decorate the luxury vessel, which boasts every conceivable facility, including basketball courts, ice rinks, a hospital, a landscaped park, and a wedding chapel. Some 55 tons of ice are produced onboard every day to supply the ship's 37 bars and 20 cafés and restaurants, and no fewer than 50,000 pieces of cutlery are housed in the main dining room.

Backward Driver

Indian taxi driver Harpreet Dev drives everywhere in reverse. His backward driving skills have become so famous in his hometown of Bhatinda that he has even been given a special government license allowing him to drive in reverse anywhere in the state of Punjab. His enthusiasm for driving backward at speeds of up to 50 mph (80 km/h) began one night in 2003 as he was returning home from a party. He discovered that, owing to a mechanical fault, only the reverse gear of his Fiat Padmini worked. He has since redesigned the car's gearbox so that it has four reverse gears and just one forward one.

Super Model

Tony Nijhuis of East Sussex, England, has built a balsa wood and plywood model airplane that weighs more than 100 lb (45 kg) and, with a 20-ft (6-m) wingspan, is as wide as a house. The model is so large it is classed as a light aircraft and has to be licensed by the Civil Aviation Authority. He spent two years and £8,000 ($12,900) constructing the 1:7 scale version of a 1950s U.S. Air Force Boeing B-50 Superfortress bomber, which has four electric motors, 96 batteries, and can reach a speed of 40 mph (64 km/h).

Extreme Devotion

These religious devotees are masters of mind over matter, performing totally unbelievable feats that require intense physical and mental discipline and endurance.

Sadhus, sometimes known as fakirs by people in the West, are predominantly Hindu mystics from India. Following an ancient practice of spiritual devotion, sadhus remove themselves from normal life and dedicate themselves to extreme physical feats, often for their entire lifetime. They often claim to be able to control pain using the power of thought, and some have demonstrated this by walking on razor-sharp blades, or piercing their flesh with metal pins. Some go for years without sitting down—or standing up.

HAND HELD HIGH

Many Hindu sadhus make a pilgrimage every four years to the Kumbh Mela festival at the Ganges River, India. This man claimed to have held one of his arms aloft, and not cut his nails, for more than 20 years.

HEAD IN THE SAND

Some Hindu sadhus—such as this gentleman photographed in the 1970s—will bury their head in the ground for extended periods of time.

ON ALL FOURS

In 1936, Robert Ripley encountered a bizarre religious ascetic at the holy site of Bodh Gaya, India. He had assumed the shape of a monkey and taken to walking on all fours at all times.

FEET OF ENDURANCE

In India, in 1923, as part of his religious devotion, this sadhu had contorted his body for so long that his leg was permanently twisted behind his back leaving his foot forever resting on his shoulder.

NAP ON NAILS

In 1907, English photographer Herbert Ponting took this picture of a sadhu in Varanasi, India. He appears to be resting quite comfortably on a bed of nails.

Ash Man

Artist Daniel Roberto Ortega from San Diego, California, turns the ashes of dead people and pets into cherished works of art. His first human cremation piece included the ashes of his late father. Bereaved relatives or pet owners send the former mortician's assistant ashes and bone fragments, together with a photograph and biography. He mixes the cremated remains into a paste, adds artifacts representing aspects of the subject's life, and then paints the resulting pattern. He dries it, then applies an acrylic finish.

Same Name

Even though he had no connection with the town, Eric Gordon Douglas, of Edinburgh, Scotland, left more than $17,000 in his will to Douglas, Isle of Man, simply because it shared his surname.

Family Church

When Daryl McClure married Dean Sutcliffe at St. Michael's and All Angels' Church in Ashton-under-Lyne, Greater Manchester, England, she became the seventh generation of her family to marry at that church. At least 11 members of her family have been married there since 1825, but the connection could date back as far as the 17th century.

Long Dead

Tokyo officials trying to update their list of centenarians in preparation for Japan's Respect for the Elderly Day in September 2010 discovered that the city's "oldest man" had actually died more than 30 years earlier. Police said Sogen Kato, who was born in July 1899 and would therefore have been 111, was in fact discovered lying in his bed in a mummified state, wearing pajamas and covered with a blanket.

You Can't Hurry Love

A couple with a combined age of 184 married in England in July 2010. After a four-year courtship, Henry Kerr, 97, tied the knot with Valerie Berkowitz, 87, in North London.

Body Snatchers

An illegally parked funeral van—with a corpse inside—was once towed away by the New York Police Department. Funeral director Paul DeNigris had parked his 2002 Dodge minivan outside the funeral home while he went inside on business, but he returned to find the vehicle—and the body in the back—had been towed to the city pound. He had to rush there to reclaim the corpse and put it on a flight to Miami, where it was headed for cremation.

Faint Pulse

Pronounced dead three hours after suffering a suspected heart attack, Jozef Guzy of Katowice, Poland, was about to be sealed up in a coffin when a funeral director detected a faint pulse. Mr Guzy, 76, was taken to hospital where mystified doctors could find nothing wrong with him, and a few days later he was allowed to go home.

Video Girlfriend

In 2009, a man in Tokyo, Japan, married his animated video-game girlfriend—who exists only in a Nintendo DS game—in a public ceremony complete with a priest, a D.J., and speeches made by friends and family.

Macabre Marriage

To mark the end of his bachelor days bridegroom Pat Vincent arrived for his wedding in London, England, in a coffin. After marrying Jacqueline Brick, he climbed back into the wooden box and was carried on a train to the wedding reception.

Age Gap

A couple who married in Guriceel, Somalia, in 2009 had an age difference of 95 years. Ahmed Muhamed Dore, who claimed to be 112, wed Safia Abdulleh, 17, making him old enough to be her great-great-great grandfather.

Grass Diet

Fifty-year-old Li Sanju of Guangdong Province, China, spent more than two years eating only leaves and grass. He said he enjoyed his unusual diet but admitted that he did smell strongly of grass.

Humongous Hummus

Chefs in Beirut, Lebanon, prepared a massive plate of hummus weighing more than 2 tons. They used 2,976 lb (1,350 kg) of mashed chickpeas, 106 gal (400 l) of lemon juice and 57 lb (26 kg) of salt to make the dish that weighed 4,532 lb (2,056 kg).

Deep-fried Beer

Texas chef Mark Zable has created a recipe for deep-fried beer. The beer is placed inside a pocket of salty, pretzel-like dough and dunked in oil heated to 375°F (190°C) for about 20 seconds. When customers take a bite, the hot beer mixes with the dough to give an alcoholic taste.

Hot Chocolate

In 2009, scientists at Warwick University, England, unveiled an environmentally friendly racing car, built partly from vegetables and powered by chocolate. The bodywork of the WorldFirst car was made from plastic bottles and scraps from airplanes, the seat from flax and soy, and the steering wheel from the waste of juiced carrots. The car, which reached speeds of 135 mph (217 km/h), used plant-oil based lubricants and could run on biodiesel made from chocolate-factory waste and stale wine.

Zebra Pizza

A pizza takeout store in Burnley, England, sells pizzas topped with the meat of zebras, crocodiles, kangaroos and buffalo, alongside more familiar flavors. Owner Arash Fard sells around 20 of his exotic pizzas every week.

Burger Candle

Columbus, Ohio-based fast-food chain White Castle offered customers a new way to sniff its produce by introducing candles that smell like its oniony Slider hamburgers.

Mega Meatball

In 2009, Nonni's Italian Eatery in New Hampshire created a meatball that weighed a colossal 222 lb 8 oz (101 kg). The giant ball of minced meat took three days to cook.

Rich Dish

A 513-lb (233-kg) tuna sold for $177,000 at an auction in January 2010 in Tokyo's Tsukiji fish market. That works out to $345 a pound.

Exotic Tea

Made from older leaves, Puer tea is renowned in China for its exotic taste and healing properties, and is so coveted that just one third of an ounce (10 g) of century-old tea can sell for $10,000.

Still Bubbly

Divers exploring the wreck of a sailing vessel 180 ft (55 m) below the surface of the Baltic Sea off the coast of Finland found 30 bottles of Champagne some 230 years old. As the bottles had been preserved in the ideal conditions of cold and darkness for so many years, experts said the Champagne tasted remarkably good despite having lost some of its fizz.

Wrap Artists

In Lewisburg, Pennsylvania, cooks used 15 lb (6.8 kg) of bacon and 175 wraps held together with about 1,200 toothpicks to create a sandwich wrap 102 ft long (31 m).

Tasty Spider

To raise funds for his school in Kent, England, headteacher Aydin Onac ate a baked Cambodian tarantula spider in front of a packed assembly. He said it tasted like burned chicken.

Jellyfish Candy

In response to an invasion of 6-ft-wide (1.8-m), 440-lb (200-kg) jellyfish, students at Obama Fisheries High School, Japan, harvested the creatures and then turned them into caramel candies.

Dig In

Some people eat the strangest things—wood, glass, metal, clothing, stones, hair, and even excrement. The Glore Psychiatric Museum in St. Joseph, Missouri, has a display of 1,446 unusual items swallowed by a patient and removed from her intestines and stomach—including 453 nails, 42 screws, and assorted safety pins, spoons, and salt-and-pepper shaker tops. She died during surgery from bleeding caused by her weird diet.

DIET OF BUGS

Mr. Zhu from Sichuan Province, China, has eaten live centipedes since he was a child. In just one month, he and his friends consumed more than 3,000 bugs and worms.

SHE'S CRACKED IT

Zhou Yuqin from Chongqing, China, says she has cured all her ailments by eating up to 50 eggshells every day for 13 years. She has even persuaded her children to copy her. When eggshells aren't enough to satisfy her appetite for the unusual, she also nibbles on sand and cullet (broken glass).

DIRT DISH

Fan Qianrong from China's Hebei Province has stayed healthy by eating soil and mud for more than 40 years. Millions of people around the world consume soil, a practice known as geophagy.

Wooden Bicycles

Max Samuelson of Cape May, New Jersey, builds functional bicycles out of wood, using as many as 120 pieces of wood in a single bike.

Motorized Unicycle

In 2009, Japanese auto manufacturer Honda unveiled a motorized unicycle designed mainly for the country's aging population. It has a series of smaller, motor-controlled wheels inside the main wheel, so that to steer the 22-lb (10-kg) battery-powered device on a busy sidewalk all you have to do is lean in the direction you want to go.

Welcome Tip

Taxi driver Don Pratt from Cornwall, England, retired from work after a grateful passenger left him a $375,000 tip in her will. Don had spent 20 years ferrying pensioner Mary Watson to and from her local stores.

Extended Journey

Given permission to drive the family pickup truck to the end of the driveway to unload trash at their home in Damascus, Oregon, a 12-year-old boy kept going for nearly 100 mi (160 km) until police eventually stopped him.

Electric Bullet

In August 2010, the Buckeye Bullet 2.5, an electric car designed by a team of students from Ohio State University, clocked an average speed of 307.7 mph (495.2 km/h) on Utah's Bonneville Salt Flats. The Bullet is powered by nearly 1,600 compact lithium-ion batteries, the kind that are used to power laptops.

Sole Owner

In 2012, 93-year-old Rachel Veitch of Orlando, Florida, finally parted with the Mercury Comet Caliente that she had bought new in 1964 and has since driven nearly 600,000 mi (965,500 km).

When is a Stratoliner airplane not an airplane?

Parking Space

An uncovered, outdoor parking space in Boston, Massachusetts, was sold for $300,000 in June 2009.

Close Encounter

A motorist in London, England, tried to avoid a fine for driving in a bus lane by claiming aliens had forced him into it.

Out to Launch

Having spent nearly 30 years building a boat in his mother's back garden in Hampshire, England, Owen Warboys finally launched the 40-ft-long (12-m) sloop in 2010. He got the 20-ton vessel out of the garden by hiring a crane that lifted it 40 ft (12 m) into the air over the house and onto a truck.

Plane Sailing

Is it a boat? Is it a plane? Actually, it's a bit of both—a plane-boat. Visitors to Fort Lauderdale, Florida, can charter Dave Drimmer's *Cosmic Muffin*, a boat recycled from movie-producer Howard Hughes' old Boeing B-307 airplane. The historic Stratoliner plane was rescued from landfill in 1969 by pilot Ken London, who bought it for $69 and spent four years removing the wings and converting it into a luxury boat. The cockpit of the original plane still houses the controls that steer the craft.

...with steering controls in the cockpit.

Five decades later, when it's a boat...

PLANEBOATS.COM

Jumbomania

Jumbo was an African elephant of monumental proportions, and he enjoyed fame on both sides of the Atlantic every bit as huge as his stature.

Jumbomania, as it was called, began in 1861 when the elephant was captured in the French Sudan and then exported to the Jardins des Plantes Zoo in Paris, France. He then moved on to London Zoo, where he became famous for giving rides to visitors. Placed under such unnatural restraints, Jumbo's patience wore thin. The elephant, whose name was based on *jumbe*, the Swahili word for "chief," became too hot to handle and he was sold to "The Greatest Show on Earth"—the Barnum & Bailey Circus based in the U.S.A. The whole British nation rose up to protest. Crowds converged on the zoo, legal proceedings against the decision began, and Queen Victoria, herself a huge fan, received 100,000 letters appealing for her to intervene. American P.T. Barnum was offered £100,000 ($160,000) in exchange for the precious elephant, but in a moment of huge showbiz drama, he refused the offer. Jumbo was to be shipped out of London for good.

WHAT HAPPENED TO JUMBO?

After Jumbo's death, the New York Times reported that taxidermists had removed the elephant's hide—which weighed 1,600 lb (726 kg) and needed 100 tons of salt and 100 lb (45 kg) of elm bark to cure it—and bones. His skeleton was given to New York's Museum of Natural History, and his heart was bought by Cornell University. The rest of his body was cremated. His stuffed hide traveled with the circus until Barnum donated it to Tufts University, near Boston (left), where Jumbo became the official mascot. He was displayed there until destroyed by a fire in 1975.

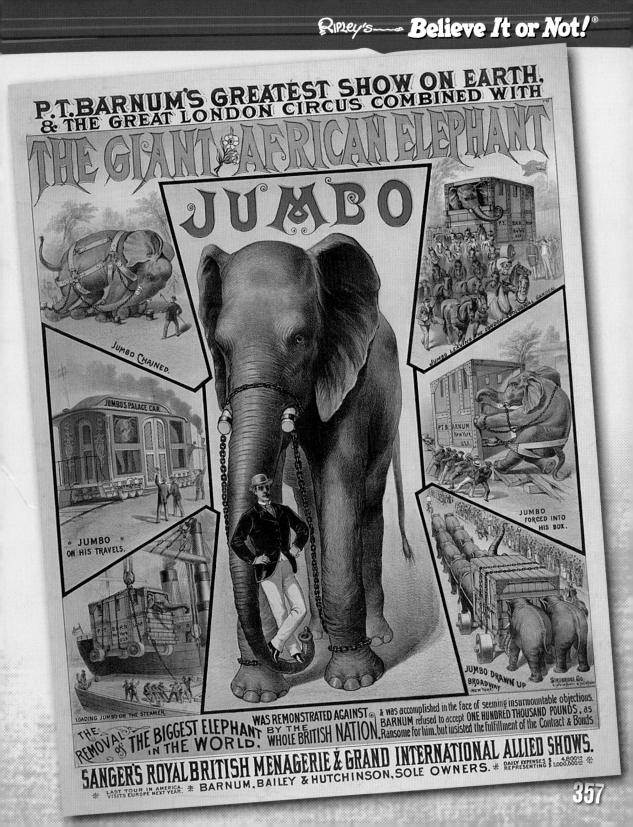

Sweet Skulls

Marina Malvada, an artist from Montreal, Canada, uses genuine human skulls—borrowed from a tribal art collector who specializes in collecting cannibal skulls—to cast life-sized skulls in chocolate. Each head is solid chocolate, takes four days to complete and is entirely edible—although at a weight of 5½ lb (2.5 kg) each, one is enough.

Barter System

In 2010, a bar owner on Estonia's Hiiumaa Island in the Baltic Sea revived the age-old barter system to allow customers to pay for drinks with goods. Tarvo Nomm agreed to sell beer in return for bundles of firewood and catches of fish to help the locals beat economic hardship.

Banana Boxers

Australian company AussieBum has unveiled a range of men's underwear made from bananas. The eco-friendly range incorporates 27 percent banana fiber, making the garments lightweight and absorbent without actually smelling of bananas.

Half-mile Pizza

In August 2010, chefs in Krakow, Poland, used 3.5 tons of flour to make a pizza measuring 3,280 ft (1,000 m) in length—that's more than half a mile (0.8 km) long!

Chocolate Shoes

Confectioner Frances Cooley from Bristol, England, sells shoes and handbags made of chocolate. She has developed a line of individual, high-heeled shoes—including zebra-striped and polka-dot versions—which she makes by hand in her own kitchen. The largest shoe is 6¾ in (17 cm) long and made from two 3½-oz (100-g) bars of Belgian chocolate.

Scott's Butter

Two blocks of New Zealand butter nearly a century old were found intact in 2009 in an Antarctic hut used by British explorer Robert Falcon Scott on his doomed 1910–12 expedition.

Nacho Tray

At Northstar Church, Frisco, Texas, more than 300 volunteers built a 3,555-lb (1,613-kg), 48-ft-long (14.6-m) tray of nachos, loaded with 2,200 lb (998 kg) of tortilla chips, 600 lb (272 kg) of nacho cheese and 250 lb (113 kg) of sour cream, as well as an extra 250 lb (113 kg) of jalapenos, 200 lb (90 kg) of shredded Cheddar cheese and 200 lb (90 kg) of sauce.

Dogs' Dinner

An ice-cream van exclusively for dogs attended a 2010 pet festival in London, England. Created by a team of scientists, the canine-friendly, K99 ice cream comes in two flavors— Dog Eat Hog World, a gammon and chicken sorbet topped with a biscuit bone and served in a cone, and Canine Cookie Crunch, dog biscuits and ice cream topped with a biscuit bone.

Soluble Gum

Scientists at Bristol University, England, have devised a nonstick chewing gum. Rev7 has the same taste and texture as normal gum, but it disintegrates over time and can be removed from shoes, hair, and other surfaces with just soap and water.

Tea Nation

Britons drink 165 million cups of tea every day—around three cups a day per person. Although Great Britain accounts for less than 1 percent of the world's population, it is responsible for about 4 percent of its tea consumption.

Testicle Cooking

At the 2010 Testicle Cooking World Championship in Ozrem, Serbia, chefs produced dishes made from the testicles of animals including bulls, wild boar, horses, sharks, ostriches, kangaroos, donkeys, turkeys, goats, reindeer and elk.

$1,000 Burger

Joe El-Ajouz's restaurant in Sydney, Australia, has a burger on the menu that costs $1,000. It weighs 210 lb (95 kg), requires 178 lb (81 kg) of minced meat, 120 eggs, 120 cheese slices, 4½ lb (2 kg) of lettuce, 16 tomatoes, 46 lb (21 kg) of bread, and 1.1 lb (500 g) of barbecue sauce. It takes over 12 hours to cook and serves more than 100 people.

Double Banana

Having bought a bunch of bananas at a grocery store in Somerset, England, Cedric Hooper got home and found that one skin in fact contained two bananas!

Fast Grub

Eating insects is so popular in Thailand that the country even has its own insect fast-food chain. Insects Inter has more than 30 outlets selling fried, crunchy grasshoppers, crickets, grubs and silkworms in 70-cent pots with ketchup or hot chili dips.

Pub Crawl

Since 1984, Stuart Ashby of West Sussex, England, has drunk more than 8,500 pints of beer in over 17,000 British pubs, from Cornwall to the Shetland Islands, in the process traveling some 25,000 mi (40,000 km).

Long Lunch

In September 2010, chefs in Italy served lunch on a table that was more than a mile (1.6 km) long. The 5,775-ft-long (1,760-m) spread was laid out for 2,700 diners and stretched from Bosco to nearby Borzano. The organizers' biggest problem was that the table required a 5,905-ft long (1,800-m) tablecloth.

Wee Dram

London-based designer James Gilpin has created whisky made from the high-sugar urine of elderly diabetic patients, including his own grandmother. Gilpin, who is himself diabetic, filters the urine by the same processes used to purify water, and in doing so removes the sugars, which are then used in fermentation. The drink, named Gilpin Family Whisky, is not for sale.

Safe Breakfast

Scientists in the U.K. have developed a breakfast that won't make you sick if you go on a roller coaster shortly afterward. It consists of yogurt mixed with blueberries and grilled bacon in a wholemeal bun with tomato. It is served with a drink of celery and carrot juice with ginger. U.K. theme park Alton Towers was so confident in the product that it offered to refund anyone who was sick on a ride after eating the breakfast.

Beers and Spirits

For more than nine months in 2009, a ghost apparently kept topping up drinkers' glasses at the Apsley House pub in Southsea, Hampshire, England. Landlady Janice McCormack complained that the specter was costing her a fortune because it was giving away her beer.

Vegetable Phobia

Vicki Larrieux of Portsmouth, England, suffers from lachanophobia, a fear of vegetables. The only vegetables she can bear to eat, touch or see are potatoes. The sight of a carrot or a pea, not just on her plate but even on grocery-store shelves, leaves her sweating and stricken with panic attacks.

Giant Cupcake

Chefs in Boca Raton, Florida, unveiled a 1,500-lb (680-kg) chocolate cupcake. It stood 4½ ft (1.4 m) high, 6 ft (1.8 m) wide, and was topped with pink frosting, handmade 5-in (12.5-cm) sprinkles, and a cherry with a circumference of 12 in (30 cm). It was baked in an oven measuring 10 x 10 ft (3 x 3 m).

Golden Curry

Restaurateurs Padma Prasad and Bhagat Saxena of Hyderabad, India, added finely ground flakes of gold and silver to create a chicken curry that costs $300 a serving.

Molto Macaroni

Chef John Folse cooked 2,469 lb (1,120 kg) of macaroni and cheese—enough for 6,500 servings—in New Orleans, Louisiana, in September 2010.

Full O Bull

The Cowtown Diner in Fort Worth, Texas, serves a chicken fried steak that weighs about 10 lb (4.5 kg) and packs a fattening 10,000 calories. The "Full O Bull," which comes complete with 6 lb (2.7 kg) of mashed potatoes and 10 slices of toast, normally costs $70—but if you can eat it solo, it's free!

Squirrel Ale

In 2010, a Scottish brewery packaged bottles of its new beer, "The End of History," inside the bodies of dead animals. BrewDog sold bottles of its strong, limited-edition Belgian ale— made with juniper berries and containing a staggering 55 percent alcohol—for $1,000 if housed inside a dead squirrel and $750 for bottles encased in a dead stoat. The limited edition 12 dead-animal bottles were hand-crafted by a Yorkshire taxidermist using only creatures that had died of natural causes.

INDEX

INDEX

ACKNOWLEDGMENTS

12 Chin Boon Leng; **14–15** Alex Smith - www.as-images.com; **16** Getty Images; **18** Richard Jones/Sinopix/Rex Features; **19** Debbie Does Cakes/Rex Features; **20** Honda Motor Europe Ltd; **22** Californiaskateparks.com; **23** Kevin Le; **24** (t/r) National Geographic/Getty Images, (t/l) SSPL via Getty Images, (t/r) Stephen L. Alvarez/National Geographic/Getty Images; **25** (b) Jae C. Hong/AP/Press Association Images, (b/r) Robyn Beck/AFP/Getty Images; **27** Barcroft Media; **28** Jayna Sullivan Photography; **30** Charles Eisenmann Collection/University of Syracuse; **31** Getty Images; **32** Reuters/Reinhard Krause; **33** Collect/PA Wire/Press Association Images; **34–35** Paul Christoforou; **37** Chris Trueman/Alexander Salazar Gallery; **38** APOPO; **39** © EuroPics[CEN]; **40–41** Theo Stroomer / Demotix; **42** Wenn.com; **43** The Cheeky/Rex Features; **44** Getty Images; **45** Charles Eisenmann Collection/University of Syracuse; **47** Jagdeep Rajput/Solent; **48** Reuters/Will Burgess; **49** Chin Boon Leng; **50** KeystoneUSA-ZUMA/Rex Features; **51** © EuroPics[CEN]; **52** (t) AP Photo, The Canadian Press, Lethbridge Herald, Ian Martens, (b/l, b/r) Gabriel Luque/Rex Features; **53** (t/l) AP Photo, The Canadian Press, Lethbridge Herald, Ian Martens, (t/r) Polaris/eyevine, (b/l) Rob Yuill/Albanpix Ltd/Rex Features, (b/r) Rob Yuill/Albanpix Ltd/Rex Features; **54** Eddie Mitchell/Rex Features; **55** INS News Agency Ltd./Rex Features; **56** Photo by Havel Ruck Projects, "Inversion". 2005, (demolished), Dan Havel & Dean Ruck, Site-specific sculptural installation, Art League Houston, Houston, Texas; **58** (b) J.D. Griggs/US Geological Survey/Rex Features, (t) David Jordan AP/Press Association Images; **59** (c/l) Ethel Davies/Robert Harding/Rex Features, (b/l, b/r) EPA/Photoshot; **60** (b/r) John Terning, (b/l) Carl McCabe; **63** Jay Fine/Caters News; **64** Photo by Havel Ruck Projects, "Inversion". 2005, (demolished), Dan Havel & Dean Ruck, Site-specific sculptural installation, Art League Houston, Houston, Texas; **65** Imagine China; **66–67** Massimo Brega, The Lighthouse/Science Photo Library; **67** Apex; **69** © Hulton-Deutsch Collection/Corbis; **71** LatinContent/Getty Images; **72** © Swim Ink 2, LLC/Corbis; **73** (l) © Rykoff Collection/Corbis, (r) © Blue Lantern Studio/Corbis; **77–79** Library of Congress; **80** EPA/Photoshot; **81** Solent News/Rex Features; **83** www.Freitag.ch; **84** Tsuzuki Minako; **85** Reuters; **86** Dmitry Dudin; **88–89** Will Hunt; **90** (l) Mark Duncan/AP/Press Association Images, (r) U.S. Coast Guard photo by Petty Officer 2nd Class Lauren Jorgensen; **91** Barcroft Media via Getty Images; **92** Malcolm Teasdale/KiwiRail; **93** (t) Barcroft Media via Getty Images, (c) © Vladone/istockphoto.com; **94–95** ChinaFotoPress via Getty Images; **96** Bloomberg via Getty Images; **98** Alain Van de Maele; **99** Rex/Wendy Connett/Robert Harding; **100** Diane Smith/www.noahs-ark.org; **102–103** Ingo Arndt/Nature Picture Library; **104** Mark Moffett/Minden Pictures/FLPA; **105** © Ch'ien C. Lee; **106** Tibo Szabo, Sue Lees, Photographer Michael Orescanin; **107** Richard Young; **108** Caters News; **110** Caters News; **111** Conny Sandland/Rex Features; **112** R. Roscoe (photovolcanica.com); **113** Luke Marsden/Newspix/Rex Features; **114–115** James Dagmore / Polaris / eyevine; **116** Caters News; **117** Nicole Kane; **118** Wenn; **120** Armin Weigel/DPA/Press Association Images; **121** Rossparry.co.uk/syndication/Doncaster Free Press; **122** Reuters/Michael Caronna; **123** © Europics; **126** M & Y Agency Ltd/Rex Features; **127** Jonathan Pow/Ross Parry Agency; **128** Diane Smith/www.noahs-ark.org; **129** © Stuart Isett / Anzenberger represented by: eyevine; **130** DR Richard Kirby/BNPS; **131** Image courtesy of Expedition to the Deep Slope 2006 Exploration, NOAA Vents Program; **132** Quirky China News/Rex Features; **135** (c) Luis Fernando Espin/Rex Features, (t) Karen Bacon/Solent News/Rex Features, (b) Michael Cenci/Solent News/Rex Features; **137** Quirky China News/Rex Features; **138** www.sell-my-photo.co.uk; **139** © Johann Opperman/solentnews.co.uk; **140** www.toadfactory.com; **141** Reuters/Wolfgang Rattay; **143** Tomas Rak/Solent News/Rex Features; **144** www.tesladownunder.com; **146–147** Akash Awasthi; **149** Akinunde Akinleye/Reuters/Corbis; **150** AP Photo/Luis Benavides; **151** Swell.com; **152** Jeffrey Cunningham; **154** Iain Ferguson, The Write Image; **155** © Wifredo Garcia Alvaro/epa/Corbis; **156** Dan Callister/Rex Features; **157** Quirky China News/Rex Features; **158** © -M-I-S-H-A-/iStockphoto.com; **162** Christian Pondella/Caters News; **164** Getty Images; **166–167** EPA/Photoshot; **169** Nick Obank/Barcroft Media LT; **170–171** Edmond Hawkins; **172** Harry Scull Jr./AP/Press Association Images; **173** Eric Lafargue /www.LPS.ch; **174–175** (t) Stephen Pond/Empics Sport; **174** Ryan Remiorz/AP/Press Association Images; **175** Ron Jenkins/Fort Worth Star-Telegram/Polaris; **176** Rex/Imagine China; **178** Nagananda Swamy; **179** www.tesladownunder.com; **180** Henrik May/ski-namibia.com; **181** AFP/Getty Images; **182–183** anthonyescapes.com; **184** The Shields Gazette; **187** ChinaFotoPress via Getty Images; **191** (t/c) NY Daily News via Getty Images, (t/r) Getty Images; **192** Xinhua/Photoshot; **193** Charles Eisenmann Collection/University of Syracuse; **194** Christine Cornege/AP/Press Association Images; **196** Collection of Jack and Beverly Wilgus; **198** © Europics; **198–199** Sinopix/Rex Features; **200** (t) Chad Grochowski, (b) Bob Huberman; **202** KPN; **203** Joey Miller; **204** Steve Gschmeissner/Science Photo Library; **205** Atlas Press/eyevine; **206** Reuters/China Daily China Daily Information Corp — CDIC; **208** Circus World Museum, Baraboo, Wisconsin; **210** Nick Afanasiev; **212** © Europics [CEN]; **213** Pictures courtesy of Steve McFarlane; **214** Mario Rosenau/Bizarre archive/Dennis Publishing; **216** Quirky China News/Rex Features; **217** EPA/Photoshot; **218** (t/r) Science Photo Library, (b/c) Scott Camazine/Science Photo Library, (b/l) Kaj R. Svensson/Science Photo Library; **220** Reuters/Paulo Santos; **221** Getty Images; **222** Chuck Nyce; **225** Asha Mandela; **228** Dennis Van Tine/ABACA USA/Empics Entertainment; **229** Anders (The Piercing Guy) Allinger www.phatpiercings.com; **230–231** Alan Humerose/Rezo.ch; **232** Yang Maoyuan; **234–235** Pictures courtesy of Craig Tracy; **236** Images courtesy of Shauna Richardson; **237** Victor Liu/Solent News/Rex Features; **239** Drew Gardner/eyevine; **240–241** Getty Images; **242** Caters News; **244–245** L.A. Pop Art www.lapopart.com; **246–247** Yang Maoyuan; **248–249** Solent News/Rex Features; **252** Ari Mahardhika/Solent News/Rex Features; **254** Insaland.com; **255** Xia Xiao Wan; **256–257** Kris Kuksi; **258** Solent News/Rex Features; **259** Ji Yong-Ho/Solent/Rex Features; **260–216** Geoffrey Robinson/Rex Features; **262** Guerra de la Paz; **263** Images courtesy of Morten Viskum and VEGAS gallery, London; **264** Fredo; **266** (t/l) Matthew Albanese, (t/r, c/r) matthewalbanese.com/Solent News/Rex Features; **267** Michael Tompert/Paul Fairchild/Rex Features; **269** Bernard Pras; **270** www.grindshow.com; **272–273** Solent News/Rex Features; **275** Dr Rev Bloodpainter; **280** DeWitt Webb/www.cfz.org.uk; **281** Fortean Picture Library; **282** Quirky China News/Rex Features; **283** Quirky China News/Rex Features; **284** Fortean Picture Library; **285** Tony O'Rahilly/Rex Features; **288** JPL/NASA; **289** Shizuo Kambayashi/AP/Press Association Images; **290–291** Fortean Picture Library; **292** Kamioka Observatory, ICRR (Institute for Cosmic Ray Research), The University of Tokyo; **294** Andy Willsheer/Rex Features; **295** © Europics; **296** Fortean Picture Library; **298** Stew Milne/AP/Press Association Images; **299** www.suzanneproulx.com; **300** © Bettmann/Corbis; **301** Pictures courtesy of Donald Estes/Natchez Cemetery; **302** www.sell-my-photo.co.uk; **303** SSPL via Getty Images; **304–305** Henrik Lauridsen, Kasper Hansen, Michael Pedersen and Tobias Wang; **306** Leon Shadeberg/Rex Features; **307** Courtesy of Caz Housey; **309** © Illustrated London News Ltd/Mary Evans; **310** © 2009 Heiner Muller-Elsner/Focus/Eyevine; **311** Quirky China News/Rex Features; **312** Claire Carter; **314** Fabi Fliervoet/Solent News/Rex Features; **315** (t) Flughafen Leipzig/Halle GmbH/DPA/Press Association Images, (b/l) Cover/Getty Images, (c/r) James D. Morgan/Rex Features, (b/r) Getty Images; **317** Barcroft Media via Getty Images; **318** Quirky China News/Rex Features; **319** Reuters/Sean Yong; **320** Pictures courtesy of Tyler Shepard sponsored by Dreyer Honda of Indianapolis, IN; **322–323** © Edward A. Ornelas/San Antonio Express-News/Zuma/Eyevine; **323** (c/r) © Val Horvath/Shreveport Times/Zuma/Eyevine; **324** Rex Features; **325** KPA/Zuma/Rex Features; **326** Annie B. Brady; **327** © Europics; **328–329** Lou Sapienza/Polaris/eyevine; **329** (b/l) Philip Makanna/Polaris/eyevine; **330** Michael Yon; **331** Roger Viollet/Getty Images; **332–333** Indy Boys Inc; **334** Wenn; **335** Kristjan Logason / Demotix; **336** Getty Images; **337** (t) Courtesy of Cookie Crum, (b/r) Reuters/Amit Gupta, (b/l) Reuters/Fayaz Kabli; **338–339** Barry Bland/Barcroft USA; **341** (t/r, t/l) East News/Rex Features, (b) Roger-Viollet/Rex Features; **342** (t) Hannes Langeder/Rex Features, (b) Manfred lang/Rex Features; **344** www.themidnightrider.com; **345** Pictures courtesy of Tyler Shepard sponsored by Dreyer Honda of Indianapolis, IN; **346** Wenn.com; **347** Ross Parry Agency; **348** (t/r) Raghu Rai/Rex Features, (b/l) Rajesh Kumar Singh/AP/Press Association Images; **349** (b) Herbert Ponting; **350** Daniel Ortega; **353** ChinaFotoPress via Getty Images; **354–355** David Drimmer; **356** Collection of the John and Mable Ringling Museum of Art Archives; **357** From the John and Mable Ringling Museum of Art Tibbals Digital Collection; **358** Marina Malvada/Rex Features; **360–361** AFP/Getty Images; **363** David Branfield www.davebranfield.com

Key: t = top, b = bottom, c = center, l = left, r = right, sp = single page, dp = double page
All other photos are from Ripley Entertainment Inc.
Every attempt has been made to acknowledge correctly and contact copyright holders and we apologize in advance for any unintentional errors or omissions, which will be corrected in future editions.